the complete
vegetarian
handbook

recipes & techniques for preparing
delicious, healthful cuisine

the complete
vegetarian
handbook

By Kathy Farrell-Kingsley

Illustrations by David Pollard

CHRONICLE BOOKS

SAN FRANCISCO

acknowledgments

Many people made this book possible and supported me in one way or another through the writing of it. Thanks to:

My colleagues and former staff of *Vegetarian Times* magazine: Cristin, Joe, Terry, Toni, Maria, Stephanie, Suzanne, Janet, Amy, Jordan, Jane, Al, Andrea, and Derek. They are the finest group of people I have ever had the good fortune to work with, and their daily e-mails kept me going through the writing and production of this book.

The many gifted vegetarian, vegan, and nonvegetarian chefs and food writers who have inspired and taught me with their creative and fabulous food: Richard Pierce, Dana Jacobi, Peter Cervoni, Lorna Sass, Myra Kornfeld, Nava Atlas, and Patsy Jamieson.

Janet Blake, who, thankfully, is never at a loss for words and has a gift for putting them on paper. David Pollard, a talented designer and illustrator and all-around great guy. My agent, Stacey Glick, for always being on top of things. The people at Chronicle Books, Bill Leblond for making my idea a reality; Amy Treadwell and Rebecca Pepper for their attention to detail; and Benjamin Shaykin for a great design.

And especially my family, David, Emma, and Caroline, for their love and patience.

Text copyright © 2003 by Kathy Farrell-Kingsley. Illustrations copyright © 2003 by David Pollard. All rights reserved. No part of this book may be reproduced in any form without written permission from the publisher.

Library of Congress Cataloging-in-Publication Data:

Farrell-Kingsley, Kathy.
   The complete vegetarian handbook : recipes and techniques for preparing delicious, healthful cuisine / by Kathy Farrell-Kingsley
      p. cm.
ISBN 0-8118-3381-X (pbk.)
1. Vegetarian cookery. I. Title.
   TX837.F285 2003
   641.5'636—dc21
                                    2002151514

Manufactured in Canada. Printed with vegetable-based inks on 100% post-consumer recycled paper.

Cover photograph by Dorey Cardinale Photography/ Stockfood.
Designed by Benjamin Shaykin.
Typesetting by Kristen Wurz.

Distributed in Canada by Raincoast Books
9050 Shaughnessy Street
Vancouver, British Columbia V6P 6E5

10 9 8 7 6 5 4 3 2 1

Chronicle Books LLC
85 Second Street
San Francisco, California 94105
www.chroniclebooks.com

For my mother and father
and their unending love and support.

contents

preface

As the former food editor of *Vegetarian Times* magazine, I was always amazed at how many letters and inquiries I would receive for cooking advice. I can empathize. Even as a professional cook I've encountered my share of kitchen disasters—from hard, under-cooked beans and dense, heavy breads to watery tofu dishes and mushy pasta. Unfortunately, most cookbooks don't explain how to do everything a recipe tells you to do or how to solve common cooking dilemmas. Unless you have culinary training or a cookbook reference collection, you are left guessing when things don't go as planned in the kitchen.

To make matters worse, cooking has changed dramatically over the last ten years. We can buy more kinds of fruits and vegetables now than ever before. Once-unfamiliar soy foods and new soy products have become mainstream. A wide variety of rice and grains now line grocery store shelves. All these new-to-market foods require different preparation methods than what we're used to. And we have less time to experiment in the kitchen to find out what works best.

This is what prompted me to write *The Vegetarian Handbook:* the need for a book that focuses on the tips and techniques that every cook interested in a healthy lifestyle needs to know. I don't cover all techniques—that would be too overwhelming, especially for novice cooks. Rather, I've chosen the cooking techniques that a vegetarian or health-conscious home cook will really use. From roasting vegetables, simmering grains, and pressing tofu to grinding flax seeds, cleaning mushrooms, and steaming tempeh, this book is filled with easy-to-follow instructions, information, and practical advice. *The Vegetarian Handbook* shows you how to cook and use some of our healthiest foods. You can look over my shoulder and see the best way to peel and seed a tomato, dissolve yeast, boil eggs, roast peppers, and caramelize onions. I also include tips for healthful cooking techniques, such as steaming, sweating, and stir-frying. And at the end of each chapter I give several recipes to illustrate the techniques covered.

I hope you enjoy this book and find that it increases your cooking skills, confidence, and enjoyment in the meatless kitchen—for that is its purpose.

—KATHY FARRELL-KINGSLEY

NOTE: *One of the things that I find so fascinating about food and cooking is that there are always discoveries being made and new things to learn. With this in mind, I invite you to e-mail me at veghandbook@aol.com with any new or different culinary techniques and/or kitchen tips that you discover.*

how to use this book

The Vegetarian Handbook is organized so that you can find information easily. It is divided into chapters by food groups, including vegetables, fruits, pasta and grains, soy foods, legumes and sprouts, nuts and seeds, and baked goods. To find a specific technique, you will need to locate the food item. Let's say, for example, that you're looking for the best way to peel and seed tomatoes. Turn to the chapter on vegetables. The foods are listed alphabetically, so you can quickly find the listing for tomatoes. Look under this heading to find techniques for preparing tomatoes. You will also find boxes of interesting and useful information related to the technique and helpful kitchen notes.

In addition, there's a chapter on general cooking techniques called Cooking Basics. Here you'll find techniques like steaming, stir-frying, making stock, and knife skills such as chopping, dicing, and slicing.

This introduction serves as a valuable reference for all cooks, novice as well as skilled. Included is a guide on essential kitchen equipment, foods to stock the vegetarian pantry, and the best way to store ingredients. In addition, there are sections on how to plan a vegetarian menu, plus menu suggestions based on the recipes in the book and a dictionary of ingredients commonly used in vegetarian cooking but not covered in the main text, like umeboshi plum vinegar and tahini.

If you don't find the answer to a question by looking under the food item, refer to the index. You're sure to find the information you need in this handbook.

introduction

essential kitchen equipment

To be able to prepare meals in your own kitchen, with your own fresh, whole-some ingredients, you need to have a few tools of the trade. You don't need the most expensive knives or pots and pans, but you do need sturdy, good-quality kitchen utensils and cookware that gives you freedom and dexterity while cooking.

Although cooks differ in their opinions about what the single most important piece of kitchen equipment is, they would probably all agree that if you are starting from scratch, you should buy the best quality you can afford. This saves you money and trouble in the long run, since well-made equipment can last almost forever.

baking equipment

Baking (cookie) sheets are usually flat metal pans with very low rims or a rim on only one end. Those without rims are designed so that the cookies can slide off them onto the waiting cooling racks. Buy heavy-duty baking sheets; thin ones will warp in the oven and cause uneven baking. Dark-colored pans absorb heat, and therefore cookies will brown more quickly when baked on them. Many home bakers prefer nonstick baking sheets. If you bake a lot of cookies, you'll want to have both nonstick and regular baking sheets. Double-layer insulated baking sheets are wonderful investments, as their construction practically guarantees that no cookie will ever have an over-browned bottom.

Standard loaf pans are 9 by 5 by 2¾ inches and are made of metal or glass. Mini loaf pans measure 6 by 3¼ by 2 inches. Metal loaf pans produce loaf cakes and quick breads with more evenly browned crusts; cakes and breads baked in glass loaf pans may brown before they are thoroughly baked.

Standard muffin tins have 12 cups, each holding 6 to 7 tablespoons of batter.

Heavy, smooth, high-quality wooden rolling pins are best for working with pie crusts and other doughs. Many bakers prefer French-style rolling pins, which taper at the ends and have no handles. Others like American-style rolling pins with handles attached to both ends that turn on ball bearings. For fine pastry work, marble rolling pins are used because they stay cool.

Although not essential, a flat, wooden shovel-like tool called a pizza peel makes transferring pizza in and out of the oven a breeze. Baking tiles or a baking stone distributes oven heat evenly and delivers a pizza crust that's crisp on the outside and chewy on the inside.

blenders and food processors

A blender or food processor is a big-ticket item that should go on your wish list. They are not essentials but are extremely useful luxuries. They allow the cook to pulverize and purée without a lot of fuss. A mini food processor is great for chopping herbs, onions, and garlic and for grinding nuts and seeds.

bowls

You'll need four or five bowls of various sizes for mixing and holding items you are setting aside. Small glass bowls are especially handy for measuring out small amounts of ingredients ahead of time.

cutting boards

A wooden cutting board is easiest to work with and best for your knives. To keep cutting boards bacteria-free, simply wash them with hot, soapy water. Since you will not be preparing any raw meat, you do not have the worries that go along with it. Bacteria can be on any type of fresh food, however, so it is still wise to clean cutting boards thoroughly after each use. Select a cutting board that is large enough to work on comfortably but small enough for you to lift easily. A good size is 12-by-15-inches.

knives

Knives are your number one kitchen tool. Sharp, sturdy knives make easy work of chopping, slicing, and dicing. They are most often made out of either stainless steel or carbon steel. Stainless-steel knives stay honed longer and keep their shine (carbon discolors on contact with many foods), but carbon knives are much less costly. Recently, ceramic knives have received a lot of attention. These knives, which are pricey, are delicate and beautifully designed.

Knives are also either forged or stamped. Forged knives are made of one piece of steel that runs from the tip of the blade to the handle. The steel is pounded into shape with a mechanical hammer. A knife that is made of stamped steel is welded together at the bolster, and the steel may or may not run the length of the handle. Stamped knives are thinner and lighter than forged blades. Forged knives are generally considered stronger than stamped ones. When selecting knives, hold them first and make sure they are comfortable and are neither too heavy nor too light.

An 8- to 10-inch chef's knife is the star of the cutlery set. It is an all-around utility knife that is most often used for chopping, dicing, and slicing. It's also good to own one serrated knife, which cuts bread and tomatoes better than a chef's knife. A small paring knife is another handy tool to have. It's great for hulling strawberries, pitting and seeding fruits and vegetables, slicing garlic cloves, removing the eyes from potatoes, and cutting heads of broccoli and cauliflower into florets. For actual paring, I prefer to use a swivel-blade vegetable peeler, and I keep several around for helpers.

A cleaver is nice if you like the feel of a heavy, substantial piece of steel in your hands, but it isn't really necessary, especially since, as vegetarians, we don't ever need to slice through bones. If you already have one, use it for chopping, slicing, and cutting through stubborn pumpkins and winter squash.

Along with your knives, you'll need a knife sharpener so you can keep your knives as sharp as possible. Contrary to what you might think, knives shouldn't be sharpened every day, only when they are dull. Electric knife sharpeners do the job effortlessly, but they are expensive, costing more than $100. Sharpening stones (which resemble bricks) are less expensive and are available in a variety of materials, sizes, and textures. They are usually slicked with either water or oil, depending upon the type. You then draw the knife over the stone from the heal to the tip, holding it at a 20-degree angle and pressing down lightly. This stroke is repeated on both sides of the knife until the blade is sharp.

Honing a knife is different from sharpening; it is done on a steel (a chrome-plated carbon steel shaft with a protective handle) to make sure the edge of the blade is aligned. The edge of a knife blade comes into repeated contact with the hard surface of a cutting board from routine chopping and slicing. This causes the blade edge to curl ever so slightly, making duller cuts. Honing the blade straightens the curl and makes the knife appear to be sharper. Professionals recommend honing a knife after every 10 minutes of use. To use a steel, set the knife blade at a 20-degree angle against the shaft and, pressing lightly, draw the blade across it from the heel to the tip. Do this about five times, then repeat on the other side of the blade.

measuring devices

Make sure you have a set of measuring cups for dry ingredients and a 4-cup glass measuring cup for liquids. Buy a set of measuring spoons; ones made of stainless steel or heavy plastic will work fine.

nonstick cookware

High-quality nonstick skillets are key for low-fat cooking, and you should have them in several sizes. With a nonstick skillet, you can cook many foods with little or no added fat. Avoid pans with flimsy coating. Although you should use plastic utensils with nonstick cookware, a good nonstick pan won't be ruined the first time it has an accidental meeting with a metal spatula.

odds and ends

An immersion blender isn't essential, but it makes puréeing soup a breeze. It allows you to purée soup right in the stockpot, as opposed to in batches in a blender. Some are also powerful enough to chop ice.

If you've never used a Crock-Pot (some call them slow cookers), you might want to try one. These handy, inexpensive devices allow you to cook all day without being at home. They make terrific stews and soups, and if you prepare the ingredients the night before, you can just turn the Crock-Pot on in the morning and be on your way. Crock-Pots come in various sizes; the most useful ones have removable inserts that can be put in the dishwasher.

A colander is necessary for rinsing vegetables and draining pasta; a swivel-blade vegetable peeler will remove the outermost skin of roots and tubers; and a stainless-steel, fine-mesh strainer is good for rinsing grains and beans, straining liquids, sifting dry ingredients, and draining pasta and noodles. A sturdy, stainless-steel cooling rack is key for holding hot cookie sheets and pots. Although funnels are seldom used, they make transferring liquids to narrow-necked containers a breeze. A mortar and pestle crushes dried herbs and whole spices; a pepper mill grinds whole peppercorns for a fresher taste; and a salad spinner quickly dries greens with centrifugal force, eliminating the tedious, wasteful process of squeezing out greens in paper towels. An egg separator is also handy for separating yolks and whites.

You must have kitchen towels and pot holders, a timer or two, and an apron so you can feel free to make a mess, and keep your clothing clean.

pots and pans

Everybody asks, "Which brand of pots and pans is the best?" The answer to that question is really that it's a personal choice. Each cook has to find a style that works for him or her. You have to consider everything, from presentation to purpose to ease of cleaning. Don't buy a whole set of cookware if it is not in your budget. To get started, you should have a large soup pot, a Dutch oven (a large lidded pot intended for slow cooking), two skillets, and a few saucepans.

Heavy-duty, thick-bottomed pots and pans won't scratch, dent, or burn as easily as thinner ones. They distribute heat more evenly, thus preventing scorching. Cast-iron pans are heaviest but demand the most care—they must be seasoned and carefully washed and dried to prevent rusting. Enamel-coated cast-iron pans eliminate the worries of rusting, but because they are cast iron, they are heavy, and their weight can make them awkward to clean. Heavy-duty anodized aluminum pans are slightly lighter, making them easier to lift and clean. Stainless-steel pans are also a good choice; choose ones made with a sturdy aluminum or copper core to help conduct the heat. Nonreactive pans are made from materials, such as enameled cast-iron, stainless steel, and ceramic, that do not react with acidic foods.

Tight-fitting lids are essential for making rice. A snug cover will keep the steam from escaping; a snug glass cover will allow you to see whether the rice is done or if you need to add more water.

You will likely use your skillets every day, and it's good to have a large 10- to 12-inch skillet, as well as a small 7-inch version. A large skillet with deep, sloping sides is great for stir-fries, eliminating the need for a wok. A grill pan will allow you to grill vegetables on your stovetop without adding much fat.

For making rice, heating up soup, or making hot cereal, a 1- or 1½-quart saucepan will fit the bill. To make pasta and stew and to boil and steam vegetables, the 3-quart size will work. When making vegetable stock, a stockpot is essential. It can also be used for making large quantities of pasta, soup, stew, or sauce.

A double boiler comes in handy for cooking foods that need protection from direct heat, such as soft polenta, custards, and sauces. It consists of a pair of stacked saucepans; the lower pan holds a few inches of simmering water that gently heats the food in the upper pot. You can also devise your own double boiler by setting a large bowl over a saucepan of a smaller dimension.

spoons and spatulas

Large, thick-handled wooden and metal spoons for stirring are important. Heavy, heat-resistant rubber spatulas in different sizes are essential for scraping bowls and pans. Bamboo utensils are excellent for stir-frying.

steamers

A steamer is great for preparing crisp, flavorful, colorful vegetables. Some steamers can even be used to prepare couscous. There are several different types. A collapsible steamer insert will work in just about any size pot.

utensils

To help move food around the kitchen, you'll want stainless-steel wire whisks in several sizes for smoothing out and mixing batters and for incorporating dry ingredients; a pancake turner or metal spatula for flipping and serving pancakes, veggie burgers, and other flat foods; a wide, flat, flexible metal spatula for spreading, splitting, and icing cakes, turning crêpes, and prodding muffins out of tins; and a stainless-steel ladle for properly serving soups, stews, and sauces.

the minimalist kitchen

If you want the bare essentials, here's what to buy:

Good 8-inch chef's knife

Large cutting board

6-quart (or larger) ovenproof pot

1-quart ovenproof saucepan with a tight-fitting cover

10-inch heavy-duty ovenproof skillet

Large mixing bowl (preferably ovenproof)

Heavy-duty baking sheet

Can opener

Wooden mixing spoon

Rubber, wooden, or metal spatula

Set of measuring spoons

Set of measuring cups

NOTE: *Buying ovenproof pots and pans eliminates the need for casserole dishes and roasting pans. In a pinch, you can even bake brownies in a skillet.*

stocking the vegetarian pantry

If you've been a meat eater until today, you probably haven't given much thought to your pantry. You know what you need for your basic meals: the same things your mother needed. A few spices like oregano and lemon pepper, some bouillon, a box of spaghetti, and a can or two of stock have been your pantry staples, along with canned tomatoes and a box of instant rice. For the vegetarian, however, the pantry takes on a new, more international look, filled with a wider variety of spices and noodles, beans, and items such as sea vegetables, with which you may be unfamiliar. But to ensure an easy transition to vegetarianism, you will need to rid your kitchen of the old standbys as well as the old notions of the "right" way to cook. You will soon create new dishes that you'll rely on again and again. You will be making delicious soups, stews, pilafs, casseroles, main-dish salads, and stir-fries. Much of what you'll need you can now buy in large supermarkets. Some of the items can be found in natural-food stores or specialty markets, such as Asian groceries. Start by looking for items in your favorite grocery store, then take what is left of your list to a natural-food store. If you look inside the pantry (and by this I also mean the refrigerator and freezer) of the vegetarian, here is what you are likely to find.

baking needs

Eating veggie means you are making a decision to eat more healthful foods. This also applies to baking.

BASICS: Whole-wheat pastry flours, unbleached white flour, baking soda, baking powder, vanilla extract, active dry yeast.

EXTRAS: Specialty flours such as brown rice, barley, and oat flour; blue cornmeal; carob powder.

beans and peas

Beans and peas come under the umbrella term "legumes," and they provide the vegetarian with a plethora of vitamins, minerals, fiber, and amino acids, the building blocks of protein. They can be used in dips and spreads, salads, soups, sauces, casseroles, veggie burgers, and croquettes. It's best to have both dried and canned beans on hand, the latter for when you are fixing a quick meal.

BASICS: Garbanzo beans (chickpeas), black beans, pinto beans, navy beans, great Northern beans, brown lentils, green split peas, kidney beans.

EXTRAS: Mung beans, black-eyed peas, black soybeans, edamame, adzuki beans, lima beans.

beverages

Organic, unsweetened fruit juices are best, as is organic coffee and chemical-free decaf. Alternatives to coffee are beverages made from grains with brand names such as Cafix, Yannoh, and Postum.

BASICS: Noncarbonated and sparkling mineral water, fruit juice, herbal teas.

EXTRAS: Amasake, vegetable juice.

breads and grains

Grains are the foundation of most vegetarian meals.

BASICS: Brown rice, including long-grain and basmati; rolled oats; barley; bulgur; couscous; cornmeal; whole-grain bread; whole-grain cereal; whole-grain crackers.

EXTRAS: Quinoa, millet, wild rice, Arborio rice, wheat berries, whole-grain pitas, whole-grain tortillas, rice cakes.

condiments and seasonings

Like herbs and spices, condiments and seasonings can transform uninspired dishes into memorable meals.

BASICS: Sea salt, soy sauce or tamari, light and dark misos, dark sesame oil, prepared mustards, vinegars (various kinds, such as balsamic, apple cider, rice), horseradish, vegetarian Worcestershire sauce, hot pepper sauce, olives.

EXTRAS: Capers, Bragg Liquid Aminos, soy mayonnaise, pickles, umeboshi plum vinegar and paste, chile paste, Szechuan hot bean paste, pickled ginger, dry sherry.

dairy and eggs

You'll want dairy products and eggs in the fridge if you're not vegan. Whole-milk dairy products contribute a smooth and creamy quality to dishes but should be used sparingly because of their high fat content. Low-fat or nonfat items are best for regular use. Eggs from free-range chickens that aren't fed hormones and antibiotics are the most flavorful. Stay away from margarine, as it is packed with trans fatty acids that contribute to heart disease.

BASICS: Skim milk, butter, low-fat soft and hard cheeses, low-fat or nonfat yogurt, eggs.

dried fruits and vegetables

Look for organic, unsulfured, preservative-free products.

BASICS: Raisins, currants, apricots, dates, figs, prunes, mushrooms, tomatoes.

EXTRAS: Apples, cranberries, cherries, bananas.

dried herbs and spices

There is no limit to what you can do with food when you combine it with the sometimes subtle, sometimes bold flavor of herbs and spices. Many cuisines of the world are primarily vegetarian, and they all use their own magical combinations. Even a workweek, 30-minute supper can easily be turned into something extraordinary using dried herbs and spices you keep in your pantry.

BASICS: Bay leaves, sage, whole black peppercorns, oregano, rosemary, basil, thyme, cumin, curry powder, cinnamon, nutmeg, chili powder, paprika, cayenne, garlic powder, crushed red pepper flakes.

EXTRAS: Tarragon, dill, coriander, cardamom, allspice, cloves (preferably whole), ground ginger, garam masala, caraway seeds, fennel seeds, herbs de Provence.

nuts and seeds

Besides adding extra crunch to salads and other dishes, nuts and seeds are full of nutrients, so make sure you always have some on hand (unsalted is best).

BASICS: Almonds, walnuts, sesame seeds, sunflower seeds, tahini.

EXTRAS: Pine nuts (pignoli), cashews, pecans, pumpkin seeds, nut butters.

oils

Buy expeller-pressed, unrefined oils if possible. Also keep on hand vegetable oil spray (nonstick cooking spray) to lower the fat content of many dishes.

BASICS: Olive oil (preferably virgin and extra-virgin), canola oil, peanut oil, and toasted sesame oil.

EXTRAS: Flaxseed oil, safflower oil, walnut oil, hazelnut oil.

pasta

Vegetarianism isn't all about pasta primavera, but noodles of all sorts help pull a meal together in a time crunch:

BASICS: Fettuccine, linguine, penne, orzo, ramen noodles.

EXTRAS: Whole-grain pastas such as corn and whole-wheat, soba and udon noodles, rice noodles, bean threads.

prepared foods

Just because you are trying to eat meatless meals doesn't mean you can't enjoy the convenience and ease of prepared foods. Look for those that are low in sodium and sugar, without additives or preservatives. Organic is always a good choice.

BASICS: Whole-grain cereals such as muesli, granola, and hot cereals; ready-made pizza crust; canned beans; canned tomatoes; soups; tomato sauce and other pasta sauces; salsas; salad dressings; frozen vegetables and fruits; fruit-sweetened apple butter, jams, and preserves; vegetable stock or powder; applesauce; prepared entrées.

produce

Certainly, the type of produce in your pantry or refrigerator will be based upon the season and where you live. Just remember that fresh produce is preferable over canned or frozen, and choose organic when you can. Try not to overbuy.

WINTER: Carrots, turnips, rutabagas, daikon radishes, beets, winter squash, onions, cabbages, citrus fruits.

SPRING: Leeks, tender lettuces, watercress, spinach, red radishes, scallions, peas, asparagus, new potatoes, rhubarb, strawberries, blackberries.

SUMMER: Tomatoes, sweet corn, beans, eggplant, zucchini, chard, okra, sweet and hot peppers, peaches, blueberries, plums, fresh herbs.

FALL: Apples, pears, cauliflower, broccoli, Brussels sprouts, kale, collards, potatoes, yams, winter squashes, pumpkins.

sea vegetables

You can call them seaweed, but sea vegetables are packed with minerals and vitamins. In some Asian societies, dried sea vegetables are used in soups and stews as well as snacked on like chips.

BASICS: Kombu, hijiki, wakame, nori.

EXTRAS: Dulse, arame.

soy foods

Soybeans are the most nutritious legumes, and they are basic to the vegetarian diet. You will find a myriad of soy products at even your local supermarket.

BASICS: Tofu in various degrees of firmness, tofu in aseptic packages, tempeh, soy milk, both plain and flavored.

EXTRAS: Soymeat products such as crumbles, frozen desserts, soy margarine, soy yogurt.

sweeteners

Many vegetarians shun refined table sugar, not only for its undesirable side effects, but because some brands are produced using animal bones. Natural alternatives abound, however.

BASICS: Pure maple syrup (grade B is all-purpose), honey, brown rice syrup.
EXTRAS: Unsulfured molasses, blackstrap molasses, date sugar, Sucanat, barley malt syrup.

thickeners

Gelatin is not an option for vegetarians, because it is made from animals, but there are many other thickeners from which to choose.

BASICS: Kudzu, arrowroot powder, agar, tomato paste.

five good reasons to buy organic

1. Organic foods taste better.
2. Buying organic produce supports small independently owned and operated family farms. It also supports the health of farmworkers and their families by affording them a safe work environment.
3. Organic farming methods, such as the use of compost and beneficial insects, enhance rather than deplete soil fertility, prevent soil erosion, and control pests without poisons.
4. Organic farming promotes biodiversity—the perpetuation of a broad variety of plant species. This simultaneously preserves consumer choice and protects our food supply over the long term.
5. Organic farming techniques prevent the problem of fertilizer runoff into surface water and groundwater.

If you're not ready go organic all at once, at least make an effort to find organic sources for the most contaminated fruits and vegetables. The Food and Drug Administration tested 15,000 food samples over a two-year period and identified the crops with the highest levels of pesticide residue. The Environmental Working Group, a nonprofit research organization based in Washington, D.C., compiled that list in descending order of toxicity. The top ten are strawberries, bell peppers and spinach (tied for second), U.S.-grown cherries, peaches, Mexican-grown cantaloupes, celery, apples, apricots, green beans, and Chilean grapes.

The lowest levels of pesticide residue were found on avocados, sweet corn, bulb onions, cauliflower, asparagus, Brussels sprouts, U.S.-grown grapes, bananas, plums, green onions, watermelons, and broccoli.

guide to storing foods

Storing the fresh food you buy is as important a consideration as actually purchasing the food. In order to eat in the most healthful way possible, one must seek out the freshest vegetables and fruits, the most colorful beans, and the tofu with the longest expiration date. But there's no use in taking them home and just plunking them in the refrigerator or the pantry to see how they fare. To keep food fresh and avoid those annoying—and expensive—extra trips to the store, you need to use basic common sense and some of these tips. Here you'll find general information about storing food, as well as details on storing specific types of food for best results.

general food storage

If you have a cool, dry area in your basement where you can store food, build some shelves in there and turn it into a pantry. The one thing that will shorten the shelf life of any food, even one that is canned or otherwise packaged, is heat.

If you don't have a pantry area in your home, be sure to store food away from stoves and ovens. If you live in a hot climate, consider buying another refrigerator for food storage and skipping the cabinets.

Many canned goods today have expiration dates on them, but as a general rule, canned goods should be kept for only a year.

Think of dried beans as produce. The fresher they are, the better they will taste and the easier they will be to cook. Dried beans take longer to cook the older they are. If you buy your beans in bulk, make sure the store has a high turnover. Bulk bins can be a great way to buy beans because you can purchase only as much as you need.

When purchasing, look for legumes with a vibrant color. Fading is a clear indication of long storage. The longer beans are stored, the less fresh they'll taste. And if their surface looks cloudy, they may also be moldy.

Refrigerate or freeze whole-grain flours and yeast.

When you purchase root vegetables, take them home and wash them. Then separate them from their green tops, leaving about one inch still attached. Wrap the greens in paper or cloth towels and place them in a perforated plastic vegetable bag. Refrigerate everything on the lowest shelf of your refrigerator or in the vegetable bin.

Buy small quantities of herbs and spices, as they lose their flavor intensity over time. Buy fresh herbs when possible; stand cuttings in water, cover loosely, and refrigerate. Keep dried seasonings in tightly closed jars away from heat and light.

Keep a supply of wrappers on hand for different storage needs (buying them in bulk at a warehouse store will save money). You should also have plenty of small and large self-sealing bags, including some suitable for the freezer; paper bags in various sizes; and glass jars (with lids) in all sizes.

Rotate your food. Use the oldest food first. Find a method of food rotation that works best for you.

storing specific foods

baking mixes: Store unopened packages in a cool, dry pantry. Refrigerate or freeze after opening. ✱ *The shelf life for most unopened mixes is 1 year; use those containing cornmeal within 9 months.*

breads: To maintain best flavor, keep breads at room temperature; refrigeration wards off mold but causes bread to dry out quickly. Store in a paper or perforated cellophane bag, clean towel, or bread box; plastic bags trap moisture, making bread soggy and susceptible to mold growth. Store flat breads, such as tortillas and chapatis, in the refrigerator for up to 5 days or in the freezer. ✱ *For longer storage, freeze breads of all types. Slice loaves and keep them, well wrapped, in the freezer for about 3 months.*

canned tomatoes: Keep unopened cans in a cool, dry pantry. Store leftovers in tightly closed glass or plastic containers in the refrigerator. ✱ *Store unopened cans for up to 2 years. Cooked leftovers will keep for several days refrigerated.*

cereals: Store unopened packages in a cool, dry pantry. Refrigerate dry hot cereals and granolas after opening. ✱ *Keep unopened instant cereal cups for up to 9 months. An unopened ready-to-eat cereal's shelf life is 6 to 12 months; use it within 3 months when opened. Unopened hot cereals keep for 12 months, 6 months once opened. Granolas keep for 6 months unopened and, when opened, for 6 months refrigerated.*

cheese: Wrap cheeses tightly in plastic or foil and refrigerate. Replace the wrappings often to discourage mold. ✱ *Fresh soft cheeses (ricotta, goat) keep for several days; harder cheeses (Cheddar, Gouda, mozzarella, Muenster, provolone, Swiss) keep for up to several weeks refrigerated. Parmesan and Romano keep for 9 to 12 months in the refrigerator.*

condiments: Store unopened vinegars, mustard, mayonnaise, hot pepper sauce, ketchup, tamari, soy sauce, and the like in a cool pantry. Refrigerate all after opening. ✳ *These items will keep for 1 year unopened and for about 6 months opened.*

cracked and rolled grains: Cracked and rolled grains are less resistant to rancidity than whole grains. Wrap them tightly and store in the refrigerator or freezer. ✳ *Unopened packaged grains will keep for 12 to 18 months. Once opened, most keep for up to 3 months refrigerated and longer frozen.*

dried beans: Store in airtight containers in a cool, dry pantry. Protect from insect infestation by burying a bay leaf in the middle of the container of beans. Refrigerate or freeze cooked beans. ✳ *Use bulk beans within 3 to 12 months of purchase. Cooked beans keep for up to 5 days refrigerated, 6 months frozen.*

dried fruits: Store tightly sealed in a cool, dry pantry; glass or rigid plastic containers are the best insurance against insect infestation. Fruit tends to dry out and harden when refrigerated, though it will keep longer. ✳ *All keep for at least 1 month in the pantry and for at least 6 months refrigerated.*

dried herbs and spices: Keep in tightly closed jars in a cool, dry, dark cupboard. ✳ *Whole herbs and spices keep longer than ground. Keep them for 1 year maximum.*

dried sea vegetables: Store in a tightly sealed container in a cool, dark pantry. Refrigerate cooked sea vegetables in tightly sealed containers. ✳ *Dried sea vegetables keep indefinitely. Once cooked, they keep for 4 to 5 days refrigerated.*

eggs: Store eggs, pointed-ends down, in their carton in the refrigerator. ✳ *Use eggs within 3 to 4 weeks. Keep refrigerated egg yolks for 1 to 2 days, whites for 3 to 4 days. Unpeeled hard-cooked eggs keep for 3 to 5 days, peeled for 2 to 3 days.*

fresh fruits: Ripen pears, peaches, plums, nectarines, apricots, bananas, and avocados at room temperature. Store unwashed ripe fruit in plastic bags in the high-humidity drawer of the refrigerator. Berries keep best in their plastic baskets inside a paper bag in the refrigerator. Citrus fruits need not be wrapped. ✳ *Storage time varies greatly. Apples and citrus fruits are particularly long-lasting and will keep for anywhere from 5 to 10 days refrigerated.*

fresh herbs: Cut ½ inch off the stem ends and stand in a container of water. Cover loosely with a plastic bag and refrigerate. ✳ *Herbs stored this way will keep for up to a week.*

fresh vegetables: Store most vegetables in plastic bags in the vegetable bin of your refrigerator. Squeeze as much air as possible out of bags containing greens. Fresh mushrooms keep best in a paper bag. To preserve flavor, do not refrigerate tomatoes. Keep onions, shallots, garlic, potatoes, sweet potatoes, and winter squash in a cool, dry pantry. ✳ *Storage time varies widely. Cruciferous and root vegetables keep for up to 5 days; peas, beans, and tender greens for up to 3 days.*

jarred tomato sauce and salsa: Store unopened containers in a cool, dry pantry; refrigerate after opening. ✳ *Unopened, their shelf life is 12 to 18 months. Opened jars will keep in the refrigerator for up to 1 week.*

miso: Keep in a tightly sealed container in the refrigerator. ✳ *It keeps almost indefinitely.*

nuts and seeds: Unshelled nuts keep best. Store in a cool, dry place. Keep shelled nuts and seeds, tightly wrapped, in the refrigerator or freezer. Whole nuts keep better than chopped or ground ones. Roasted nuts are especially perishable. ✳ *Keep unshelled nuts for 2 or 3 months, longer if refrigerated. Refrigerated shelled nuts and seeds keep for 3 to 6 months, depending on the variety; you can freeze them for up to 1 year. Use roasted nuts within 1 month.*

oils: Cooking oils keep best in opaque glass containers stored in a cool, dry place. Flavoring oils (sesame, chile) should be refrigerated. ✳ *Oils high in monounsaturated fats (olive, canola) keep for up to 4 months in the pantry. Oils composed primarily of polyunsaturated fats (safflower, corn) keep for up to 2 months. If you plan to keep any oils longer than that, or if you live in a warm climate, it's best to refrigerate them and use within 1 year.*

pasta: Store dried pasta in a cool, dry pantry. Refrigerate fresh pasta tightly wrapped. ✳ *Use fresh pasta within 2 days. Keep dried egg noodles for up to 6 months, other dried pasta for up to 18 months.*

soymilk: Keep unopened, aseptically packaged soymilk in a cool, dry pantry. Close containers securely and refrigerate after opening. Soymilk sold in the refrigerated section of the store should be kept in the refrigerator. All soymilk is sold with an expiration date. ✳ *After it is opened, soymilk will keep for several days refrigerated.*

sweeteners: Store white sugar, brown sugar, and date sugar tightly wrapped in a cool, dry pantry. Keep honey, molasses, barley malt, and rice syrup in tightly sealed containers, preferably glass, at room temperature. Transfer maple syrup in tins to glass jars to avoid an off flavor, and refrigerate to prevent fermentation. ✳ *White and brown sugar keep indefinitely at room temperature.*

Date sugar, honey, molasses, and refrigerated maple syrup will keep for at least 1 year; barley malt and brown rice syrup for 6 months.

tempeh: Keep in the refrigerator or freezer. ✳ *Opened or sealed, use it by its expiration date or freeze it. Frozen tempeh keeps well for several months.*

tofu: Refrigerate water- and vacuum-packed tofu before opening; unopened, aseptically packaged tofu doesn't need refrigeration. Once opened, store tofu immersed in water in a tightly covered container in the refrigerator. Change the water daily. Keep freeze-dried tofu in a cool, dry pantry and wrap tightly once opened. ✳ *Packaged tofu comes with an expiration date. Once opened, it will keep for about a week when stored properly. Freeze all but silken types in a plastic bag or container (without water) for up to 6 months. Use opened freeze-dried tofu within 4 months. After opening, it will keep for several days refrigerated.*

vegetable and fruit juices: Keep bottled, canned, and boxed juices in a cool pantry. ✳ *Unopened bottles and cans keep for 1 year; boxed juices keep for 6 to 9 months. Frozen juices keep for 8 to 12 months. Once opened, juices keep for 7 to 10 days refrigerated.*

whole-grain flours: Store in airtight, moisture-proof containers, preferably in the refrigerator or freezer to prevent the natural oils in the bran and germ from turning rancid. ✳ *Whole-grain flours will keep for up to 3 months unrefrigerated and for 6 months refrigerated. Refined flours will keep about twice as long. Most unopened packaged flours will keep for up to 1 year; use cornmeal and rice flour within 9 months.*

whole grains: The oil-rich germ of whole grains makes them susceptible to rancidity. Grains will keep longer if refrigerated or frozen. If not freezing, store raw grains in clean, airtight glass or rigid plastic containers in a cool, dry, dark place. ✳ *Most unopened packaged grains will keep for up to 1 year; use rice within 9 months. It's best to buy small quantities. Once opened, most are usable for 6 months if stored in a cool, dark area; use brown rice and quinoa within 3 months.*

meatless menu planning

Many people who want to put more meatless meals on their table or who are new to the world of vegetarianism begin with the same perplexing question: How do I replace meat on my plate? It's hard for us to discard the image of the standard American dinner trilogy of meat, potatoes, and a vegetable. Yet the answer is simple if you remember this—you don't have to replace the meat.

In other words, vegetarian meal planning isn't about finding something to replace the meat. It's about opening yourself up to a world of other menu ideas. Build your meals around a variety of whole-grain pastas, noodles, and breads, plus a broad selection of vegetables and fruits. High in complex carbohydrates, vitamins, and minerals, these foods will fill you up and provide all the fuel your body needs without overloading your system with protein, fat, and cholesterol.

One mistake that many new vegetarians make is replacing meat with a cheese- or egg-based dish. Cheese and eggs, like meat, are filling and high in protein, making them seem to be ideal meat substitutes. The problem is that they are too much like meat: They provide much more protein, fat, and cholesterol than you need. Used in small quantities as a garnish, they're fine. But don't overdo them.

Many new vegetarians worry needlessly about designing meals that have adequate protein. In most cases, these fears are groundless. With few exceptions, both meat eaters and vegetarians alike in this country consume more than enough protein. The current Recommended Dietary Allowances for protein are 63 grams for adult men and 50 grams for adult women. You can easily consume these amounts without even thinking about it.

Here are several ideas to get you started.

the joys of soy: Meat substitutes can help make the transition to a vegetarian diet really easy. There is a whole new generation of meat-like soy products on the market that provide us with appealing possibilities for meatless meals. Among the many types of soymeat from which you can choose, crumbles and frozen soymeat are perfect for turning out quick meals. Crumbles resemble chopped meat. Supermarkets sell them both refrigerated, in the produce section, and frozen. There are also frozen soymeats that resemble chicken or turkey. Made from soy fibers specially processed to be chewy like cooked meat, they will absorb the flavor of any sauce, and they come in bite-size pieces, chunks, and whole "breasts" to slice or shred. Also look for this type of soymeat in ready-to-eat frozen entrées. They have never been more abundant. Stock up on a few for days when you're stymied or just don't want to cook.

around the world: Vegetarian cuisines are enjoyed all over the globe. Asian countries have made a culinary art out of using minimal amounts of meat. You can go one step further and remove the meat altogether. Stir-fried vegetables over a bed of rice can be filling and satisfying. Or you can toss in cubes of tofu or tempeh for the meat if you prefer. There are as many versions of stir-fries as you have the imagination to create: You can toss in any combination of vegetables, noodles, nuts, beans, and sprouts and serve it over brown rice, millet, couscous, kasha, or any other grain. Include a cool dish, such as a marinated vegetable or citrus salad, on the side.

Many Italian dishes are vegetarian naturals. Pasta in its myriad forms can be the basis for any number of great meals. Penne can be topped with a tomato sauce enriched with steamed broccoli and mushrooms or other vegetables, or tossed with spinach that has been sautéed with onions and spices. Tubular pastas and shells can be stuffed with mixtures of ricotta, garlic, parsley, and Parmesan cheese and topped with a light tomato sauce. Risottos are especially good made with wild mushrooms, asparagus, spinach, or butternut squash. And pizza can be the basis for as many topping combinations as you have the imagination to create. Don't be restrained by the belief that pizza has to have cheese; with a hearty sauce and lots of vegetables, you won't miss it. And then there are the Middle Eastern, Latin, Thai, Indonesian, and Indian cuisines to turn to.

dynamic duos: Beans and grains appear together in many cuisines. Circle the globe and you'll find Hoppin' John (black-eyed peas and rice), *pasta e fagiole* (macaroni and beans), and refritos (mashed beans) and tortillas, to name just a few. And there are so many more combinations that you can create, such as noodles with peanut sauce and curried chickpeas over bulgur. Not only do these combos taste great, but together they form a complete protein (containing eight of the essential amino acids). Accompany any of these combinations with steamed or sautéed vegetables for a complete, nutritious meal.

Soup and salad are also satisfying, especially in the cold-weather months. Hearty bean or barley soups and other substantial soups go well with crisp salads; lighter soups can be teamed with heartier salads, such as pasta- or bean-based salads.

backwards meal: Breakfast items can make excellent suppers. Homemade buttermilk pancakes or waffles with fresh berries and soy sausages are a favorite any time of day. Omelets, frittatas, and poached eggs can also fill the dinner bill. Potato-vegetable hash or potato pancakes sprinkled with tamari and a dollop of yogurt are easy and satisfying.

copycat: There's no better way to gather good menu ideas than by imitating meals you've enjoyed in restaurants and creating variations on those themes. Also, many vegetarian cookbooks and magazines suggest menus and, of course, provide the recipes to help you put them together.

think ahead: Planning meals in advance makes it easier to eat a varied diet. It will also save you time shopping because you won't have to run to the store every day for this or that. And well-planned meals make cooking easier during the week, because you don't have to worry about what's for dinner.

don't forget dessert: Dessert can be an essential part of a meal's satisfaction and nutritional value. Try making a bread- or rice pudding from a previous day's leftovers. Or have a baked apple (take out the core and fill it with raisins and a drizzle of maple syrup). Dried fruit can be stewed into an iron-rich compote, flavored with orange zest and cinnamon or cardamom. Of course, there's always the decadent route: cookies, cakes, pies, and the like. But these, too, can make a respectable contribution to a meal, particularly if you make them with whole grains, natural sweeteners, fresh fruit, and a minimum of fat.

It doesn't matter whether you're organizing a holiday feast for twenty or just planning family dinners for the week; with practice and a commitment to the ideas outlined here, you'll soon be a menu making pro.

menu suggestions

Spinach-Mushroom Omelet
  (page 262)
Roasted potatoes
Apple-Oat Squares (page 143)

Banana Soy Smoothie (page 188)
Cinnamon-Apple Waffles (page 241)
Date-Nut Bread (page 235)

Lentil and Escarole Soup (page 203)
Wheat Berry Waldorf (page 172)
Pita bread
Fresh melon with gingersnaps

Eggplant Caponata (page 108)
Winter Squash Risotto (page 171)
Mixed Greens with Lemon-Mint
  Vinaigrette (page 64)
Fruit sorbet

Potato, Fennel, and Celery Root
  Soup (page 109)
Roasted Vegetable Ratatouille
  (page 117)
Olive and Herb Flatbread (page 236)
Biscotti

Vegetable potpie
Wasabi Mashed Potatoes (page 112)
Mixed Greens with Goat Cheese
  (page 110)
Lemon curd dip with cherries and
  berries

Guacamole (page 142)
Three-Bean Chili (page 202)
Cornbread
Mango with coconut sorbet

Steamed Artichokes with Herb
  Vinaigrette (page 59)
Pasta with Tempeh Bolognese
  (page 185)
Garlicky Broccoli Raab (page 111)
Lemon Cornmeal Cake (page 139)

Hearty Corn Chowder (page 107)
Portobello Burgers with Pesto-
  Pepper Mayo (page 118)
Asparagus and Roasted Bell Pepper
  Salad (page 104)
Peach Crunch Pie (page 243)

Tomato-Basil Bruschetta (page 114)
Tuscan Pasta and Vegetables
  (page 116)
Hazelnut-Fig Bread (page 214)

the vegetarian dictionary

Here are descriptions of ingredients and cooking terms that those interested in eating a vegetarian diet should be familiar with.

all-purpose flour: This flour may be bleached or unbleached, but regardless of the processing, it always appears bright white, and either will behave as well as the other. Which to buy is a personal preference; bleached flour is more processed than unbleached. White flour is milled from the endosperm of the wheat berry, which surrounds the center of the grain and contains no oil.

almond milk: As a measure-for-measure substitute for dairy milk, almond milk can be used in many recipes. It is simply a mixture of ground almonds and water. Almond milk is often considered the best of the nut milks because of its delicate flavor. It can be purchased in aseptic containers at natural-food stores or made at home by blending raw almonds and water and straining well. Do not allow almond milk to boil, as it will separate.

amaranth: This small herb seed is higher in calcium and phosphorus than any other grain except millet. It also boasts a high amount of protein and lysine, an essential amino acid rarely found in vegetable matter. There are two main ways of cooking amaranth: One is to toast the seeds in a dry skillet until they pop into miniature popcorn. Popped amaranth adds a crunchy, mildly spicy flavor to soups, stews, and vegetables. The other method is to cook the seeds with a liquid to create a mixture resembling grits that makes a delicious side dish or stuffing.

amasake: Similar to rice milk, amasake is a Japanese sweetener or drink made from sweet rice, millet, or oats and *koji* (mold) starter. The mixture ferments into a thick liquid. Hot or cold, amasake is a delicious beverage, and it contributes a gentle sweetness and wonderfully moist texture to baked goods. It is also called amazake.

anaheim chile: Interchangeable with the New Mexico chile, the Anaheim chile is light green, with a sweet taste and just a hint of heat. Anaheim chiles are available fresh or canned and are often stuffed or used in salsas.

ancho chile: A dried 3- to 4-inch-long chile that is deep reddish-brown. Its flavor is sweet and fruity, and it can range in heat from mild to pungent. When it's fresh and green, it is called a poblano chile.

arrowroot: Used for thickening, arrowroot is a starchy flour from the root of a tropical American plant. It can be substituted measure-for-measure for cornstarch, although it is less processed than cornstarch, so it is a good choice for those who try to eat only whole foods. To use, mix it with cold water before adding it to the recipe, and bring it to a boil.

ayurveda: The ancient Indian science of life and self-healing.

baking powder: A leavening powder that is a mixture of alkaline and acid. It will leaven a batter without the addition of an acidic ingredient. Double-acting baking powder, the kind used in our recipes and also most available to the consumer, reacts with liquid to initiate the leavening process and then again in the oven when the batter is exposed to heat.

baking soda: An alkaline powder used for leavening. In order to perform its leavening magic, baking soda must react with an acid, such as sour milk, buttermilk, yogurt, citrus juice, or molasses.

barley: A hardy grain, barley is larger and plumper than other grains except corn. It is rich in protein, niacin, thiamin, and potassium. Barley with the bran layer peeled off is called pearl barley and is lower in fiber, protein, fat, and minerals than whole barley.

barley malt syrup: A dark sweetener made from germinated barley that has a consistency slightly thicker than molasses. Sometimes called malted barley syrup, it can replace honey or molasses in most baked goods. Pure barley malt syrup tastes much like molasses and is about half as sweet as white sugar. It contains simple sugars, B vitamins, and protein. Refrigerate this syrup to keep it from fermenting. It is sold in natural-food stores.

beat: To stir with a quick, steady motion to incorporate air into batters and doughs while mixing the ingredients together. May be done by hand with a whisk or spoon or, more commonly in baking recipes, with an electric beater.

black beans, fermented: Sometimes called salty black beans, these small black soybeans are preserved in salt. They are used to flavor Asian-style dishes after being soaked in water for 30 minutes and finely diced.

black bean sauce: A pungently flavored, bottled Chinese condiment made from fermented black beans, rice wine, and garlic. Chiles are also sometimes an ingredient.

blanch: To plunge food in boiling water briefly and then into cold water. Blanching is usually used for vegetables and fruits to loosen their skins and heighten their color and flavor.

Bragg Liquid Aminos: A flavoring that tastes like, and is a substitute for, soy sauce or tamari. It contains amino acids and is available bottled in natural-food stores.

brown rice flour: Flour made from ground brown rice. It has a slightly crunchy texture and a mild, nut-like flavor. Although it is a good substitute for wheat flour, it contains no gluten, so bread made from rice flour doesn't rise. It works well in quick breads. Once opened, brown rice flour should be stored in the refrigerator to prevent spoilage.

brown rice syrup: A syrup used as a sugar substitute in sweets and desserts, also called rice malt. It is a thick, liquid sweetener, with a mild taste, that is made by combining cooked brown rice with dried sprouted barley and culturing the mixture until it converts some of the rice starch into maltose and glucose. Refrigerate brown rice syrup to prevent surface molding. Use it as you would barley malt. You may also find brown rice syrup powder; substitute it for refined sugar, cup for cup.

brown rice vinegar: Vinegar made from fermented brown rice. This Japanese vinegar has a smooth, mellow flavor and low acidity.

buckwheat: Usually eaten in its roasted form, called kasha, or ground into a flour, buckwheat is technically not a grain but a member of the rhubarb family. It contains all eight essential amino acids and is a good source of calcium, vitamin E, and the B-complex vitamins.

bulgur: Parched, steamed, and dried wheat berries. This grain is popular in Middle Eastern cooking and is a good source of protein, phosphorous, and potassium.

cane syrup: A thick, very sweet, liquid sweetener is made from sugarcane and is used in Creole and Caribbean cooking. Look for it in specialty markets.

cardamom: A relative of ginger and native to India, this aromatic spice is used widely in Scandinavian and Indian cooking. It comes ground or in a pod containing small black seeds. The pods can easily be crushed with a mortar and pestle to release the spicy-sweet seeds, whose flavor diminishes as soon as they are ground.

carob powder: The dried, roasted, ground pulp of pods from a Mediterranean evergreen known as the locust tree. It is used as a substitute for cocoa powder due to its chocolate-like flavor, and is caffeine-free. It is sold in natural-food stores and specialty markets.

chai: A tea made in the Indian tradition. This luscious drink is a peppery-sweet mix of black tea, spices, and milk. It can be enjoyed warm or iced. For vegans, some brands of chai are made with soymilk.

chickpeas: Also called garbanzo beans, these legumes are available dried, canned, and ground into flour. Dried chickpeas are notoriously hard and benefit from being soaked before cooking. They have a satisfying nutty flavor and chewy texture.

chile oil: A vegetable oil infused with the flavor of chile peppers. Chile oil is orange-red in color and can be found in small bottles in Asian markets or large supermarkets. All you need is a drop to add a spicy kick to dishes.

chile paste: A concentrated, thick, red paste made of ground chiles, garlic, and a little oil. It is used to flavor Chinese dishes and is sold in small jars in most supermarkets and Asian specialty stores. Chile paste keeps indefinitely when refrigerated.

chinese five-spice powder: True to its name, Chinese five-spice powder is a pungent mixture of ground cinnamon, cloves, fennel seed, star anise, and Szechuan peppercorns. It is available in Asian markets and supermarkets.

chipotle chile: A smoked jalapeño chile pepper, great for adding a sweet, smoky flavor to foods. It is available dried and pickled, as well as canned and bottled in adobo sauce.

chutney: A condiment, served with Indian curries, made with fruit such as mango, vinegar, sugar, and spices. It has a sweet and spicy flavor.

coriander seed: The ripe, dried fruit of the coriander plant, used as a spice. The seeds have the flavor of lemon, sage, and caraway. Whole coriander seeds are used in pickling and mulled wine; the ground spice can be found in curries, soups, and baked goods. Although the leaves of the coriander plant are known as cilantro or Chinese parsley, the seeds and leaves do not impart the same flavor.

crimp: To seal two pastry edges by pinching them together to form a decorative edge.

cumin: An essential ingredient in most chili powder, cumin is a spice with a strong, aromatic, and slightly bitter taste. It is available whole or ground.

curry powder: Curry powder is a blend of numerous spices and is used to flavor many dishes, particularly those referred to as curries, inspired by the cooking of India. Not all curry powders are identical, but most commercially available ones include ginger, cumin, turmeric, pepper, cayenne, and coriander.

cut in: A term that refers to incorporating a cold, solid fat into a dry ingredient, such as flour, until the mixture resembles coarse crumbs. Most cooks use either two kitchen knives, a pastry blender, or their fingertips to cut fat into flour.

date sugar: This dark brown, sugary-textured substance consists simply of ground dried, pitted dates, and it contains iron, potassium, and other minerals and vitamins. Sprinkle date sugar on cereal and use it for baking, though be aware that it tends to burn as a topping. You may want to blend coarse date sugar to a finer texture or dissolve it in water when making batters. Substitute it for refined sugar, cup for cup.

dehydrated sugarcane juice: Granulated sugarcane juice is a natural food substitute for refined white sugar. The sugarcane juice is dehydrated by being spun at a high temperature through a vacuum tunnel and then milled into a powder. Sucanat, short for "sugarcane natural," is a popular brand. Mexican *piloncillo* and Indian *jaggery*, sometimes available in ethnic markets, are similar unrefined sugars. Look for organic products, because dehydration concentrates pesticides and other chemicals used on sugarcane in the field. Substitute dehydrated cane juice for refined sugar, cup for cup.

dredge: To lightly coat a food with flour, cornmeal, bread crumbs, and the like. Often a food is dredged before being browned or fried.

dust: To cover food on one side or a work surface with a light sprinkling of a dry ingredient, such as flour, cornmeal, or bread crumbs.

Egg Replacer: The brand name for a powdered combination of starches and leavening agents that bind cooked and baked foods in place of eggs. It is sold in natural-food stores and large supermarkets.

farro: A grain that looks like light brown rice, with a nutty taste reminiscent of oats and barley. It lacks the heaviness of other whole grains, and hence is attractive to restaurateurs, who often use it in risotto-type dishes. Rich in fiber; magnesium; and vitamins A, B, C, and E; farro is also easily digested and low in gluten and therefore a good choice for those who are sensitive to wheat.

fermented black beans: See *black beans, fermented.*

flaxseed: Small, brown glossy seeds that are a rich source of omega-3 fatty acids. Also called linseeds, they can be ground and added to baked goods, sauces, and dressings. Flaxseeds are also pressed into an oil.

flute: To make a decorative edge on a pie shell or another pastry, usually in a scalloped pattern.

fold: To combine two mixtures with different densities, such as beaten egg whites and creamed batter, so that they lose neither air nor volume.

garam masala: A northern Indian blend of dry-roasted, ground spices used to add spicy heat to dishes. Typically it includes black pepper, cinnamon, cloves, coriander, cumin, cardamom, dried chiles, fennel, mace, nutmeg, and other spices. Look for it in specialty markets or large supermarkets.

gelatin: For vegetarians, gelatin is a minefield. Ordinary gelatin is an animal by-product. It's a clear, tasteless thickening agent made from beef and veal bones, cartilage, tendons, and other tissue, or from pigskin. Vegetarian gelatin, which is made without animal by-products, from plant gums, is available at some specialty and natural-food stores and by mail order. Also, some kosher gelatins are animal-free. Read ingredient labels carefully to be sure.

ginger: A staple of Indian and Asian cooking, the ginger plant is grown for its aromatic, knobby root. When the root is sliced, it imparts a peppery, slightly sweet, spicy flavor that is subtle yet unmistakable.

granulated maple syrup: Also known as maple sugar or dehydrated maple syrup, granulated maple syrup is just that: the sap from a maple tree that has been boiled until it is almost entirely evaporated. The result is a granulated sweetener that is twice as sweet as granulated white sugar and imparts a luscious maple flavor. It's best used sparingly, as it is costly, but a little goes a long way. Specialty stores or mail-order houses are the best sources for granulated maple syrup.

grits: Anyone who has traveled in the South has encountered grits on a breakfast menu. Any coarsely ground grain such as corn, oats, or rice is known as grits or, sometimes, hominy grits. Grits are cooked with water or milk, baked or boiled, and served as a side dish or as a hot cereal.

groats: Any hulled crushed grain, such as barley, buckwheat, or oats, is known as groats. Although the terms "groats" and "grits" are used interchangeably, groats are generally more coarsely ground than grits. Buckwheat groats are the most widely used groats, and are also known as kasha. They are cooked in a manner similar to rice. Groats are used in cereals, as a side dish, or as a thickener for soup.

hoisin sauce: Used to flavor Chinese dishes, hoisin sauce is a thick, brown sauce that is both sweet and spicy. It is made from soybeans, garlic, spices, and chile peppers and is available in cans, jars, and bottles.

hominy: Dried white or yellow corn kernels from which the hull and germ have been removed. It is sold dried, canned, and ready to eat. When ground it is called hominy grits.

hummus: A dip or spread made from chickpeas blended with lemon juice, garlic, olive oil, and tahini (sesame seed butter), hummus has moved into the mainstream of American supermarkets. It is great with a vegetable platter or used on a fresh vegetable wrap.

isoflavin: A class of flavonoids (compounds found in plants) that may help prevent hormone-related cancers such as breast cancer.

jalapeño chile: Of all the hot chile peppers, jalapeños may be the best known. They are smooth and dark green, 1 to 2 inches long, with a rounded tip. The seeds and stems are extremely hot and should be removed (it's best to do this wearing plastic gloves). Add a small amount to soups, stews, salsas, and chilis if like your food extra-hot. Jalapeños are also available bottled in brine or pickled.

Job's tear: This grain looks like large pearled barley. The bead-like seeds, which Christian legend asserts grew from the tears of Job, were used for necklaces and rosaries in ancient Persia.

kamut: The word "kamut" comes from the ancient Egyptian word for wheat, but the grain itself is 2 or 3 times the size of wheat berries. Ounce for ounce, it is higher in protein and minerals than most other grains and is also easier to digest. With a pleasant chewiness and distinct buttery taste, this grain is very low in fat.

kasha: See *groats*.

kudzu: Used to thicken soups, sauces, and puddings, kudzu is a white, starchy powder made from the root of the kudzu plant.

lacto: A classification of vegetarianism that includes dairy products but not meat, poultry, fish, or eggs.

lacto-ovo: A popular choice for new vegetarians, this classification of vegetarianism includes dairy and eggs but not meat, poultry, or fish.

lemongrass: A key ingredient in Thai cuisine, lemongrass is a long, thin, gray-green herb that has a sour-lemon flavor and fragrance. It is used to make tea and to flavor soups and other dishes and can be found fresh, dried, or bottled in Asian markets and large supermarkets.

light soy sauce: This variety of soy sauce, used to flavor many dishes, is lighter in color and flavor than traditional dark soy sauce. It is not "lite" in the sense of being sodium-reduced. Traditional soy sauce is a dark, salty liquid made by fermenting boiled soybeans and roasted wheat or barley.

liquid smoke: Commonly used to impart a smoky flavor to sauces, liquid smoke is bottled hickory smoke flavoring.

maple sugar: See *granulated maple syrup*.

maple syrup: It takes 30 to 40 gallons of maple sap containing 3 percent sucrose to produce 1 gallon of 65 percent sucrose syrup. Look for pure maple syrup; "maple-flavored" syrup consists primarily of sugar or corn syrup and usually contains artificial coloring and flavoring. Buy organic maple syrup to avoid formaldehyde and chemical antifoaming agents and mold inhibitors. Refrigerate maple syrup in a glass jar to prevent it from acquiring a metallic taste or fermenting. Highest-grade (AA or fancy) maple syrup has the sweetest, most delicate flavor and is best used as a topping.

millet: A tiny, round, yellow grain, millet has a slightly nutty and mild flavor. It is gluten-free, easily digestible, and contains abundant minerals, vitamins, and protein. When cooked, millet swells to a fluffy texture.

mirin: A sweet Japanese cooking wine made from rice that adds a subtle flavor to stir-fries. A light, sweet white wine can be substituted for mirin.

molasses: The thick syrup that remains after sugar crystals are removed during the sugar-refinement process. Exceptionally dark, strong-flavored blackstrap molasses derives from the final phase of sugar extraction. About half as sweet as white sugar, it is rich in calcium, iron, and B vitamins. If not organic and unsulfured, blackstrap molasses may also contain high concentrations of pesticides and sulfur dioxide, an allergen for some people. Unsulfured molasses has a less assertive flavor than blackstrap molasses and is about two-thirds as sweet as sugar.

mung beans: These small, round beans have a dark green skin wrapped around a yellow seed. Native to India, these beans are widely used in Asian cooking. They have a slightly sweet flavor and soft texture.

nutritional yeast: Nutritional yeast is a dietary supplement and condiment that has a taste ranging from meaty to nutty to cheesy. It is a good source of protein, iron, and several B vitamins. It can be added to soups and casseroles or sprinkled on toast, popcorn, or spaghetti.

oat milk: A measure-for-measure substitute for dairy milk that is made from oats and water.

palm sugar: Also called *jaggery*, palm sugar is a coarse, unrefined sugar made from the sap of various palm trees or from sugarcane juice. It is primarily used in India. It comes in two forms: one with a soft, honey-butter texture and one with a harder, cake-like texture. The softer version is used as a spread, and the harder form can be crushed for sprinkling on foods. See also *dehydrated sugarcane juice.*

pasilla chile: These chile peppers are generally 6 to 8 inches long and 1 to 1½ inches in diameter. Pasillas are dried, brownish-black chiles used primarily in sauces and known for their hot, rich flavor. In their fresh form, they are called chilaca chiles.

pesto: There are many variations of pesto, a popular sauce in Italy, but all have the same base: fresh basil, garlic, and olive oil, often with grated Parmesan or Romano cheese and pine nuts added. Pesto is simple to make at home or can be purchased in fresh and bottled forms at most supermarkets. While pesto is most often used to flavor pasta, it is also delicious as a topping for baked potatoes and as a spread in sandwiches.

phytochemical: A biologically active substance in plants responsible for giving them characteristics such as color, flavor, and disease resistance.

pinch: A very small amount, usually less than ⅛ teaspoon.

poblano chile: When stuffed with cheese and cooked in an egg batter, poblano chiles are the basis for the famous Mexican dish, chiles rellenos. These peppers are dark green, shiny, and curvaceous, about the size of an elongated green bell pepper, with a heat scale that is medium to hot. Dried, they are known as ancho chile peppers.

preheat: To turn on the oven about 20 minutes before baking to allow it to reach the correct temperature. Broilers are also preheated.

proof: In baking, this term refers to testing yeast to make sure it is alive and capable of leavening bread dough.

purée: To blend in a blender, process in a food processor, or pass though a food mill until food is smooth and lump-free. The term also refers to the food that has been puréed.

pumpkin seed oil: Pumpkin seed oil is a robustly flavored oil made from roasted pumpkin seeds. Because of its strong flavor, it is often used as a condiment or in combination with milder oils. Look for it in specialty food shops.

quinoa: A quick-cooking grain native to the Andes. Its small, disc-shaped seeds are rich in calcium and protein. When cooked, it has a delicate nut-like flavor and a light texture, with a slight crunch. Readily available in health-food stores and supermarkets, quinoa has been laboriously scrubbed free of saponin, a sticky substance that coats the seeds. However, it is recommended that you thoroughly rinse it again before cooking.

rice milk: A lightly flavored alternative to dairy milk, this beverage is made from rice and water and can be used measure-for-measure for dairy milk.

rice paper wrapper: The rice paper wrapper is an edible, translucent film made from water and the pith of a tropical shrub called the rice paper tree. Rice flour is also sometimes used. Rice paper is used to wrap foods such as Thai spring rolls and can be prepared by soaking or deep-frying.

rice vinegar: Common in Asian cooking, rice vinegar has a subtle, sweet flavor.

rice wine: Made from fermented glutinous rice, this wine is popular in Asian cooking. Japanese rice wines are sake and mirin.

roux: A classic mixture of flour and fat that is slowly cooked over low heat and then used to thicken soups and sauces.

saffron: The world's most expensive spice, saffron is a flavoring derived from the purple crocus. It lends a yellow color and distinctive taste to dishes. Fortunately, a little goes a long way.

scald: To heat liquid until it almost boils and just begins to form tiny bubbles around the rim of the pan

score: To make elongated shallow cuts in meat or fish or on loaves of bread.

scrape down: To use a rubber spatula or spoon to remove batter, whipped cream, or another mixture from the sides of the bowl during mixing.

seitan: A chewy, meat-like, high-protein food made from boiled or baked wheat gluten. You can make it yourself or purchase it in dry mixes or prepared and either chilled or frozen in natural-food stores. Its flavor varies according to the spices and herbs with which it's cooked.

serrano chile: A small, slightly pointed chile with a hot, savory flavor. As serrano chiles age, their green color gives way to scarlet and then to yellow. They are available fresh, canned, pickled, packed in oil, and in carrot and onion mixtures. Dried serranos are called *chiles secos*.

sesame oil: Oil expressed from sesame seeds. It comes in two basic types—light and dark. Lighter varieties are good for making salad dressing and sautéing; dark sesame oil, which burns easily, is drizzled on Asian dishes as a flavor accent after cooking.

sherry vinegar: Vinegar made from sherry, a fortified wine originally from southern Spain. Some sherries are dry and light; others are sweeter and darker.

shred: To cut food into flat strips, using a knife or a shedder.

sift: To remove lumps and aerate dry ingredients by passing them through a mesh sifter or strainer.

simmer: To boil very gently so that the liquid produces small, occasional bubbles around the edges of the pan and across the surface of the liquid.

soy isolate powder: See *soy powder*.

soy powder: A ground, concentrated source of soy protein. Soy powder is an easy way to add soy to one's diet, as the powder can easily be incorporated into other foods, such as shakes or smoothies.

soy sauce: A dark, salty liquid made by fermenting boiled soybeans and roasted wheat or barley. Used extensively in Asian cuisine, soy sauce flavors soups, sauces, and marinades. It comes in many varieties, ranging in color from light (weaker) to dark (stronger) and in consistencies from thin to very thick. Several brands are low in sodium.

spelt: A grain that is native to southern Europe, spelt has a subtle, nutty flavor and is higher in protein than wheat and rich in iron. And because it is gluten-free, it is good for people with wheat sensitivities.

star anise: Native to China, star anise is a spice with a flavor slightly more bitter than that of regular anise seed. It can be found whole in Asian markets and natural-food stores and as a ground ingredient in Chinese five-spice powder.

stevia: Used as a sweetener for centuries in South America, stevia has more recently become a popular sweetening agent in Japan and other Asian countries. Derived from the leaves of yerba dulce, or "sweet leaf," a shrubby herb indigenous to Paraguay and Brazil, this exceptionally sweet substance tastes 10 or more times sweeter than sugar—and up to several hundred times sweeter in its extracted form. Just ½ teaspoon of white stevia powder equals the sweetening power of 1 cup of sugar.

tahini: A thick, smooth paste made of ground sesame seeds, tahini is a staple of Middle Eastern cuisine.

tamari: A naturally brewed soy sauce that contains no sugar and is available wheat-free. It has a more subtle flavor than soy sauce, but is salty.

teff: The smallest grain, teff is popular in Ethiopian cooking. It is particularly high in calcium and iron. Of the three varieties, white, red, and brown, white is the mildest.

textured vegetable protein (TVP): Known among vegetarians as a "meat replacer," TVP is a dehydrated soy product that, when reconstituted, resembles meat. It is sold plain and flavored and minced, in flakes, and in chunks.

thai curry paste: Available in Asian markets and specialty food shops, curry paste is a blend of curry powder and other spices, vinegar, and oil or clarified butter.

triticale: A nutritious whole grain that is a hybrid of wheat and rye. It has a nut-like, sweet flavor.

turbinado sugar: Sugar made from the first crystallization of cane juice, retaining some of the molasses, which accounts for its golden-brown color. It contains no more nutrients than table sugar and is best used for general baking needs.

turmeric: A spice with a bitter, pungent flavor and intense yellow-orange color, turmeric is the root of a tropical plant related to ginger. It is used mainly to add both flavor and color to food and is popular in East Indian cooking. It is an essential ingredient in curries.

umeboshi plum paste: A thick condiment made from Japanese sour plums that are salted, sun-dried, and aged. It contains iron, calcium, minerals, vitamin C, and enzymes and is believed to aid digestion.

umeboshi plum vinegar: A mild Japanese vinegar made from pickled, slightly sour umeboshi plums.

vegan: The most complete type of vegetarianism. Vegans do not eat animal products of any type, including meat, poultry, fish, dairy, eggs, or honey.

wasabi: The Japanese version of horseradish, wasabi comes from the root of an Asian plant. It is used to make a green-colored condiment that has a fiery, pungent flavor. It comes in both paste and powdered forms.

well: A hollow depression in dry ingredients into which liquid ingredients are added before being incorporated into the dry ingredients.

wheat berries: Whole grains of wheat. These need a while to cook and have a great chewy texture. The flavor will vary according to the variety.

wheat bran: The outer covering of the wheat kernel, which is separated for wheat flour during milling. Wheat bran is a rich source of dietary fiber.

wheat germ: The vitamin-, mineral-, protein-, and oil-rich embryo of the wheat berry. It has a nutty flavor and is available toasted and in its natural form.

wheatgrass: Often juiced as a health tonic, wheatgrass is the young green from grain plants.

whole-wheat pastry flour: Ground and sifted wheat that is fine-textured and soft, with the high starch content needed for tender cakes and pastries. Whole-wheat pastry flour is made from whole-wheat flour, which contains the wheat germ.

whip: To beat with a whisk or beater until the mixture increases in volume.

white wheat flour: White wheat flour is milled from the white wheat berry, as opposed to regular whole-wheat flour, which is milled from the red wheat berry. White wheat flour has a lighter, sweeter taste than whole-wheat flour. It is available in specialty food shops or by mail order.

wild rice: Not a rice at all, but a grain harvested from grass that grows in marshes along the banks of freshwater lakes. The grains are blackish in color and have a nut-like flavor and chewy texture when cooked.

wonton skins: Thin sheets of dough made from flour and eggs and used to make Chinese dumplings (wontons) and egg rolls. They can be purchased in most supermarkets and Chinese markets, and usually come in both square and round shapes.

worcestershire sauce: A marinade and condiment developed in India by the English. Because its ingredient list includes anchovies, it is not vegetarian, but vegetarian versions are available at natural-food stores. Worcestershire sauce also contains garlic, soy sauce, tamarind, onions, molasses, lime, vinegar, and other seasonings.

yeast extract: Popular in English cuisine, yeast extracts are bottled, brownish-black pastes used to flavor tea sandwiches or soup bases. They have a very salty flavor and are available in specialty markets.

Most vegetarian cooking is based on just a small number of techniques. Once you understand these basic skills, reading recipes and cooking will begin to fall into recognizable patterns and make more sense. In this chapter you will find careful explanations of some healthy cooking basics, followed by some recipes chosen to help you learn by doing.

cooking basics

measure ingredients

Accurate measuring can sometimes make the difference between success and failure when preparing a recipe. Baking, for example, requires exact amounts. Using too much flour in a baked good will make the texture dry and coarse, and too little will produce flat or wet results. All recipes call for specific amounts so the ingredients will interact in certain ways. Upsetting the balance will affect the final result.

butter

Many times the tablespoon increments printed on butter wrappers do not line up correctly. The best way to measure butter is to unwrap it and mark the halfway point. Then mark the midpoint of each half, and then the midpoint of each quarter. It should now be marked into eighths. Each increment is 1 tablespoon. For melted butter or other solid fats, measure in solid form, then melt.

dry ingredients

Use stainless-steel or plastic measuring cups for dry ingredients. A liquid or glass measuring cup isn't accurate for dry ingredients because it cannot be leveled off.

baking powder or soda: Dip a measuring spoon of the correct size into the container, then sweep the away excess with the edge of the package lid, or with a knife or small spatula.

brown sugar: Pack brown sugar firmly into a dry measuring cup. Use the bottom of a smaller cup to tamp and press the sugar into the larger cup. Level the sugar with a knife. The sugar should hold its shape when turned out of the cup.

chopped foods, granulated sugar, and spices: Lightly fill a measuring spoon or cup of the correct size with the ingredient, then sweep away excess with a knife or small spatula.

flour: Because flour tends to pack down, aerate it before measuring by stirring lightly with a fork. Dip the measuring cup into the flour (don't tap or bang the cup). Sweep away the excess with a straight-edged utensil like the flat edge of a knife blade or frosting spatula (a).

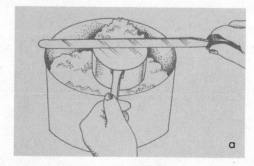

The top should be level with the cup. If a recipe calls for sifted flour, sift the flour using a sifter or just a sieve and then gently fill the measuring cup.

liquid ingredients

When measuring liquids, use a glass measuring cup with calibrations marked on the inside of the glass. Place the cup on a level surface and pour in the liquid. To get an accurate reading, bend down to check it at eye level.

sticky ingredients

For easy removal of sticky ingredients, like honey, molasses, and syrups, from measuring cups, lightly coat the cups first with nonstick cooking spray and use a rubber spatula to scrape the food out.

basic measures

1 tablespoon = 3 teaspoons	1 gallon = 4 quarts / 8 pints / 16 cups
¾ tablespoon = 2¼ teaspoons	1 quart = 2 pints / 4 cups
½ tablespoon = 1½ teaspoons	1 pint = 2 cups
⅓ tablespoon = 1 teaspoon	1 pound = 16 ounces
Pinch = less than ⅛ teaspoon	¾ pound = 12 ounces
1 cup = 16 tablespoons	⅔ pound = 10⅔ ounces
½ cup = 8 tablespoons	½ pound = 8 ounces
⅓ cup = 5½ tablespoons	⅓ pound = 5⅓ ounces
¼ cup = 4 tablespoons	¼ pound = 4 ounces

cut vegetables

Recipes use many different terms for chopping vegetables, including mince, chop, slice, dice, julienne, and shred. Each has its own technique, and all are easily mastered with a little practice. And keep in mind that using a well-sharpened knife makes all the difference in the world.

chop and mince: To chop generally means to cut into coarse or fine pieces, and to mince means to chop very finely.

1. Place the knife over a pile of food to be chopped, with one hand grasping the handle and the other hand holding the tip on the cutting surface.

The point always stays on the cutting surface. Rock the knife up and down rapidly, moving it to cover the whole pile of food (b).

2. Gather the vegetable pieces together with your knife and continue to chop until the food is reduced to the desired size.

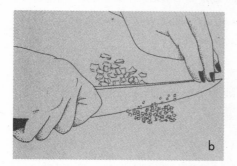
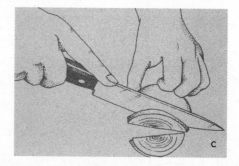

slice: In this technique, you cut the vegetables into discs of even thickness

1. Peel the vegetable, if necessary. If you are cutting a round or oval vegetable, cut a thin slice from one side so the vegetable will sit flat on the cutting surface. Hold the vegetable firmly with one hand, with your fingertips curved under so you do not cut yourself and so the knife slides up and down against the knuckles (c).

2. Slice, moving the fingers back as a guide for the knife to determine the thickness of the slices.

dice: To dice is to cut the food into uniform cubes. This is done when appearance is important. There are different sizes of dice, including small (¼-inch squares), medium (½-inch squares), and large (¾-inch squares).

1. For long vegetables, peel if necessary, then cut in half crosswise. Cut lengthwise into ½-inch-thick slices. Stack 2 or 3 slices at a time and cut into ¼-inch strips. Turn and chop horizontally into small dice (d).

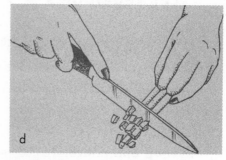

2. For round vegetables, peel if necessary, then cut off the rounded sides of the vegetable so it is square. Cut the square into ½-inch slices. Reassemble the slices and cut them lengthwise into strips (e). Turn the square and cut through the strips crosswise to make medium dice (f).

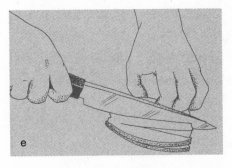

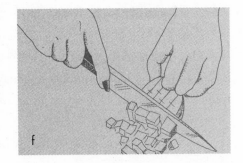

julienne: This classic French cooking technique means to cut into fine strips.

1. For long vegetables, peel if necessary and cut into 2-inch lengths. Stand each length on end and hold firmly with your fingertips. Slice as thinly as possible (g). Stack 2 or 3 slices together and cut into fine strips.

2. For round vegetables, peel if necessary, and then cut into thin slices. Cut each slice into fine strips.

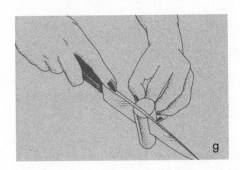

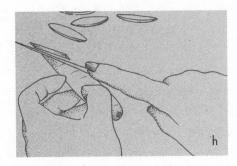

cut on diagonal: Vegetables for stir-fries and sautés are often cut on the diagonal to expose a larger surface to the heat so that the vegetables will cook quickly.

1. Hold the knife almost parallel to the length of the vegetable and slice at an angle. The knife can be held straight or at an angle to the cutting board (h).

shred: Leafy vegetables and herbs are frequently cut into shreds.

1. For round heads such as cabbage, cut into halves, and then cut out the core. Place each half cut-side down on a work surface and cut into thin vertical slices.

2. For long vegetables such as bok choy, cut into thin crosswise slices.

3. For leaves like lettuce, spinach, and basil, roll the leaf lengthwise. Cut crosswise into thin slices. This is also called chiffonade.

chop fresh herbs

A garden isn't required to enjoy the flavor of fresh herbs, since all varieties of fresh herbs are available in markets today. But store-bought herbs are expensive and an essential part of good cooking, so it makes sense to know how to preserve and best use them.

Because fresh herbs are highly perishable, buy them only as they are needed.

Mince or chop herbs (see page 45) just before using, because the aromatic flavors are quickly lost as the volatile oils are released. The delicate flavors are also easily dissipated by heat, so it's best to add fresh herbs near the end of cooking. Use the leaves only, as the stems are tough and woody. Stems can be used in preparations where they are removed or strained at the end, like a stock or a sauce.

fresh vs. dried herbs

Because the oils in the leaves becomes concentrated in the drying process, dried herbs are generally more flavorful than the same amount of fresh. A general rule of thumb to follow is that ¼ teaspoon crumbled dried herbs equals 2 teaspoons chopped fresh herbs.

To dry fresh herbs, rinse and pat thoroughly dry. Set the herbs on a rack in a warm, dry place for about 1 week. Crumble the leaves and store in an airtight container or small jar with a tight-fitting lid. Label and date the containers and store in a cool, dark place. Dried herbs will retain their fragrance for up to 6 months.

KITCHEN NOTES

:: When buying fresh herbs, be sure to choose those that have a fresh scent and bright color.

:: The refrigerator is a little too cold for most herbs, so the best way to store them is as you would flowers. Put their stems in a container of water and leave at room temperature for up to 2 days.

:: The easiest and best way to cut fresh chives is to snip them to the desired size using small scissors.

stir-fry

When it comes to fast food, stir-fries might well be the first kind that was invented. Developed by the Chinese centuries ago, this technique involves cooking bite-sized pieces of food quickly over high heat in a small amount of oil. The food is cooked by both the heat of the pan and the heat of the oil. It's an ideal way to preserve the colors, flavors, textures, and nutrient in foods.

equipment

Stir-frying begins with a wok or stir-fry pan that has deep, sloping sides. This design allows food at the bottom to cook rapidly over intense heat, while other ingredients along the sloped sides can cook more slowly or be kept warm.

The most traditional type of wok is a 14-inch carbon-steel pan with a wooden handle and a rounded bottom. This classic wok, however, was not designed for use in a home kitchen, and its rounded bottom cannot be brought close enough to the heat source to reach the correct temperature. For home cooking, a flat-bottomed wok or stir-fry pan works best. You can find flat-bottomed woks in a variety of shapes, sizes, and metals, such as stainless steel, anodized aluminum, and nonstick.

Although recipe details will vary, the same technique applies to all stir-fried dishes.

1. Prepare all your ingredients in advance. This is helpful due to the quick pace of stir-frying. Make the sauce, if required, and set it aside. Chop all the ingredients and arrange in separate bowls so they can be easily tossed into the pan.

2. Heat a wok over medium-high heat for 1 minute, and then add oil in a thin stream around the inside rim of the pan. As the oil slides down the hot sides of the pan, it both heats and coats the sides to keep food from sticking. You want the oil really hot so the ingredients will cook quickly.

3. Add any seasonings for the dish, such as chopped garlic, fresh ginger, or onions, and stir constantly with a Chinese-style spatula (a long-handled utensil with a slightly curved blade) or wooden spoon. Continuous stirring is necessary to ensure that all the uncooked pieces have contact with the bottom of the pan. Cooking the seasonings separately flavors the oil.

4. As the seasonings become aromatic, add the vegetables, beginning with those that will take the longest to cook; keep stirring. Add the vegetables a handful at a time to avoid reducing the temperature of the pan. As these vegetables cook, scoop and toss them so they cook evenly. Scoop from the center out to the sides so the vegetables will fall back to the bottom. Keep the oil hot enough to sear the vegetables. Do not overload the wok; cook the vegetables in batches, if necessary.

5. Add liquid seasonings or sauce after the main ingredients have cooked. Adding the liquids too soon will result in braised food rather than stir-fried. Push the vegetables up the side of the wok and pour the liquids or sauce into the bottom of the pan; stir until thickened, then stir well with the other ingredients. You may need to cover the wok briefly at this point to allow the ingredients to steam.

6. Remove the wok from the heat; taste and adjust the seasonings.

season a carbon-steel wok

Woks made of carbon steel are usually the least expensive, but they tend to rust if not used often and properly cared for. If you do purchase one of these, you will need to season it before you use it. First, use a mild detergent to scrub off the protective coating; then rub the inner surface with oil and place it in a 300°F oven for 45 minutes. Don't worry about the wooden handles; they may darken in color but will otherwise be unharmed. After each use, wipe the wok out and gently scrub it in very hot water; do not use soap. Dry the wok over a medium-hot burner. Rub the inside with vegetable oil and wipe out the excess. In time your wok will become virtually nonstick and will darken to a deep brown.

sauté

Sautéing is one of the simplest ways to cook and a good technique for preparing a wide variety of vegetables. It calls for briefly cooking food in a small amount of fat over fairly high heat, thus evaporating the water in the vegetables and concentrating their flavors. The high heat also seals in the vegetables' natural taste.

equipment

For successful sautéing, a heavy-bottomed skillet or a sauté pan with sloping sides is essential so the heat will be evenly distributed over its surface and the food will cook without scorching. Be sure to use a pan that is just large enough to hold the food in a single layer without crowding. If it is too large, the juices released from the foods will run to the edges and burn, and if it is too small, the food will steam in its juices rather than sauté.

1. Add enough oil or butter (or a combination) to the skillet to lightly coat the bottom. Heat the pan over medium-high heat until hot. It's important to let the pan get very hot, or the food will absorb too much oil, stick to the bottom, and begin to stew in its own juices.

2. Add the vegetables and cook by tossing or stirring them until lightly browned. Tossing the ingredients in the pan is a technique used by chefs. It is not hard to do and is worth the practice for the home cook. Grasp the handle of the skillet with both hands and move the pan back and forth. Lift up slightly on the backward pull to make the vegetables jump and redistribute themselves (i).

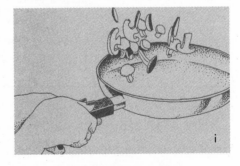

i

KITCHEN NOTES

:: Chopped and diced vegetables can be easily tossed or stirred. Sliced vegetables are a little more cumbersome; a spatula works well for these.

:: Potatoes need to be partially cooked or blanched (see page 31) before sautéing.

:: Vegetables that exude a lot of water, such as zucchini and mushrooms, are best sautéed over very high heat to quickly evaporate the liquid.

:: Foods can first be coated in flour or a breading mixture to give them a crisp coating.

steam

As our interest in eating healthy increases, so does the popularity of steaming foods. This technique involves simply cooking with the heat of steam. The food is placed on a rack in a pan above boiling liquid. The pan is tightly covered to keep the steam in. It's a quick and easy cooking method that locks in flavors, preserves more nutrients, and gives foods a wonderfully moist texture.

equipment

Several types of steamers are available. The type most commonly used by home cooks is the collapsible stainless-steel steamer basket that can be adjusted to fit into different sizes of saucepans. Chinese bamboo steam baskets are convenient because they come in a range of sizes and can be stacked to steam several foods at once. There are numerous other steaming devices, such as perforated racks, ceramic bowls, trivets, and inserts that fit into pots, poachers, and roasting pans. Most well-stocked kitchen shops will carry several kinds and sizes. You can also always improvise a steamer by setting a metal colander or strainer in a large saucepan and covering it.

1. Bring at least 1 inch of water to a boil in the base of a steamer. The boiling water should be at least 1 inch from the bottom of the steamer basket so the steam can circulate and the bubbling water cannot reach the food.

2. Arrange the food in a single layer in the steamer basket for even cooking. Be sure the water is boiling before you add the food.

3. Cover the pot tightly to keep the steam in, and steam the food until tender. When checking for doneness, uncover the pot as briefly as possible. Tilt the lid away from you to avoid releasing a cloud of steam into your face.

4. Check the bottom part of the steamer occasionally to be sure the water does not boil away. If the water level gets too low, add boiling water.

KITCHEN NOTES

:: Cut the food into pieces that are about the same size, for even cooking.

:: For added flavor, steam foods over a vegetable stock, or add herbs and other seasoning to the boiling water.

:: When using stackable steamers, remember that the food in the upper levels will drip onto the food below, so be sure they are compatible. Also, place the food that will take the longest to steam closest to the source of the steam.

:: Remember, each time you remove the cover of the steamer to check the progress of cooking, steam escapes, so add a few minutes of cooking time.

braise

Although braising is a technique that has long been associated with turning economical cuts of meats into fork-tender morsels, this method of cooking also works well with vegetables. Slow cooking in just a small amount of liquid imparts a delicious, melting tenderness and a caramel glaze to vegetables—and fruits. Leafy vegetables, such as endive, cabbage, root vegetables, and fennel, lend themselves well to this technique of cooking.

equipment

For even heating, a heavy pan with a tight-fitting lid is important. A flame-proof casserole of enameled cast iron or stainless steel, also called a Dutch oven, is ideal. It's best to use a wide pan, so that the liquid evaporates and thickens gradually.

1. In a deep, flameproof pan, over medium heat, heat just enough oil to prevent the vegetables from sticking. Add the vegetables and cook, stirring often, until they begin to brown.

2. Add enough liquid to come about one quarter of the way up the vegetable. (Adding too much liquid will turn the dish into a stew.) Water, stock, juice, and wine are common choices. Stir with a wooden spoon, scraping loose any caramelized bits on the bottom of the pan.

3. Cover the pan and simmer over low to medium heat on the stove-top, or bake in a 300° to 325°F oven, until the liquid is evaporated and the vegetables are very tender. Check the pan often to make sure it isn't dry before the vegetables are cooked. Add a little more liquid if necessary. If any liquid is left after the vegetables are completely cooked, uncover the pan and cook for about 10 minutes to evaporate the liquid.

deglaze

The technique of deglazing is used in several cooking methods, such as braises, stews, and sautés. It involves cooking food over high heat to form a golden crust. The juices that are drawn to the surface are condensed and browned, giving the crust an enticing flavor and leaving caramelized bits in the pan. While the pan is still hot, a liquid is added to it and the browned bits are scraped loose and stirred into the liquid where they dissolve, adding richness and depth of flavor.

make a stock

Many cooks are intimidated by the idea of making their own stock, but in fact there are few dishes that are easier to prepare. You don't have to follow a recipe, and there are no tricky techniques to a master. The secret to good soup is a good stock, and this is especially true for vegetarian soups.

There are basically two kinds of stocks that vegetarians should know how to make: a mild, clear stock and a rich, dark brown one. Each has its own uses. The clear stock, usually made with onions, leeks, celery, and herbs, is good for pale soups and other light-colored, delicate-flavored dishes. Brown stocks are made by roasting the vegetables first, to give the stock a richer flavor and darker color. They are good for robustly flavored soups and hearty-tasting dishes.

This is an all-purpose clear vegetable stock. For a recipe for brown vegetable stock, see page 63.

1. In a large, heavy stockpot, bring 2 ½ quarts of chopped vegetables (such as onions, leeks, garlic, carrots, celery, potatoes, greens, cabbage, corn cobs, and fennel), ½ cup chopped fresh herbs (such as basil, oregano, and parsley stems), bouquet garni (see the box below), and 4 quarts of water to a boil.

2. Skim off any foam that rises to the surface. Reduce the heat and simmer, uncovered, until the stock is well flavored, 1 to 2 hours. Add water as necessary to keep the vegetables covered, and skim as needed.

3. Season to taste with salt, pepper, and tamari sauce if desired. Strain the stock through a fine sieve set over a large bowl, pressing on the vegetables with the back of a spoon to extract as much liquid as possible. Discard the solids.

4. Cool the stock to room temperature, then transfer to airtight containers and refrigerate for up to 5 days or freeze for up to 6 months.

KITCHEN NOTES

:: Avoid using strong-tasting vegetables such as broccoli, cauliflower, and Brussels sprouts in your stock, as they can overpower the flavor.

:: Beets will turn the stock red, and asparagus will turn it green.

:: For a thicker stock, strain the stock and purée the pressed vegetables in a food processor. Stir the purée back into soup and then strain again.

bouquet garni

A bouquet garni is a bundle of herbs added to stocks, soups, and stews for flavor and aroma. They can be purchased at specialty stores, but it's also easy to make your own. The classic French bouquet garni includes parsley stems, fresh thyme sprigs, and bay leaves. Simply tie the herb stems together with kitchen twine, or tie them into a neat bundle in a square of cheesecloth.

make a vinaigrette

Many cooks claim that if you know how to make a good vinaigrette, you know how to cook. That's not to say, however, that everyone agrees on what makes a good vinaigrette.

Basically, all vinaigrettes are made of oil, vinegar, and seasonings. The classic proportion of oil to vinegar in a vinaigrette is 4 to 1. But personally, I prefer a ratio of 3 to 1. Knowing how to make a vinaigrette really comes down to tasting and adjusting the ingredients to your liking.

You can vary the basic dressing by using different kinds of oils and vinegars or by adding shallots, mustard, garlic, herbs, capers, or olives.

To make a vinaigrette, in a small bowl, whisk together 1 part vinegar with salt, pepper, and any seasonings to taste. Slowly whisk in 3 parts oil. Taste and add more salt and pepper, if needed. The vinaigrette can be refrigerated for up to 1 week. Whisk well before using.

olive oils

Americans are finally learning what Mediterranean cultures have known for centuries: Olive oil not only tastes sublime, but it's good for you as well. This fruity oil is now considered a good guy in the war against fat, because it is monounsaturated and contains cholesterol-lowering properties.

Olive oil is available in several different grades, according to the degree of acidity. The first cold pressing of the olive gives the finest, fruitiest oil, naturally low in acid. These cold-pressed, low-acid oils are called extra-virgin. Subsequent pressings use heat, which yields oil of lesser quality and a higher level of acidity. Olive oil is then classified (in order of acid level) as super-fine, fine, or virgin.

The best way to select olive oil is by its color and flavor. Deep-green oils are produced from less mature olives and have a pungent fruit flavor. Golden oils, pressed from ripe olives, offer a mellower, smoother flavor. Both are good quality; it's all a matter of taste. Keep in mind that price is not always a good indication of quality.

Heat affects the flavor of cold-pressed extra-virgin olive oil, so it doesn't make sense to cook with these oils. Save them for cold dishes like salads and for drizzling onto cooked food before serving. For cooking, use a mild, virgin olive oil. Store olive oil in a cool dark place for up to 6 months or in the refrigerator for up to 1 year.

pad thai

SERVES 4 / Pad Thai is one of the most famous stir-fry dishes. As the name implies, it originated in Thailand. It's a fascinating mix of flavors and textures—crunchy bean sprouts and nuts set off by soft noodles.

8 ounces dry rice noodles or linguine

¼ cup fresh lime juice

2 tablespoons tamari or soy sauce

2 tablespoons light brown sugar

1 to 2 teaspoons hot chile sauce

1 tablespoon water

1 tablespoon peanut oil

3 cloves garlic, minced

1 to 2 teaspoons peeled, minced fresh ginger

1 medium carrot, peeled and cut into narrow strips

1 bunch green onions (white and light green parts), sliced

1½ cups mung bean sprouts

¼ cup chopped fresh cilantro leaves

2 tablespoons chopped dry-roasted peanuts

1 lime, sliced (optional)

In a large bowl, soak the rice noodles in warm water to cover until they are limp and white, about 20 minutes.

In a small bowl, mix the lime juice, tamari, brown sugar, chile sauce, and water. Set aside.

In a wok or large, deep skillet, heat the oil over high heat. Add the garlic and ginger and stir-fry for 30 seconds. Add the carrot and green onions and stir-fry for 1 minute.

Add the lime juice mixture to the skillet. Drain the noodles and add to the wok, tossing them with tongs until they soften and curl, about 1 minute. Add the sprouts, cilantro, and peanuts. Divide the mixture among 4 serving plates and serve with lime slices, if desired.

chinese green beans

SERVES 6 / Green beans are quickly stir-fried and receive a zesty flavoring from ginger, garlic, sesame oil, and soy sauce. This recipe can also be made with blanched broccoli florets or asparagus.

½ teaspoon salt

1 pound green beans, ends trimmed

2 tablespoons tamari or soy sauce

2 tablespoons water

1 teaspoon cornstarch

1 teaspoon brown sugar

1 teaspoon dark (Asian) sesame oil

¼ teaspoon crushed red pepper flakes

1 tablespoon peanut oil

1 teaspoon minced garlic

1 teaspoon peeled, minced fresh ginger

Fill a large bowl with ice and water and set aside. Bring a large saucepan of water to a boil. Add the salt, and then drop in the beans and cook for 3 to 5 minutes. Drain the beans in a colander, and immediately plunge them into the ice water. Drain again, spread them out on paper towels, and pat them dry.

In a small bowl, mix the tamari, water, cornstarch, brown sugar, sesame oil, and red pepper flakes until the cornstarch is dissolved.

In a wok or large, heavy-bottomed skillet, heat the peanut oil over medium-high heat. Add the green beans and stir-fry for 3 minutes, or until the beans are very hot and start to char in spots. Add the garlic and ginger and stir-fry for 2 minutes. Pour in the tamari mixture. Toss the beans over the heat for 1 minute, until evenly coated and glazed. Serve hot.

steamed artichokes with herb vinaigrette

SERVES 4 / Steaming is a good way to cook artichokes because it locks in flavor and nutrients. Eating artichokes in this manner is a casual affair; there is no substitute for your fingers (see How to Eat an Artichoke on page 67).

4 medium artichokes
1 medium lemon, cut in half
½ teaspoon salt

herb vinaigrette
2 tablespoons white wine vinegar
1 tablespoon fresh lemon juice
½ cup olive oil
2 tablespoons minced fresh herbs, such as tarragon, basil, and dill
Salt and freshly ground pepper

Cut off the stem of each artichoke so it stands upright. Next, cut off the top fourth of the artichoke. Break off and discard the small leaves from the bottom. Snip off the thorny leaf tips. Rub the cuts with lemon juice to prevent discoloration.

Pour 1 inch of water into a large pot and bring to a boil. Place the trimmed artichokes, stem-ends up, in a steamer basket and carefully set the basket in the pot. Sprinkle with the ½ teaspoon salt. Cover and steam over medium-high heat until tender, about 40 minutes, or until the outer leaves pull away from the base without much effort.

Meanwhile, make the vinaigrette: In a small bowl, whisk together the vinegar, lemon juice, and oil until well blended. Stir in the herbs and salt and pepper to taste.

Remove the artichokes with a slotted spoon. Drain them upside down in a colander.

To serve, place each artichoke on a serving plate with a small bowl of the vinaigrette.

spicy vegetable sauté

SERVES 4 / An unusual combination of cauliflower, potatoes, spinach, and carrots comes together nicely in this simple yet spicy dish. It's seasoned with a blend of Indian spices, including coriander, turmeric, and cumin.

1 tablespoon butter

1 tablespoon olive oil

1 medium red onion, thinly sliced

1 small head cauliflower, quartered and thinly sliced, including stem

1 clove garlic, minced

½ teaspoon ground turmeric

1 teaspoon ground cumin

1 teaspoon ground coriander

6 small red potatoes, cubed and steamed

1 bunch spinach (about 1 pound), stemmed

1 small carrot, peeled and grated

2 tablespoons fresh lemon juice

Salt and freshly ground pepper

In a large skillet, heat the butter and oil over medium-high heat. Add the onion and cook, stirring often, until beginning to brown, about 5 minutes.

Add the cauliflower and cook, stirring often, until it begins to brown in a few places. Add the garlic, spices, and potatoes. Reduce the heat and cook, stirring occasionally, until heated through, about 5 minutes.

Add the spinach and carrot. Cover and cook until the spinach is wilted, about 1 minute. Stir in the lemon juice. Season with salt and pepper to taste and serve hot.

braised fennel

SERVES 4 TO 6 / Whisking a little Dijon mustard into the braising liquid just before serving thickens it and adds a boost of flavor.

4 medium fennel bulbs
1 tablespoon olive oil
2 leeks (white and light green parts), rinsed well and sliced
¼ cup finely chopped shallots
½ cup dry white wine
1½ cups clear vegetable stock
Salt and freshly ground pepper
2 teaspoons Dijon mustard

Trim the stalks from the fennel bulbs, reserving the fronds. Trim the bottoms of the bulbs and tough outer layers. Cut each bulb lengthwise into 8 wedges.

In a Dutch oven or large, deep skillet, heat the oil over medium heat. Add the leeks and shallots and cook, stirring often, until softened, about 5 minutes. Add the wine. Increase the heat to medium-high and simmer for 2 minutes. Add the fennel wedges, stock, and salt and pepper to taste. Bring to a simmer. Reduce the heat to low, cover, and simmer until the fennel is tender, 20 to 25 minutes.

With a slotted spoon, transfer the fennel to a plate. Add the mustard to the liquid in the pan and cook, whisking often, until the mixture is blended and slightly thickened. Return the fennel to the pan, spooning the liquid over the wedges. Cook just until the fennel is heated through. Garnish with chopped fennel fronds before serving.

mushroom bisque

SERVES 4 TO 6 / Every vegetarian cook should have at least one good mushroom soup recipe in his or her repertoire. This one is a low-fat, purée-style bisque that can be as elegant or simple as you want. Like most soups, it can be made ahead of time. You may need to thin the soup with additional stock or water and to re-season it at serving time.

1 tablespoon olive oil

1½ pounds cremini mushrooms, cleaned, trimmed, and chopped

4 ounces fresh shiitake mushrooms, cleaned, stems removed, and sliced

½ cup minced shallots

½ cup dry sherry

6 cups homemade brown vegetable stock (facing page)

1 teaspoon chopped fresh thyme leaves

½ teaspoon salt

½ teaspoon freshly ground pepper

1 tablespoon Dijon mustard

1 cup plain low-fat yogurt

Sliced green onion tops for garnish

In a large pot, heat the oil over medium heat. Add the mushrooms and shallots and cook, stirring often, until the mushrooms begin to soften, about 5 minutes. Add the sherry, stock, thyme, salt, and pepper. Bring the mixture to a boil. Reduce the heat to medium-low and simmer, stirring occasionally, for 15 minutes. Whisk in the mustard until well blended.

Purée the soup until smooth, using an immersion blender or food processor. Return the soup to the pot, if necessary, and stir in the yogurt until well blended. Ladle the soup into serving bowls and garnish with sliced green onion.

brown vegetable stock

MAKES 6 CUPS / Roasting the vegetables intensifies the flavor of this basic vegetable stock.

4 medium carrots, peeled and cut into ½-inch-thick slices
2 medium parsnips, cut into ½-inch-thick slices
1 large onion, cut into 1-inch pieces
1 large leek (white part only), well rinsed and cut into ½-inch pieces
1 small celery root, peeled and cut into ½-inch pieces
4 cloves garlic, peeled
Olive oil for coating
8 cups water
1 teaspoon salt
¼ teaspoon peppercorns
10 parsley stems
6 sprigs fresh thyme
2 bay leaves

Preheat the oven to 425°F. In a large bowl, combine the carrots, parsnips, onion, leek, celery root, and garlic and coat lightly with olive oil. Transfer the vegetables to a shallow roasting pan large enough to hold the vegetables in a single layer. Roast the vegetables, stirring and turning them with a spatula every 10 minutes, until they are tender and lightly colored, about 40 minutes.

Transfer the roasted vegetables to a large pot. Add the water, salt, peppercorns, parsley, thyme, and bay leaves. Bring the mixture to a boil. Skim off any foam that rises to the top. Reduce the heat and simmer, partially covered, until the stock is well flavored, 1 to 1½ hours. Add more water as necessary to keep the vegetables covered, and skim as necessary.

Strain the stock through a fine sieve set over a large bowl, pressing on the vegetables with the back of a spoon to extract as much liquid as possible. Discard the solids. Cool the stock to room temperature, then transfer to airtight containers and refrigerate for up to 5 days or freeze for up to 6 months.

mixed greens with lemon-mint vinaigrette

SERVES 4 / Slightly tart, this vinaigrette also suits cucumber, spinach, and Belgian endive.

lemon-mint vinaigrette
1 small clove garlic, minced
2 tablespoons fresh lemon juice
½ teaspoon grated lemon zest
5 tablespoons extra-virgin olive oil
1 tablespoon chopped green onion (white and light green parts)
1 tablespoon chopped fresh mint leaves
Salt and freshly ground pepper

12 ounces mixed greens (about 8 cups)
12 kalamata olives, pitted and halved
8 yellow or red cherry or teardrop tomatoes

TO MAKE THE VINAIGRETTE: In a small bowl, whisk together the garlic, lemon juice, and lemon zest. Slowly whisk in the oil until well blended. Stir in the green onion, mint, and salt and pepper to taste.

TO ASSEMBLE THE SALAD: In a large bowl, mix the greens, olives, and tomatoes. Add the vinaigrette and toss to coat. Transfer to serving dishes.

An unprecedented variety of fresh vegetables is available to the U.S. consumer today. Improved methods of transportation and advanced technology provide us with vegetables that are in better condition than ever before. Supermarkets now offer items including unusual greens and lettuces, fresh wild mushrooms, and regional specialties such as okra, chile peppers, and tomatillos. In addition, local farmers' markets are springing up across the country, offering us a bounty of seasonal and, many times, organic produce.

With their ever-increasing variety, availability, and healthful appeal, vegetables have taken on a new importance in our diets. Naturally low in fat and high in vitamins and fiber, they offer today's nutrition-conscious consumers endless options.

vegetables

artichokes

There is no need to be intimidated by artichokes. According to classic culinary technique books, preparing and cooking them can be a laborious task. But I've found that all those steps aren't absolutely necessary and that whole artichokes can be relatively easy to prepare. Steaming is an easy way to cook any size artichoke, from the whole globes to babies and trimmed hearts.

best way to cook artichokes

to prepare whole artichokes for steaming: First clean them by soaking them in cool water for 5 to 10 minutes. Cut off the stem of each artichoke with a chef's knife. Break off and discard the small leaves from the bottom. Snip off the thorny leaf tips. Next, cut off the top quarter of the artichoke.

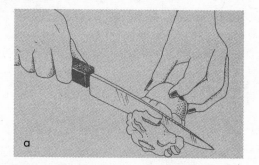

to prepare artichoke hearts for steaming: First cut off the stem end and top quarter of the artichoke. Bend back and snap off the outer leaves, leaving the thick bottom portion attached to the base. Continue snapping off the leaves until you reach the inner cone of pale purple-tipped leaves.

With a small knife, slice off the cone at its base (a). Smooth the outer surface of the artichoke heart by shaving it with a paring knife (b). You can halve the raw heart to remove the inedible center, known as the choke, or you can cook it first, then halve it and remove the choke. In either case, using a spoon, scrape away the fuzzy choke (c). This step is not necessary if you're using baby artichokes.

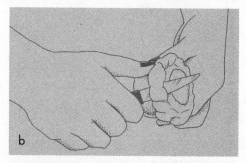

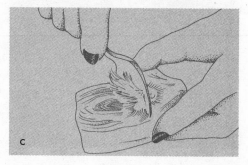

to steam: Pour 1 inch of water into a large pot and bring to a boil. Place trimmed artichokes, stem-ends up, or artichoke hearts in a steamer basket and carefully set the basket in the pot. Sprinkle with ½ teaspoon salt. Cover and steam over medium-high heat until tender, about 40 minutes for large whole artichokes, about 25 minutes for baby artichokes, about 30 minutes for large hearts, and about 15 minutes for baby hearts. Whole artichokes are cooked when the outer leaves pull away from the base without much effort. Artichoke hearts are done when a toothpick or skewer inserted into the stem end goes in easily. Remove the artichokes from the pot with tongs and serve.

KITCHEN NOTES

:: Look for artichokes with a deep green color that are heavy for their size and have compact leaves. The leaves should "squeak" when pressed together.

:: Store unwashed artichokes in a perforated or loosely closed plastic bag in the refrigerator for up to 4 days.

:: A steaming apparatus, such as a collapsible basket or bamboo rack, is helpful but not necessary. You can also use the stems and artichoke trimmings as a rack.

eating an artichoke

To eat an artichoke, begin by snapping off an outer leaf with your fingers. If there is a sauce, dip the leaf's base into it, and then, holding the tip of the leaf, bite down on the fleshy part at the base and draw it through your teeth. When all the leaves have been removed, you'll find a tightly closed cone of purple-tipped, pale green leaves. Remove these thin leaves by pulling the cone away with a sharp twist of your wrist (do not eat them). Using a spoon, scoop out and discard the fuzzy core called the choke. The remaining heart can be eaten with a fork and knife.

asparagus

If you attended culinary school, you most likely learned the French way to cook asparagus: Snap off the ends, peel the spears, tie them into bundles with kitchen twine, and cook them in boiling salted water until tender. Although this is the way I was taught, over the years I've stopped peeling and bundling, and I have discovered that steaming is easier, producing spears with good color, texture, and taste.

best way to cook asparagus

Asparagus stems will snap off in just the right spot if you hold them correctly. Hold the asparagus about halfway down the stalk; with the other hand, hold the cut end between the thumb and index finger, about an inch or so up the stalk. Bend the stalk until it snaps. Discard the stem ends, or save them for a pot of asparagus soup.

In a large pot, bring 1 inch of water to a boil. Put the asparagus in a steamer basket and carefully place the basket in the pot. Cover and steam over medium-high heat until the asparagus spears bend slightly when picked up, 4 to 5 minutes for asparagus under $\frac{1}{2}$ inch in diameter, 5 to 6 minutes for thicker spears.

Drain and serve the asparagus right away. If you won't be serving the asparagus right away, plunge the spears immediately into ice water to stop the cooking process. (You can cover the cooled, drained asparagus and refrigerate it overnight.)

to peel or not to peel?

The question of whether to peel asparagus or not really comes down to personal preference. Some cooks believe that peeled spears are less flavorful than unpeeled, while others claim that peeled asparagus has a more tender, delicate flavor. I've concluded that asparagus is worth peeling only when it is large and fibrous, or when you want an especially elegant presentation.

To peel asparagus, cut the stalks to uniform lengths. Hold the tip of a stalk in your hand and, using a swivel-blade peeler, lightly peel down the length of each stalk.

white vs. green

Very popular in Europe, white asparagus comes from the same plant as the green variety, but it is grown under mounded dirt without exposure to sunlight. Compared to growing green asparagus, the cultivation of these slender white stalks is slower and more arduous, requiring 20 to 25 percent more labor, resulting in a higher price tag. The white variety also tends to be stringier and to have a slightly more bitter taste.

KITCHEN NOTES

:: Regardless of whether the spears are thick or thin, look for ones with a vibrant green color and tightly braided tips. The stalks should feel brittle enough to snap between your fingers.

:: To store asparagus, cut off the stale ends and stand the stalks in about 1 inch of cool water. Refrigerate, uncovered, for up to 2 days.

beets

We've become so accustomed to eating canned beets in America that many of us never try fresh beets at all. That's a shame, because fresh beets are infinitely better, with a distinctive sweet, pungent flavor and crisp texture that's lost in the canning process. This vibrant-colored vegetable is more versatile than you might think. You can shred them and add them to salads; slice them warm, toss with butter and serve as a side dish; or marinate them to serve as part of an antipasto plate. Puréed roasted beets make a great dish. And of course, beets are a time-honored basis for soups, included ruby-hued borschts both hot and cold.

Although there are many ways to prepare beets, I've found that roasting is the best all-purpose method. There's almost no preparation involved, and roasting concentrates the flavors and juices and gives the beets a firm, creamy texture.

best way to cook beets

Trim all but the last inch of the stems from the beets. Wash the beets well and trim any roots. Pat the beets dry and wrap them in foil. Roast them in a 400°F oven until tender when tested with a skewer and thin knife, about 1 hour for medium-sized beets. Open the foil and let the beets cool slightly. Use paper towels to hold the warm beets and rub them gently to remove the skins.

beyond red

Although beets used to be thought of as only red, they now come in a variety of colors, shapes, and sizes. Probably the most popular of these new beets is the Chioggia (key-OH-ja), also know as the bull's-eye or candy-stripe beet because of the way its flesh has alternating bands of red and white. There is also the sunny golden beet. It has a milder flavor than most red beets, and the color doesn't bleed the way the red varieties do. Beyond the regular red beets, there are the really large Mangle and Lutz varieties, with stems that are about 2 feet long and vegetables that are wonderfully juicy, and baby beets such as Pronto and Kleine Bol.

:: If you can, purchase beets with the greens attached. Buying them this way will ensure that they are fresh, since the greens have a limited shelf life. There is also the added benefit of the greens themselves, which can be cooked like spinach or chard.

:: Cut off the leaves, keeping a 2-inch portion attached to the root to prevent the juices from bleeding. Store the leaves in a plastic bag in the refrigerator for up to 2 days. Trimmed raw beets can be stored for up to 10 days in the refrigerator.

:: Wash beets gently. Don't scrub them vigorously or you may break the skin. Beets are easier to peel after cooking, when the skins will slip off easily.

:: Red beet juice stains whatever it touches. When combining beets with other foods, keep the beets separate until the last minute, then gently toss them in.

broccoli

It's no wonder that broccoli is one of the most popular vegetables in this country. A good-quality selection is available year-round, and it ships so well that it's often one of the freshest-looking vegetables in the supermarket produce section. Beyond that, it's easy to cook, lends itself to many kinds of preparations, and rates at the top of the nutrient density chart, containing a rich supply of vitamins C and A, potassium, folate, iron, trace minerals, and cancer-fighting phytochemicals called indoles.

best way to cook broccoli

It's best to treat broccoli like a two-part vegetable, preparing the stalks and florets differently. Cut the florets from the stalks, leaving about 2 inches of the stalks attached. Separate the florets into smaller sections, if desired. Using a vegetable peeler, remove the fibrous skin from the stalks. You can cut the stalks in a variety of ways, slicing, chopping, and even shredding them. In large, wide saucepan, bring about 1½ inches of water to a boil. Add the broccoli stalks, then put the florets on top of the stalks so they are not sitting in the water. Cover, reduce the heat to medium, and cook until both the stalks and florets are tender, about 5 minutes. Drain and serve.

KITCHEN NOTES

∷ Select broccoli with tightly closed flowers that have no signs of yellowing. Avoid heads with wilted leaves or large, woody stems.

∷ Avoid buying precut florets and crowns, where freshness and nutrients may be lost.

∷ Broccoli needs air circulation; too much moisture will cause decay. Keep it in a perforated or loosely sealed plastic bag in the refrigerator for up to 1 week.

cabbage

One of the oldest vegetables cultivated by humans, cabbage grows well in almost any climate and is enjoyed all over the world. There are basically three kinds of heading cabbage—green, red, and savoy. The green and red varieties have tightly compacted round heads, while the crinkly leaves of the savoy cabbage are loosely furled.

best way to shred cabbage

Cabbage is best known for its use in coleslaw. To prepare cabbage for this preparation or to use it raw in salads, cut the head in half through the core. With a sharp knife, cut down on both sides of the V-shaped cored and remove it. Place the halves, cut-sides down, on a cutting board. Cut them in half lengthwise, then cut crosswise into thin slices.

best way to cook cabbage

Steaming wedges is a simple yet delicious way to prepare all types of cabbage. Discard any wilted or damaged outer leaves from the cabbage. Cut the head in half lengthwise, then cut each half into wedges, including part of the core.

Bring at least 1 inch of water to a boil in the base of a steamer. Arrange the cabbage wedges in a single layer in the steamer basket. Cover the pot tightly and steam until the cabbage is tender, 5 to 8 minutes. Transfer the wedges to a cutting board and cut away the core from each piece. Transfer the cabbage wedges to serving plates.

chinese cabbage

Several types of Chinese cabbage are available in supermarkets today, including bok choy and napa. Bok choy comes in an elongated head with thick white stalks and pale green, rounded leaves with white veins. It can range in size from 8 to 18 inches long; as a rule, the smaller types tend to be more tender. To prepare bok choy, trim about ½ inch from the base and discard any wilted or damaged leaves. Cut the bok choy into small pieces. It's good quickly sautéed or stir-fried and can be used raw in salads.

Napa cabbage comes in an elongated, tightly packed head with white stems and large, crinkled, pale green leaves. It has a mild flavor and is often used raw in salads and for stir-fries. To prepare, trim away any brown or wilted leaves.

KITCHEN NOTES

:: Choose cabbage heads that feel heavy for their size, with firm, fresh-looking leaves.

:: Savoy cabbage is best for stuffing and rolling because the leaves are more pliable.

cauliflower

It's puzzling that most of the cauliflower in the United States is sold during the cool-weather months, because good-quality cauliflower is available year-round. In fact, there are many great ways to serve it during the summer. The secret, whenever you buy it, is to purchase it fresh, when its flavor is mild and delicate. Old cauliflower can have an assertive, cabbagy flavor. I'd lay odds that those who consider it too strong haven't tasted it properly cooked and truly fresh.

best way to cook cauliflower

to cook cauliflower whole: Cut off the large outer leaves (small ones need not be removed). Cut off the heavy stem base. Cut a large, conical piece from the remaining stem to hollow it out so it will cook evenly. Set the cauliflower stem-end down in a heavy pot containing ¾ inch of boiling salted water. Cover tightly and cook over medium heat until tender, about 10 minutes.

to cook florets: Turn the cauliflower stem-end up and cut off the heavy base. Slice the large branches from the main stem (peel and slice this stem to cook with the florets). Cut the branches into small, bite-sized pieces. Put the florets, stems, and branches in a steamer basket set over simmering water. Cover tightly and cook until tender, about 7 minutes.

KITCHEN NOTES

:: When buying cauliflower, look for a mass of tightly packed florets nestled in a halo of crisp, leafy greens. It should feel heavy for its size and have a pleasant smell. Avoid cauliflower with wilted greens or a surface marred by brown speckles.

:: As hardy as it looks, cauliflower is actually quite delicate and can develop a strong, cabbagy taste and smell if stored too long. It will, however, keep, refrigerated and unwashed, for 2 days. Cauliflower bruises easily and needs oxygen, so wrap it in perforated plastic. Store wrapped heads stem-end up to prevent condensation on the curd, which decays and discolors quickly.

:: Above all, be careful not to overcook cauliflower, as it will quickly turn mushy.

two in one?

Green cauliflower, or broccoflower, is not a cross between cauliflower and broccoli, as the name would lead you to believe. Rather, it is just a green variety of cauliflower, bred from seeds that originated in Italy.

celery root

The celery root has never inspired love at first sight. Rough skinned, gnarled, and knotty, it wears an ugly outer cloak that belies its interior majesty. Beneath the rough exterior lies a creamy, white vegetable with a delicious celery-parsley flavor that can be enjoyed in many ways. And with just a few calories, the celery root has almost as much protein as potatoes and 5 times the amount of fiber and calcium.

Also known as celeriac, celery root happily accepts a variety of treatments. The raw vegetable can be julienned and used in salads or tossed with the French classic sauce rémoulade, which is a blend of Dijon mustard, mayonnaise, and sometimes herbs and capers. When diced, celery root is a flavorful ingredient for sautés and stews, and when puréed it makes a wonderful soup and can add new interest to mashed potatoes.

best way to cook celery root

Scrub the vegetable with a brush. Cut off the roots at the bottom and the stalks at the top so you can set it flat. Quarter it, and, using a sharp paring knife, peel off the skin. Although many cookbooks warn that peeled celery root darkens and must be plunged into a bowl of water with a little lemon juice, I find this unnecessary if you are going to use the vegetable right away.

KITCHEN NOTES

:: Select small to medium celery roots that are firm and seem heavy for their size. Big, lighter ones may have a spongy, dry texture. The bumps and crevices on their surface and their unruly roots are normal. Look for ones with the smoothest skin because they will be easier to peel.

:: To store, remove the stalks and roots of the celery root but do not peel it. Wrap in plastic and refrigerate for up to 2 weeks.

corn on the cob

All of the corn grown for human consumption in the United States is classified as sweet (other common types are field—used for flour, feed, and syrup—and popcorn, used for just that). At the market, there are three types of sweet corn that dominate, and they are distinguished by the amount of sugar they contain. In ascending order of sweetness, there is standard, sugar-enhanced, and super-sweet. All three varieties offer white, yellow, and bicolored kernels, but it is the type of corn rather than the color that determines its sweetness. There is considerable debate as to whether our love of sweetness has gone too far. Some think that corn has become too sweet and sugary, losing that old-fashioned "corny" flavor. But supersweet corn is the best seller nationwide.

best way to cook corn on the cob

When cooking corn, it's important to remember that heat speeds the conversion of sugar to starch, so the longer you cook corn, the tougher and starchier it's going to be.

Remove the husks and silks from the corn. Bring a large pot of water to a boil. When the water is boiling, add the corn and begin timing. (Do not add salt, which toughens the skins of the kernels.) The freshest and sweetest varieties will need the shortest cooking time, about 2 minutes. Older and more mature corn may need 6 to 8 minutes. Drain and serve with butter, salt, and pepper to taste.

NOTE: *Some cooks replace part of the corn cooking water with milk, but I've found that this mixture seemed to mask the flavor of the corn. Other cooks add a pinch of sugar to the water, which is fine for standard corn but unnecessary with the new, sweeter varieties on the market.*

best way to grill corn on the cob

Prepare a charcoal grill until the coals are medium-hot (when you can hold your hand 5 inches above the grill surface for only 3 seconds), or preheat a gas grill to medium-high. For standard and sugar-enhanced corn, peel back the husks but leave them attached at the base. Discard the tough outer layer and remove the silk. Replace the inner husks to completely cover the kernels. Tear off a piece of the husk about 1 inch wide and tie the husks together at the tip to keep them firmly closed. If you are using supersweet corn, discard the husks and silks and wrap each ear in foil.

Grill the corn, turning the ears occasionally, for 10 to 20 minutes. The cooking time will depend on the tenderness of the corn and the heat of the grill. As the corn grills, the husks will become charred and may split apart, exposing some kernels. Test by piercing a kernel with the tip of a paring knife; it should go in easily but still have some "pop" to it. Typically, corn on the cob takes between 6 and 8 minutes to grill.

Transfer the grilled corn to a platter and remove and discard the charred husks. Season with butter, salt, and pepper to taste, and serve right away.

To roast the corn, place it in a preheated 450°F oven and roast for 6 to 8 minutes with the husks on, or for 3 to 5 minutes husked.

NOTE: *Some cooks suggest soaking the husks in water before grilling. I've found that this technique ends up steaming the corn on the grill and you lose some of the wonderful smoky, grilled flavor.*

best way to remove corn kernels

Stand an uncooked ear of corn on its end in a shallow bowl and slice the kernels off with a sharp, thin-bladed knife. This technique produces whole kernels that are good to add to salads and salsas. If you want to use the corn kernels for soups, fritters, or puddings, you can add another step to the process. After cutting the kernels off, reverse the knife and, using the dull side, press it down the length of the ear to push out the rest of the corn and its milk.

pick the best

When choosing corn, whatever the variety, the best is simply the freshest. Ask the grower when it was picked or, if that's not possible, just use your nose. Fresh corn will smell fresh.

• Look for ears that are tightly closed, with bright green husks.

• The ends of the corn silk should be golden brown, not pale, an indication that the corn was picked too early.

• The stem end of the corn should be pale and moist, not woody.

• Don't peel back the husk. If you do, the corn will dry out. Instead, feel through the husk for plump, resilient kernels.

• Store corn in the refrigerator in an airtight bag, and husk it just before cooking. Standard and sugar-enhanced are best eaten within a day. The supersweets can be kept longer because they have 2 to 3 times more sugar and will retain much of their sweetness for up to 48 hours.

eggplant

Although the Purple Globe variety is the most prominent, an assortment of eggplants can be found at ethnic groceries, farmers' markets, and well-stocked supermarkets. You can find eggplants with names like Neon, which has magenta skin, and Easter Egg, which is a small, creamy white cylinder. Of the two most common long eggplants, the Chinese is a lighter shade of purple than its Japanese cousin. Italian eggplants are small, soft, and purple. Southeast Asian eggplants come in a wide variety of colors and sizes, ranging from tiny green ones that grow in clusters to perfectly round ivory and yellow varieties.

best way to prepare eggplant

Many cooks salt sliced eggplant and let it sit for an hour or so to reduce its bitterness. However, this step can be skipped in most cases because bitterness is not an inherent quality in eggplant. A bitter eggplant is overripe. The exception is when you are preparing eggplants for frying, in which case you may want to salt them to draw out their excess moisture before cooking. Rinse off the salt and pat dry before using.

Whether you peel an eggplant or not is up to you, as the skin is perfectly edible. Keep in mind, though, that overripeness and long storage do make the skin tough, and cooking will not soften it. In these cases, it is a good idea to remove the skin with a swivel-blade peeler.

KITCHEN NOTES

:: When buying any kind of eggplant, look for firm, taut, shiny skin, with no shriveled or soft areas, and a bright green cap. The eggplant should feel heavy, and the flesh should bounce back slightly when gently pressed.

:: If not stored properly, eggplant will quickly develop a spongy flesh and tough skin. To avoid this, store whole eggplant unwrapped in the refrigerator and use within 3 days.

:: When you cut open an eggplant, the seeds should be barely visible. If there are a great number of dark seeds, the eggplant is overripe.

fennel

Versatile and well loved by the Italians, fennel is prized for its crisp, juicy texture and almost sweet flavor, reminiscent of licorice. Every part of the vegetable can be used in cooking. Its feathery greens, which resemble sprigs of fresh dill, are frequently used as fresh herbs, and the tender white bulb is served both raw and cooked in a variety of ways. (Fennel seed, used as a spice, comes from another variety of fennel.) It's high in vitamin A and is an excellent source of potassium and calcium.

best way to cook fennel

Rinse fennel under cold running water and pat it dry. Peel off any outer stalks that are discolored, bruised, or dry. Cut the stalks off flat across the top of the bulbous part, then cut that part in half to rinse. Trim the root end and then slice the bulb according to your recipe. The feathery fronds at the top can be chopped fine for garnishes and flavorings.

KITCHEN NOTES

:: Select fennel bulbs with firm white bases and fresh-looking fronds. Avoid fennel that feels spongy or looks shriveled. Press gently at the root end of the bulb; it should not feel soft.

:: For storing, remove the fronds, which dry out quickly. The bulb can be covered loosely with plastic wrap and refrigerated for up to 4 days.

garlic

Preparing garlic is an essential step in many recipes, and one that few home cooks know how to do properly. However, all you need to know are a few simple techniques and you will have mastered this culinary task.

best way to peel and mince garlic

Put a garlic clove on a cutting board. Hold the flat side of a chef's knife over it and lightly pound to loosen skin. Pull off the skin and trim the root end.

to chop garlic: Use a sharp paring knife to slice it lengthwise, but do not cut through the root end (d). Then slice crosswise to chop the garlic into small pieces (e). Gather the chopped garlic into a pile with the blade of a chef's knife and chop finely. With the palm of one hand, hold the tip of the knife on the cutting surface and grasp the handle with other hand. Rock the knife up and down rapidly, swiveling the blade across the pile of garlic.

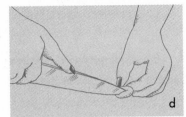

to make garlic paste: Position the flat side of a chef's knife over the garlic and hit the blade vigorously with heel of your hand to crush the clove (f). Sprinkle the garlic with a little coarse salt, then crush the garlic with the side of a chef's knife, a small amount at a time, leaning on the side of the knife with your fingers or the heel of your hand, until a paste forms (g).

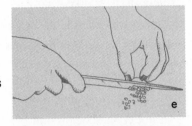

KITCHEN NOTES

:: When buying garlic, look for firm, tightly closed heads.

:: If garlic has sprouted, you can still use it in a pinch. Just remove the green shoots.

:: The way you prepare garlic affects the intensity of its flavor in a dish. For example, if you crush the garlic into a paste, the flavor will be more pronounced. If you want a subtler flavor, try slicing or coarsely chopping the clove.

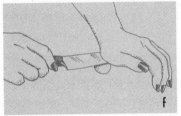

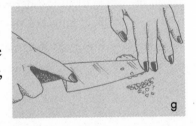

roasting garlic

Roasted garlic can be spread onto slices of crusty bread or used as a flavoring for dressing and sauces. To roast garlic, peel away as much of the papery skin from a head of garlic as possible. When it becomes difficult to remove the skin, you have removed enough. Next, use a sharp knife to slice off about ½ inch from the tip of the garlic head, so that the cloves are exposed. Place the head in an 8-inch square of aluminum foil. Drizzle with ½ teaspoon of olive oil. Wrap the head loosely in the foil and put it in a small baking dish. Roast it at 450°F until the garlic is very soft, about 30 minutes. Let the packet cool, then remove the foil. Squeeze out the softened garlic by hand or with the edge of a chef's knife, starting from the root end and working toward the tip.

green beans

Once considered the most dependable frozen vegetable, the green bean is now treated with the same reverence as other fresh vegetables. And today you may find several beans beyond the stringed variety at well-stocked supermarkets and farmers' markets, like yellow wax, flat Romanos, very thin beans known in French as *haricots verts*, and Chinese yard-long beans that do live up to their name and come in 3-foot-long pods. Collectively, these beans are known as snap beans.

best way to cook green beans

Blanching ensures maximum flavor and color; this technique works well for both hot cooked beans and beans that will be served cold in salads or as crudités. Trim the stem ends from the green beans, leaving the pointed ends intact, if desired. Most fresh beans today do not require stringing, as the fibrous string has been bred out of them. Bring a large saucepan of water to a boil. (You will need about 3 quarts of water for 1 pound of beans.) Add ½ teaspoon salt, and then drop in the beans and cook until tender but still crisp, 3 to 5 minutes. Drain the beans in a colander and serve hot.

If you will be using the beans in a salad, blanch them as directed. Fill a large bowl with ice and water and set aside. Immediately plunge the beans into the ice water. Drain again, spread them out on paper towels, and pat them dry.

KITCHEN NOTES

:: Look for green beans that have a bright green color rather than faded or yellowish ones. Fresh-picked beans should be a little fuzzy and should make a "snap" sound when broken in half.

:: Store unwashed beans in a loosely closed plastic bag in the refrigerator for up to 3 days.

:: Green beans lose their bright green color when combined with an acidic ingredient such as lemon juice or vinegar.

greens for cooking

Leafy greens of all types are surprisingly simple to cook, add great flavor and
texture to meals, and, with one or two exceptions, are easy on the budget.
Broadly speaking, greens can be divided into two categories: tender and hardy.
Tender greens—spinach, chard, and beet greens—have a mild flavor and cook
quickly. Tougher greens such as kale, mustard greens, collards, and turnip
greens, have a stronger flavor and require extra cooking to tenderize.

best way to cook greens

Remove any leaves that are yellow or wilted, and remove any tough, fibrous
stems. All greens grow close to the ground, so they can harbor dirt and sand.
For very sandy greens, plunge them into a sink filled with cold water, then
swish gently to dislodge dirt. Lift the greens from the water, so the grit remains
in the bottom. Drain the sink, add more water, and repeat as needed until the
water is clear. Leave the washed greens damp (this liquid is especially needed
to create steam if you are wilting greens in a covered pan).

For tender greens, place the green, damp from washing, in a heated
deep skillet. Cover and cook over medium-high heat, stirring occasionally, until
the greens are wilted but are still bright green, about 5 minutes. Uncover and
season to taste with salt and pepper. Cook over high heat until the liquid evaporates, about 2 minutes more. Serve right away, with lemon wedges, if desired.

Hardy greens are too tough to be simply wilted; they require extra
treatment. Bring a pot of water to a boil. Add the greens and boil for 1 to
2 minutes. Drain. In a large, deep skillet, heat a little olive oil or butter. Add
the greens and sauté until tender, about 5 minutes.

KITCHEN NOTES

:: Look for crisp, fresh-looking leaves with a good bright green (or red) color.
Yellow or brown is a sign of age. Avoid greens with wilted, decayed, or
blemished leaves. The stems should look sturdy and freshly cut.

:: Keep greens in a plastic bag in the refrigerator crisper. It's fine if they're damp
but they shouldn't be wet, because wetness encourages rotting. Don't wash
the greens until you are ready to use them. Tender greens will keep for up to
2 days, tougher greens for up to 4 days.

greens glossary

beet greens: The red-veined leafy tops of beets, beet greens have a mild, slightly sweet, cabbage-like flavor. Buy them attached to beets (small beets have the most tender greens) or in bunches by themselves. Steam or sauté as a side dish, add to soups such as borscht and stews, or use in vegetable and grain dishes. They can replace spinach or chard in any recipe.

broccoli raab: This bitter, medium-sharp-flavored green has skinny stems, leafy greens, and small bud clusters. All parts are edible. Look for closed florets, without yellow flowering. It is excellent sautéed, braised, or stir-fried, or blanched and added to pasta sauces.

chard: Sometimes called Swiss chard, this is one of the mildest-flavored cooking greens, with a beet-sweet flavor. Chard has a thick center rib and large red or green leaves. The stalks have a delicate, celery-like taste, while the leaves have a spinach flavor. If the stalks are thick, remove them and cook for a little longer than the leaves. Sauté, steam, or braise as a side dish, or add to soups, main-dish pies, and stews. Try young chard in wilted salads. Chard can replace spinach in recipes.

collards: The big, leathery, deep-green leaves of collards have a strong cabbage taste that mellows to mild and slightly sweet if properly cooked. Be sure to cook them long enough to soften the stems, or they will be chewy and unpleasant. Choose young, thin-stemmed collards for the sweetest taste. Use as a vegetable side dish or add to soups and bean stews. Collard greens are available year-round, but are best in the late fall. Kale is a good substitute.

dandelion greens: One of the most nutritious greens around, dandelion greens are available cultivated as well as wild. The bright green, jagged-edged leaves have a tart-bitter taste, which benefits from preblanching. If you pick your own, do so in early spring before the flowers blossom, and be sure they have not been treated with pesticides. The smaller the leaves, the better. Use in wilted salads, pasta dishes, soups, quiches, and frittatas.

escarole: This slightly bitter green with a sweet edge has broad, wavy, tough-textured dark green leaves on the outside and pale green, tender leaves in the center. The leaves turn silky-soft when cooked. An Italian favorite, it is good in soups, pastas, rice dishes, and savory pies.

kale: This common salad-bar garnish is in fact as versatile as spinach. The thick, ruffled, blue-green leaves can be tough, but they turn tender and almost sweet when cooked. Look for young leaves with stems no thicker than a pencil for the best texture. Kale's mild cabbage taste is good in stir-fries, soups, stews, and main-dish pies.

mustard greens: Along with turnip greens, these are considered to have the sharpest bite. The large, bright green, frilly-edged leaves have a nippy, bitter mustard flavor. They are best cooked with other, milder greens or sweet vegetables to mellow the strong taste. Small, young leaves can be added to salads for a radishy note. For a less pungent flavor, substitute escarole, kale, or Swiss chard.

spinach: One of the mildest and most versatile of greens, spinach is good in everything from wilted salads to omelets, soups, and quiches. Choose young spinach with small leaves and thin stems over older spinach with big leaves and thick stems. Spinach can be cooked quickly in just the water clinging to its leaves from rinsing.

turnip greens: These light green leaves have a slightly prickly texture and a bitter, peppery taste. In the South, they're traditionally braised in stock for hours. Along with mustard greens, these are one of the most inexpensive choices. They can be used in any kale recipe.

greens for salad

Much of the magic of a good salad comes in the way the greens are handled. Salad greens, such as tender lettuces, arugula, baby spinach, and watercress, are delicate and should be handled with care. Rinsing the leaves under a running faucet may not remove all the dirt and ends up bruising the greens.

best way to prepare salad greens

Remove and discard any bruised or wilted leaves. Fill the sink two-thirds full with cold water. Separate the leaves from the lettuce head, if necessary, and place them in the sink without crowding. Gently swish the leaves around in the sink to loosen the grit and dirt. Allow the greens to sit in the water for 5 to 10 minutes, depending on how dirty or dehydrated they are. Place a large colander over a kitchen towel. Lift the greens from the sink to the colander and let drain for 5 minutes.

A salad spinner is good for drying sturdy greens like radicchio, endive, and oakleaf lettuce; just be sure not to overfill it. Spinners are too hard on more-fragile greens. Spread these out on kitchen towels or several layers of paper towels and pat dry. Any water clinging to the leaves will dilute the dressing and prevent it from coating them properly.

KITCHEN NOTES

:: If you won't be using the salad greens right away, roll them loosely in paper towels and place in a plastic bag. Store in the refrigerator for up to 3 days.

:: Buy young greens, which have the sweetest flavor and most tender leaves. Choose bunches with leaves that are small enough to serve whole—that way, they'll be reliably mild flavored and tender.

salad greens glossary

arugula (ah-ROO-guh-lah): A peppery, nutty-tasting green with smooth, tender leaves. Perks up all salads, including potato, grain, and pasta salads. Also try it cooked in pasta sauces, soups, and omelets. It lasts only a day or two; to keep it longer, store it with its roots in a glass of water, and cover the leaves with a plastic bag.

belgian endive (AHN-deev): The long, creamy-whitish leaves of this salad favorite are crisp and bittersweet. Look for compact, nearly white heads; green can indicate slight bitterness. It's also delicious braised in stock, baked, or brushed with olive oil and grilled.

curly endive (AHN-deev): The large, bunchy head has tough, sturdy, bitter-tasting dark green leaves. The inner leaves are tender and less pungent; try mixing them with milder greens in fresh salads. Also try chicory in wilted salads, pasta sauces, soups, and stews.

frisée (free-ZAY): The fine, lacy leaves are pale green, curly, and tender. Their flavor is slightly bitter and is best tempered with milder greens in salads. It's also delicious sautéed in olive oil and dressed in a mustard vinaigrette for a French-style wilted salad.

mâche: The narrow, dark-green leaves of the corn salad plant are used fresh in salads or steamed and served as a vegetable. Also called field salad and lamb's lettuce.

mesclun: A popular salad mixture of young, small greens, such as baby lettuces and miniature greens such as chard, endive, and arugula. It is expensive, but a treat. Use as soon as possible after purchase.

mizuna: A feathery Japanese mustard green with deeply serrated dark green leaves and thin, juicy white stalks. It adds a mild mustard flavor and crunchy texture to salads, stir-fries, and Asian soups.

radicchio: Italy's premier winter salad green, this gorgeous magenta-colored member of the chicory family has a distinctive bitter bite. It's not cheap, but a little goes a long way in mixed salads. It's also good braised, added to stir-fries and sautés, or brushed with olive oil and grilled.

sorrel: A favorite in France and England, sorrel has small, dark green leaves with a unique sour, almost lemony taste. Use it raw in mixed salads or cooked in soups, sauces, stews, and casseroles.

watercress: The spicy, peppery-tasting leaves and stems add crunch to salads and sandwiches. It's also good cooked in soups, stir-fries, and sauces. Store as you would arugula, and use soon after purchase.

leeks

While other members of the onion family generally have an assertive flavor, leeks are sweeter and milder tasting, melding well with other flavors and keeping a subtle profile. They can be used in everything from terrines to tarts. You can grill, braise, sauté, stew, or even deep-fry them to use as a garnish.

best way to clean leeks

Leeks are notorious for harboring lots of sand and dirt in their many layers, so they must be thoroughly rinsed before using. Cut off all but 1 inch of the dark green tops and trim off the root end of each leek. Remove any discolored outer layers. Then, starting at the top of the stalk, cut it in half lengthwise to within ½ inch of the base (h). Holding the stalk at the top, rinse under cold running water, fanning out the layers and rubbing the stalk with your fingers to make sure all traces of dirt are removed (i).

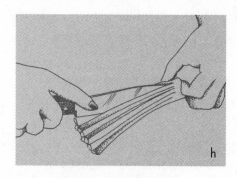 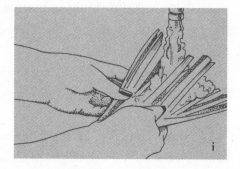

KITCHEN NOTES

:: Choose leeks with stalks that are flexible and no bigger than 2 inches across the base (large ones can be woody and dry). Look for ones that have long white bases and rich, dark green tops. Avoid any that have tinges of brown.

:: Untrimmed and unwashed, leeks will keep in the refrigerator, loosely wrapped in plastic, for up to 2 weeks. Freezing is not recommended.

mushrooms

Almost all types of mushrooms are very absorbent and will soak up any moisture that's available. Moisture causes mushrooms to decay rapidly (and makes them slimy), so the single most important aspect when cleaning them is not to soak them in water.

best way to clean mushrooms

Before you clean mushrooms, trim off the ends of the stems and any clumps of dirt that may be clinging. A soft-bristled brush or damp cloth can usually clean most of the dirt off of mushrooms. If the mushrooms are a little damp, use a clean cloth to dry them.

The one exception to using water is cleaning morels. They may need to be soaked and rinsed if they have lots of sand embedded in their pitted caps. Drain and let them dry on paper towels before cooking. Enoki and oyster mushrooms don't usually need cleaning.

keep the stems

....

Don't discard the stems of fresh mushrooms like shiitake and portobellos. Use them instead to flavor stocks, soups, and stews. Wrap them in a square of cheesecloth and add them to a simmering liquid. The stems will release their flavor in about 20 to 30 minutes; then the cheesecloth bundle can be discarded.

KITCHEN NOTES

:: Purchase mushrooms with firm caps and stems that have no bruises or spots.
:: Store immediately in the refrigerator in plastic or paper bags for up to 4 days. Do not wash mushrooms until ready to use, since moisture and warm air cause spoilage

Many people don't think of mushrooms as having a lot of nutritional value. But they are high in protein and many vitamins and minerals, particularly zinc. The shiitake mushroom, native to Japan and China, is gaining a lot of attention for its cholesterol-lowering and cancer-fighting effect. Scientists have found that the meaty-textured fungi contain a substance (eritadenine) that can lower cholesterol levels by blocking the absorption of cholesterol into the blood. This "magical" mushroom has also been shown to stimulate the immune system and improve circulation.

mushroom glossary

These mushrooms, many cultivated and some wild, can be found in produce sections today.

beech: A medium-sized tan- or ivory-capped mushroom with a firm, crunchy texture and sweet nutty flavor.

black trumpet: A trumpet-shaped mushroom that is considered a great delicacy. They have a charcoal gray exterior and can be purchased from some specialty produce markets.

blewit: A lavender-brown wild mushroom with a slightly fruity and nutty flavor. They are grown commercially in France.

chanterelle: These relatively expensive, trumpet-shaped mushrooms have a light, nutty flavor and a somewhat chewy texture. They are a golden orange color and range in size from 1 to 3 inches across. Chanterelles are available dried and canned year-round and can be found growing wild in parts of the Pacific Northwest and the East Coast. You may find some fresh chanterelles at your local market; look for those that are plump and spongy. They toughen when overcooked.

cremini: Related to white mushrooms but with an earthier flavor, cremini mushrooms are tan to rich brown in color. They are also called brown or Italian brown mushrooms.

enoki: Cultivated enoki are white, with little button caps and long, slender stems. Their flavor is mild and pleasant but not assertive. As with the white button mushroom, it is safe to use the cultivated variety raw in salads; however, the flavor is fuller when cooked.

hen-of-the-woods: A feathery brown mushroom with a dense, edible core; the stem is tender and firm with a mild flavor. Their size ranges from 1 inch across to as large as a basketball.

lobster: Lobster mushrooms grow wild in the Pacific Northwest. Their red-orange color is similar to that of a cooked lobster, hence their name. They have a crunchy texture and delicate flavor.

matsutake: A highly prized wild mushroom that is foraged in the Pacific Northwest. They have firm, creamy white caps with a pine-floral scent and flavor.

morel: The yellow morel, which also grows wild, is now cultivated and is considered to have the best flavor. The black morel is not yet cultivated. Morels have short, thick stems and long, honeycombed caps. Their texture is somewhat chewy, but the flavor is a cross between caraway and sweet peppers. Use the caps and well-trimmed stems.

oyster: This mushroom has a smoky gray cap with a silky texture and subtle, oyster-like flavor.

pompoms: These mushrooms resemble large powder puffs. Their texture is extremely firm and their flavor is somewhat like lobster when cooked. Use the entire mushroom.

porcini: Porcini mushrooms, popular in Italian cooking, are wild mushrooms also known as cèpes. Pale brown, with a smooth, firm, meaty texture and a hazelnut-like flavor, they are seldom available fresh in the United States but are often available dried in specialty markets. Dried porcini must be reconstituted for 20 minutes in water before use.

portobello: A close relative of the white button mushroom, the portobello is actually a giant cremini. A favorite for their meaty flavor and texture, these large mushrooms are tan or brown with relatively flat caps that reach 6 inches across. They can be grilled whole or sliced, and make a hearty main dish as burgers. If desired, scrape off the black gills inside the bottoms with a small paring knife.

shiitake: Used in traditional Japanese cuisine, shiitake mushrooms are rich and woodsy in flavor and have an umbrella-shaped brown cap. In most cases, you'll find them dried; these must be reconstituted for 20 minutes in hot water before use. The stems are edible only in small mushrooms. Larger ones have woody stems.

straw: Small oval mushrooms with a marbled pattern. They are usually available canned, and should be drained and rinsed before using. Fresh straw mushrooms should be beige and firm to the touch.

white button: The ordinary flavorful, inexpensive domestic mushroom that's available everywhere.

wood ear: Also called cloud ear or tree ear, these black mushrooms have crumpled and convoluted shapes. They are sold fresh or dried and are commonly used in Asian dishes. Soak the dried mushrooms in hot water for 3o minutes, and clean them carefully. Look for them in Asian markets or specialty food stores

onions

Perhaps no vegetable is used more in cooking than the onion. Its flavor varies from sweet to strong depending on the variety. Large sweet varieties, such as Walla Walla, Vidalia, and Maui onions, are best appreciated raw. Small pearl onions (about 1 inch in diameter) are good for pickling, creaming, and adding to stews. Larger onions may be white, yellow, red, or purple. Chives, leeks, green onions, and shallots are also members of the onion family.

best way to chop an onion

Chopping an onion is one of the most frequently used kitchen skills—and the most poorly executed—by home cooks. Use the same technique for chopping onions and shallots.

Using a paring knife, remove the stem end from the onion and peel away the skin and first underlying layer. Trim the root end, but leave the root intact. Using a chef's knife, cut the onion in half lengthwise from the stem to the root end. Place each half cut-side down on a cutting board. With the tip of the knife, make a series of lengthwise parallel cuts, leaving the root end intact (j). Working from the stem end, make 2 or 3 diagonal cuts toward the root end, still leaving the root end intact (k). Starting at the stem end, make even crosswise cuts all the way through the onion, making a uniform dice.

To chop the onion more finely, secure the top of the knife tip with your guiding hand. Keeping the tip of the knife against the cutting board, raise and lower the knife's heel (the back of the knife) firmly and rapidly (l). Continue chopping until it is as fine as you need.

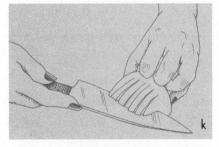

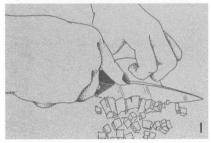

best way to caramelize onions

When onions are cooked a bit, they start to lose their sharp flavor. And when cooked until their natural sugars caramelize, the transformation goes even further. The onions darken into a rich, golden brown and take on a delicious sweetness. Caramelizing isn't difficult, but it does take some time and a watchful eye. The results are worth the effort, however.

Cut onions in half vertically, place them cut-sides down on a cutting board, and slice into thin slivers. For 3 cups sliced onions, heat 1 tablespoon oil over medium-high heat. Add the sliced onions and cook, stirring occasionally, for 5 minutes. Continue cooking, stirring often, for 15 to 20 minutes, or until the onions are a deep golden brown. Three cups sliced raw onions will yield one cup caramelized onions.

KITCHEN NOTES

:: Onions need a lot of space to caramelize, so be sure your skillet is large enough. Use a 12-inch skillet to caramelize 3 cups of sliced onions.

:: The onions should be a deep golden brown, but not burned, so watch them closely.

:: Stir the onions occasionally during the first 5 minutes, then more frequently for the remaining 15 to 20 minutes. The onions need to keep moving so they don't burn.

chopping shallots

Shallots grow in clusters of several small bulbs. They have a mild onion flavor and are used for sauces, salad dressings, and soups. To chop a shallot, separate the bulbs, remove the papery skin, and chop the same way as an onion.

peppers

At one time, the only type of pepper you could find at the grocery store was the green bell variety. But now a vast and colorful selection of the capsicum family fills produce bins. The green bells are joined by sweet red, yellow, white, and purple varieties. Other sweet peppers include the cubanelle, pimiento, and sweet banana. And right alongside these are a multitude of hot peppers, from the tiny serrano to the large, mild poblano.

best way to core and seed peppers
Using a small, sharp knife, cut around the stem end of the pepper. Pull out the inner core and seeds. Scrape out the white fibers. The pepper is ready to be stuffed, sliced, or chopped.

roasted peppers
Roasted bell peppers are one of the delights of the Italian kitchen. With a bit of patience, they really are easy to do. Their sweet smoky flavor, silky texture, and bright color adds pizzazz to salads, pasta dishes, soups, sauces, and sandwiches. You can season them with garlic, olive oil, and herbs and serve them for an appetizer.

You can roast any color bell pepper, but the red ones have the sweetest, most intense flavor. Yellow and orange ones are milder in flavor, and the green, purple, and brown varieties have a slightly different, less sweet flavor and do not keep their colors as well. You can also roast fresh chile peppers.

best way to roast peppers
Adjust the oven rack so the peppers are as close to the heating element as possible without touching it. Preheat the broiler.

Line a jelly-roll pan with foil. Cut the peppers in half, and remove the stems and cores. Put the peppers, cut-sides down, on the pan and press them down with the palm of your hand to flatten them (m). Broil the peppers until the skins are charred and puffy and the flesh is still firm, 8 to 10 minutes.

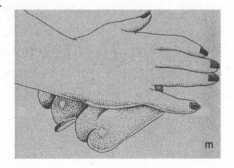

As individual peppers become blackened and blistered, remove them to a medium bowl with tongs. Cover the bowl with foil and let the peppers steam in their own heat for 15 minutes or more. This helps to further loosen the skins.

Set a strainer over a bowl. Holding a pepper over the strainer, peel away the skins with a small, sharp knife. Place the peeled peppers in a second bowl and repeat with any remaining peppers. When finished, strain the juice from the first bowl over the peppers.

KITCHEN NOTE

:: Once roasted, peppers will keep in the refrigerator for up to 3 days. Put them in an airtight container and pour the juices over them. They can also be frozen for up to 6 months. Thaw frozen peppers in the refrigerator overnight.

chile peppers

Chile peppers belong to the same family as sweet peppers, but their distinguishing feature is the presence of a compound called capsaicin, an oily substance located in the seeds and membranes. The main concern when working with fresh chiles is removing the seeds and membranes.

best way to seed a chile pepper

Capsaicin can burn sensitive skin, so be sure not to touch your face or rub your eyes when handling these peppers. If you have sensitive skin, it's best to wear rubber gloves when removing the seeds and oil-bearing membranes from chiles. Slit the pepper open lengthwise and, holding it under running water, remove the membrane with a paring knife and rinse away the seeds. Pat the peppers dry.

chile varieties

There are over 200 varieties of chile peppers, and purchasing them can be very confusing. Each variety can go by several different names, and these can change from region to region. And to make matters worse, you'll more than likely find them labeled as just hot peppers in supermarket produce sections. Here's a basic rule of thumb for buying chile peppers: the smaller, the hotter.

potatoes

Potatoes can do more than round out a meal or fill up a dinner plate. They're one of the most versatile and nutritious vegetables that cooks have at their fingertips. Potatoes are quite high in complex carbohydrates and have virtually no fat and no cholesterol. In addition, they are full of vitamin C (especially the skin), high in minerals such as potassium, loaded with fiber, and low in sodium. And as growers provide us with a broader range of varieties, there are potatoes to appeal to every palate and cooking need.

When deciding on what type of potato to use, the most important consideration is the texture of its flesh. When cooked, potatoes are either firm and waxy, starchy and mealy, or somewhere in between. Varieties that have a waxy texture, like red-skinned and Yellow Finn potatoes, are best for boiling, steaming, and making salads because their firm flesh holds its shape well. Starchy varieties, such as russets, will cook up with a mealy, fluffy texture and are good for baking, mashing, or frying. Yukon Gold and Kennebec potatoes are good all-purpose varieties.

best way to peel potatoes

Use a swivel-blade peeler to remove the peel. Use the point of a sharp knife to remove any small eyes or blemishes in the potato, and cut off any damaged or green patches

best way to bake potatoes

Scrub russet potatoes. Get them really clean so you can eat the skin. Pierce the skin several times with a fork to let steam escape. Bake at 350°F for 1½ hours. The result is a potato that has great flavor and a light and fluffy texture. In addition, the skin will be crisp and chewable. Use this method for sweet potatoes and yams as well, but reduce the baking time to 45 minutes to 1 hour, or until tender.

In a time crunch, pierce the potatoes several times and microwave on High for 5 minutes, then finish them in a 350°F oven for 10 minutes. The oven helps crisp the skin and dry out the flesh so it's not dense and gluey.

best way to mash potatoes

The variety of potato you choose makes a significant difference in the quality of the dish. Russet potatoes, like Idaho, have a high starch content and will mash to a fluffy, light texture. In addition, the low water content of these potatoes allows them to absorb soymilk, milk, cream, or butter without becoming wet or gummy. Yukon Gold potatoes are another good choice for mashing. Their yellow flesh makes creamy mashed potatoes with an almost buttery flavor.

Peel potatoes and cut them into 2-inch chunks. Put them into a saucepan and cover with cold water. Add 1 tablespoon salt. Bring to a boil. Reduce the heat and simmer until the potatoes are tender when tested with a knife, 15 to 20 minutes. Drain them in a colander. Return the potatoes to the pan. Using a potato masher, mash the potatoes with butter (use about 2 tablespoons butter per 1 pound of potatoes). Stir in some warm milk until they are the desired consistency. Season to taste with salt and pepper. Serve hot.

To mash potatoes using an electric mixer: Transfer the hot, drained potatoes to a bowl. Mix on medium speed until most of the lumps have disappeared, about 1 minute. Add butter (2 tablespoons per pound) and beat until blended. Slowly add warm milk and beat on low speed until blended. Season to taste with salt and pepper.

KITCHEN NOTES

:: Choose fairly clean, smooth, firm potatoes. For even cooking, pick potatoes that are about the same size. Do not select ones with wrinkled skins, soft dark spots, cut surfaces, or green areas. Green spots mean they have been exposed to light; cut the spot off before cooking to eliminate bitterness.

:: Potatoes are more fragile than you might think, so handle them carefully to prevent bruising. Keep them unwashed in a cool, dark, well-ventilated place. If stored in a place that is too hot, the sugar will convert to starch and the potatoes will lose their natural sweetness.

:: Potatoes baked in foil will taste more steamed than baked, with skin that is limp and chewy and flesh that is dense and overly moist.

:: Never try to whip potatoes in a food processor or you will have a gluey mess.

:: Ideally, mashed potatoes should be served freshly made, but this is not always possible. Mash them up to 1 hour before serving, reserving one-third of the milk. Place them in a heatproof bowl, set over a pan of barely simmering water. Pour the reserved milk over the top. Just before serving, stir the milk into the potatoes.

tomatoes

Many recipes call for you to peel and seed tomatoes because tomato skins can become tough and the seeds can impart a bitter taste during cooking. However, these techniques are not nearly as time-consuming as they sound.

best way to peel and seed a tomato

The skin of a fully ripe tomato is easy to remove because you can almost effortlessly peel it away with a paring knife. Tomatoes that are not at their peak of ripeness, however, require a little more attention. Submerge these tomatoes in boiling water for 15 to 30 seconds. Remove with a slotted spoon and peel them while they are still warm.

After removing the skin, cut out the core of the tomato with a serrated knife and slice the tomato in half. Then, holding one half of the tomato over a bowl, gently squeeze out the juices and seeds. Use your finger to scrape out any remaining seeds from the seed cavity.

best way to dry tomatoes

Preheat the oven to 225°F. Cut large tomatoes into slices or quarters; small tomatoes, like cherry or grape, can be dried whole. Line baking sheets with parchment paper to keep the tomatoes' juices from sticking to the pans. If desired, you can sprinkle the tomatoes with chopped fresh herbs, salt and pepper, and other spices.

Bake until the edges begin to shrivel and dry and the center still remains a little juicy, 2 to 4 hours. Store dried tomatoes in an airtight container in a cool, dry place for up to 1 month.

KITCHEN NOTES

:: Think of tomatoes as a fruit (they are actually berries). Buy them a few days ahead and let them ripen at home, just as you would bananas or avocados. Try to eat them at their peak; overripe tomatoes lose nutrients.

:: Choose smooth, unblemished tomatoes that feel heavy for their size and have firm, not mushy, flesh.

:: Never refrigerate tomatoes. Cold temperatures kill their flavor and stop the ripening process. Instead, leave unripe tomatoes in a basket on a counter, stem-sides up and away from direct sunlight (which destroys vitamins A and C). Or put them in a closed paper bag to speed up the process.

winter squash

The thick-skinned squash of winter are a collection of edible gourds that have been allowed to ripen on the vine instead of being harvested at an immature stage, as is customary with summer squash. Dozens of types of winter squash are grown, the more common varieties being acorn, butternut, hubbard, buttercup, delicata, and pumpkins. Most have dense orange-yellow flesh, but their texture can vary considerably when cooked, from smooth and creamy to more fibrous and watery.

best way to cook winter squash

For most cooks, one of the major hurdles to cooking winter squash is cutting it in half. You can always use a heavy chef's knife or a cleaver and exert some pressure. An easier method is to partially bake the whole squash until it is soft enough to yield easily to a knife. Place the squash in a 350°F oven for 15 to 20 minutes, or until the skin is easily broken by pressing with a thumbnail. Remove the squash, cut it in half, and, using a spoon, scoop out the seeds and fibrous tissue. The squash is now ready to prepare as your recipe directs.

spaghetti squash

When cooked, the flesh of the spaghetti squash produces golden, spaghetti-like strands that are crisp yet tender, with a mild nutty flavor that's perfect for sauces. Partially bake the squash as directed in the instructions for cooking winter squash. Cut it in half, discard the seeds, and place the halves cut-side down in a baking dish. Add water to the dish to a depth of ½ inch. Bake at 350°F until tender when pierced with a fork, about 30 minutes. Remove the squash from the water and let it cool slightly. Scrape the inside of the squash with the tines of a fork to remove the strands.

cooking techniques

grilled vegetables

Americans are beginning to discover that vegetables, like other foods, take on a completely different character when cooked on a grill. The natural sugars in vegetables caramelize when grilled, imparting a depth and richness that no amount of sautéing could ever achieve, and it's so simple to do.

best way to grill vegetables

Vegetables have no natural fat, so they must be marinated in an oil-based marinade or brushed with some oil before they go on the grill to keep them from sticking to the grill rack. To ensure even cooking, turn the vegetables often and regulate the heat. Large vegetables can be sliced or cut into chunks so they cook evenly. Other vegetables, such as artichokes, broccoli, cauliflower, potatoes, and fennel, will not cook through on the grill before the outside burns and must be boiled for a few minutes and drained before they are ready to be grilled. Kebabs are an easy way to grill vegetables because they save you from having to turn the vegetables individually. The "Grilling Vegetables" chart on page 102 describes how to prepare and grill various types of vegetables.

grilling vegetables

vegetable	preparation	grilling time
Asparagus	Trim ends; blanch spears for 4 minutes	3 minutes
Bell peppers	Stem, seed, and cut into large pieces	5 minutes
Broccoli	Cut into large pieces; blanch for 3 minutes	5 minutes
Eggplant	Cut into 1-inch slices	5 minutes
Endive	Halve lengthwise	6 minutes
Fennel	Cut bulb into 8 wedges	12 minutes
Garlic	Leave head unpeeled; blanch for 20 minutes	15 minutes
Leeks	Trim and halve lengthwise	5 minutes
Mushrooms	Leave whole; skewer if necessary	5 minutes
Onions	Cut into ½-inch slices	5 minutes
Potatoes, small new	Blanch for 10 minutes; cut in half	10 minutes
Potatoes, sweet	Cut into ½-inch slices	12 minutes
Summer squash	Cut into ½-inch slices	5 minutes
Tomatoes, cherry	Skewer	3 minutes
Tomatoes, plum	Cut in half lengthwise	3 minutes
Zucchini	Cut into ½-inch slices	5 minutes

grilling tips

Essential tools for grilling include a pair of large sturdy tongs and a large flat metal spatula for turning food, a long-handled basting brush, a fine-meshed grill topper to prevent vegetables and other small items from falling through the openings in the grill rack, a selection of wooden or metal skewers for kebabs, and a stiff wire brush for cleanup.

Before heading outside, assemble everything you will need at the grill on a baking sheet or tray. In addition to the tools listed above, don't forget a small tub of water, some paper towels, a kitchen towel, a timer, and a clean platter to hold the cooked food.

To add complexity to your barbecue, add bunches of dried herbs such as bay leaves, thyme, rosemary, sage, or lavender. Other aromatics include grapevine cuttings and wood chips, including mesquite and applewood

roasted vegetables

There was a time when the word "roasted" on a menu was invariably followed by "loin of pork" or "leg of lamb." But that's all changed now, as all manner of roasted vegetables show up on menus and tables.

Roasting implies a higher heat than baking. This fast cooking method seals in the vegetables' juices and caramelizes the sugars on the outside, deepening the flavors. Vitamins and flavors remain in the food instead of leaching out into the cooking liquid, as they do when braised or boiled.

best way to roast vegetables

Cut vegetables into uniform size. Generally, smaller is better (½-inch dice, ½-inch-thick slices, or ¼-by-1-inch-long strips). Put the vegetables into a large bowl and lightly coat with vegetable oil or melted butter. The fat helps them to form a crisp outer coating and seal in the flavors. Transfer the vegetables to a shallow roasting pan or baking sheet with sides, large enough to hold the vegetables in a single layer.

Roast the vegetables at 425°F, stirring and turning them with a spatula every 10 minutes or so until they are fork-tender and lightly colored. They should not appear burnt. Season the vegetables with salt and pepper to taste.

KITCHEN NOTES

:: Select the freshest vegetables possible; roasting intensifies their flavor, so they must be good at the outset.

:: Use mushrooms and tomatoes sparingly. The flavor of mushrooms will become overpowering, and tomatoes will give off liquid that could make the other vegetables mushy.

:: Herbs and spices can enhance the flavor of roasted vegetables. Add them when you are coating the vegetables with oil or butter.

asparagus and roasted bell pepper salad

SERVES 4 / You'll be hard-pressed to come up with a more enjoyable way to eat asparagus than this simple salad. For some added flavor, garnish with Parmesan shavings.

1 small yellow or red bell pepper
1 pound asparagus, trimmed
2 tablespoons red wine vinegar
½ teaspoon Dijon mustard
6 tablespoons olive oil
1 tablespoon chopped fresh chives
½ teaspoon grated lemon zest
Salt and freshly ground pepper

Preheat the broiler. Line a pie pan with foil. Cut the bell pepper in half and remove the stem and core. Put the bell pepper in the pan and press it down with the palm of your hand to flatten it. Broil until the skin is charred, 8 to 10 minutes. Remove it to a small bowl. Cover the bowl with foil and let steam for 15 minutes.

Using a sharp knife, peel the charred skin from the bell pepper, then cut it into thin strips.

In a large pot, bring 1 inch of water to a boil. Put the asparagus in a steamer basket and carefully place the basket in the pot. Cover and steam over medium-high heat until the asparagus spears bend slightly when picked up, 4 to 5 minutes for asparagus under ½ inch in diameter, 5 to 6 minutes for thicker spears.

In a small bowl, whisk together the vinegar and mustard. While still whisking, add the oil, chives, and lemon zest, then season to taste with salt and pepper.

Cut the asparagus into 2-inch pieces. In a medium bowl, combine the asparagus, and roasted bell pepper strips. Pour the vinaigrette over the vegetables and toss to mix. Serve warm or at room temperature.

roasted beets with orange dressing

SERVES 4 / Roasting beets brings out their natural sweetness. The sweet-tangy flavor of the orange dressing makes a wonderful accompaniment.

1 bunch medium beets (about 2 pounds), leaves trimmed, leaving 1 inch of stem intact

orange dressing
2 tablespoons orange juice
1 tablespoon balsamic vinegar
1 teaspoon Dijon mustard
1 tablespoon chopped fresh herbs, such as tarragon or dill
1 medium shallot, minced
⅓ cup extra virgin olive oil
Salt and freshly ground pepper

Preheat the oven to 400°F. Scrub the beets well and trim any roots. Pat the beets dry, wrap them in foil (2 to 3 beets in each package), and place on a baking sheet. Roast until tender when tested with a skewer or thin knife, about 1 hour. Open the foil and let the beets cool slightly.

Meanwhile, make the dressing: In a small bowl, whisk together the orange juice, vinegar, mustard, herbs, and shallot. Slowly drizzle in the oil, whisking vigorously until well blended. Season to taste with salt and pepper and set aside.

Use paper towels to hold the warm beets and rub them gently to remove their skins. Cut the beets into ¼-inch-thick slices and transfer to a medium bowl. Whisk the dressing and pour it over the beets, tossing to coat. Serve the beets at room temperature or chilled.

braised red cabbage

SERVES 8 / Based on a traditional German recipe, this red cabbage dish is both sweet and sour at the same time.

> **1 head red cabbage, cored and thinly shredded (about 10 cups)**
> **½ cup, plus 2 teaspoons clear vegetable stock or water**
> **1 large Granny Smith or other tart cooking apple, cored and coarsely chopped**
> **1 tablespoon packed light brown sugar**
> **1 teaspoon salt**
> **¼ teaspoon freshly ground pepper**
> **2 teaspoons all-purpose flour**
> **1 tablespoon cider vinegar**

In a large pot, combine the cabbage and ¼ cup of the stock. Cover and cook over medium heat, stirring occasionally, until the leaves are wilted, 5 to 7 minutes.

Stir in another ¼ cup of stock, the apple, brown sugar, salt, and pepper. Cover and cook, stirring 3 or 4 times, until the cabbage is almost tender, about 10 minutes.

Meanwhile, in a small cup, mix the flour with the remaining 2 teaspoons stock. Stir in the vinegar. Add to the cabbage, stirring to coat. Cook for 2 to 3 minutes, or until slightly thickened. Serve hot.

hearty corn chowder

SERVES 6 / This hearty soup has a rich, smooth texture, even though it contains no cream. The flavor depends on the quality of the corn, so be sure to use the freshest and sweetest ears you can find.

2 tablespoons vegetable oil

2 medium carrots, peeled and chopped

2 stalks celery, chopped

1 medium onion, chopped

1 leek (white part only), well rinsed and chopped

2 cups fresh corn kernels (4 medium ears)

1 medium russet potato, peeled and chopped

4½ cups clear vegetable stock

2 tablespoons chopped fresh basil leaves, or 2 teaspoons dried

1 teaspoon chopped fresh thyme leaves, or ¼ teaspoon dried

Salt and freshly ground pepper

In a large pot, heat the oil over medium heat. Add the carrots, celery, onion, and leek and cook, stirring often, until the vegetables are softened, about 10 minutes.

Add the corn, potato, stock, basil, and thyme. Bring to a gentle boil over medium-high heat. Reduce the heat to medium-low, cover, and simmer until the potato is tender and the liquid has reduced to just cover the ingredients, about 30 minutes.

Purée the mixture, using an immersion blender or food processor, until almost smooth but still a little chunky. Season to taste with salt and pepper.

eggplant caponata

MAKES 5 CUPS / With its complex flavor and texture, this classic Mediterranean dish is delicious served as an appetizer over toasted bread slices. Caponata is good served warm or at room temperature, and it tastes even better when the flavors have been allowed time to meld.

2 medium eggplants (about 2½ pounds), cut lengthwise into ½-inch-thick slices

1 tablespoon olive oil, plus more for brushing

1 small onion, finely chopped

1 medium red bell pepper, cored, seeded, and chopped

1 clove garlic, minced

1 can (15 ounces) Italian plum tomatoes

¼ cup (about 20) niçoise olives, pitted and chopped

1 tablespoon drained capers

½ cup red wine vinegar

2 teaspoons sugar

¼ teaspoon crushed red pepper flakes

¼ cup chopped fresh basil leaves

Preheat the broiler. Brush the eggplant slices with olive oil. Broil the eggplant slices about 4 inches from the heat source until they are soft and slightly charred, 4 to 6 minutes per side. Set aside to cool.

In a large skillet, heat 1 tablespoon oil over medium heat. Add the onion and bell pepper and cook, stirring occasionally, until tender, about 7 minutes. Add the garlic and cook, stirring often, for 1 minute. Add the tomatoes with their liquid, olives, and capers. Cook, stirring occasionally and breaking up the tomatoes with a spoon, until the liquid is slightly reduced, about 7 minutes.

Meanwhile, roughly chop the eggplant. Add the eggplant to the tomato mixture and cook, stirring occasionally, for 1 minute. Stir in the vinegar and sugar and cook, stirring occasionally, until most of the liquid evaporates and the mixture thickens, about 10 minutes. Remove from the heat and stir in the red pepper flakes and basil. Serve warm or at room temperature.

potato, fennel, and celery root soup

SERVES 6 / The anise-like flavor of fennel makes it a perfect partner for potatoes and celery root in this creamy soup. It is equally at home served to guests for a special occasion or to family for a casual weeknight meal.

2 medium bulbs fennel

1 tablespoon olive oil

2 stalks celery, chopped

1 medium onion, chopped

½ cup dry white wine

5 cups clear vegetable stock or canned stock

1 medium celery root, peeled and coarsely chopped

1 medium potato, peeled and coarsely chopped

4 cloves garlic, peeled

Bouquet garni made with 5 stems flat-leaf parsley, 2 sprigs fresh thyme, and 1 bay leaf, tied with cooking twine

Salt and freshly ground pepper

Trim off the fennel stalks, reserving the fronds. Trim the bottoms of the bulbs and tough outer layers. Coarsely chop the bulbs.

In a large pot, heat the oil over medium heat. Add the chopped fennel bulb, celery, and onion and cook, stirring often, until the vegetables are softened, about 7 minutes. Add the wine, increase the heat to high, and boil until almost all of the liquid has evaporated, about 5 minutes.

Add the stock, celery root, potato, and garlic and bring to a gentle simmer over medium heat. Add the bouquet garni, reduce the heat to medium-low, and simmer until the vegetables are very soft, about 45 minutes. Discard the bouquet garni.

Purée the soup using an immersion blender or food processor until almost smooth but still a little chunky. Season to taste with salt and pepper.

Coarsely chop the reserved fennel fronds. Ladle the soup into warmed shallow bowls, sprinkle with the chopped fronds, and serve hot.

mixed greens with goat cheese

SERVES 6 / Pan-grilled goat cheese, combined with greens, is a French bistro favorite.

4-ounce log fresh goat cheese
½ cup plain dry bread crumbs
¼ teaspoon dried thyme
¼ teaspoon salt
⅛ teaspoon freshly ground pepper

vinaigrette
2 to 3 tablespoons red wine vinegar
1 teaspoon Dijon mustard
¼ cup extra-virgin olive oil
Salt and freshly ground pepper

6 cups mixed salad greens, torn into bite-sized pieces
2 tablespoons olive oil

Cut the goat cheese log into six ¾-inch slices. On a sheet of wax paper, mix the bread crumbs, thyme, salt, and pepper. Press both sides of each cheese slice into this mixture. Set aside.

TO MAKE THE VINAIGRETTE: In a small bowl, whisk together the vinegar, mustard, and oil until well blended. Season to taste with salt and pepper.

TO ASSEMBLE THE SALAD: Place the salad greens in a large salad bowl. Add the vinaigrette and toss to coat. Divide the salad among 6 serving plates.

In a medium skillet, heat the oil over medium heat. Add the coated cheese slices and cook for 1 to 2 minutes on each side, or just until the cheese begins to melt and spread slightly. Using a spatula, transfer one slice to each dressed salad. Serve right away.

garlicky broccoli raab

SERVES 6 / This is a popular way to serve broccoli raab in southern Italy. This green is known for its slightly bitter flavor; blanching it first gives it a milder taste.

1 bunch broccoli raab (about 1 ¼ pounds), stems trimmed and tough leaves removed

3 tablespoons olive oil

2 teaspoons minced garlic

1 tablespoon fresh lemon juice

Salt and freshly ground pepper

Bring a large pot of water to a boil. Blanch the broccoli raab just until tender, about 3 minutes. Drain and set aside.

In a large skillet, heat the oil over medium heat. Add the garlic and cook, stirring often, until it turns a pale golden color, about 1 minute. Add the broccoli raab and increase the heat to medium-high. Add the lemon juice and salt and pepper to taste and stir well. Cook, stirring often, until the greens are heated through, about 3 minutes. Serve hot.

wasabi mashed potatoes

SERVES 6 / Available in paste and powdered forms, wasabi has a distinct, pungent, horseradish-like flavor. Although it's usually associated with Japanese cuisine, it is finding many exciting new applications, such as these mashed potatoes.

2½ pounds russet potatoes, peeled and cut into 2-inch pieces
1 teaspoon salt, plus more to taste
6 tablespoons butter
2 to 3 teaspoons wasabi powder
½ cup low-fat or whole milk, warmed
Salt and freshly ground pepper

Put the potatoes into a large saucepan and cover with cold water. Add the salt and bring to a boil. Reduce the heat and simmer, uncovered, until the potatoes are tender when tested with a knife, 15 to 20 minutes.

Drain the potatoes in a colander. Return them to the pan. Using a potato masher, mash the potatoes with the butter. Add the wasabi powder and warm milk and mash or stir the potatoes until smooth and fluffy. Season to taste with salt and pepper, and serve hot.

twice-baked spinach potatoes

SERVES 8 / These twice-baked potatoes are stuffed with spinach and cheese for a perfect winter lunch or brunch treat. The potatoes can be made up to one day ahead. Cover tightly with plastic wrap and refrigerate. Bring them to room temperature before baking.

> 4 large russet potatoes, scrubbed
>
> 3 tablespoons olive oil
>
> 2 cloves garlic, minced
>
> 1 bag (10 ounces) fresh spinach, large stems removed
>
> ½ cup plain low-fat yogurt
>
> Salt and freshly ground pepper
>
> ¼ cup grated Parmesan cheese

Preheat the oven to 350°F. Pierce the skin of each potato several times with a fork. Bake the potatoes until tender, about 1½ hours. Let them cool slightly.

Meanwhile, in a large skillet, heat 1 tablespoon of the oil over medium heat. Add the garlic and cook, stirring often, until fragrant, about 30 seconds. Add the spinach and cook, stirring occasionally, just until wilted. Remove from the heat.

Cut the potatoes in half lengthwise and, using a spoon, scoop the flesh out into a medium bowl, leaving a ¼-inch-thick shell. Using a fork, mash the potatoes in the bowl. Add the yogurt, the remaining 2 tablespoons olive oil, and the spinach mixture and stir until blended. Season to taste with salt and pepper.

Spoon the mixture into the potato shells, mounding slightly. Put the filled potatoes on a baking sheet and sprinkle some grated Parmesan cheese over each. Bake until the tops are golden and the potatoes are heated through, about 25 minutes. Serve hot.

tomato-basil bruschetta

SERVES 6 / Bruschetta is a simple but superb Italian appetizer of thick slices of toasted bread that can be served with a variety of toppings. Fresh, ripe tomatoes, basil, garlic, and olive oil make an easy yet delicious topping.

1½ pounds ripe plum tomatoes, seeded and chopped
⅓ cup chopped fresh basil leaves
1 small clove garlic, minced
2 tablespoons extra-virgin olive oil
1 tablespoon balsamic vinegar
1 teaspoon fresh lemon juice
Salt and freshly ground pepper
6 slices crusty bread, ½ to ¾ inch thick, grilled or toasted

In a medium bowl, combine the tomatoes, basil, garlic, oil, vinegar, and lemon juice and mix well. Season to taste with salt and pepper.

Cut the grilled bread slices in half. Spoon the tomato mixture over the bread and serve.

braised winter squash and root vegetables

SERVES 6 / Root vegetables take on a slightly sweet flavor when braised. Serve these with a grain like brown rice, quinoa, or bulgur.

1 tablespoon olive oil

1 tablespoon butter

2 medium leeks, trimmed, rinsed, and chopped

2 cups peeled, diced carrots

2 cups peeled, diced parsnips

1 teaspoon sugar

1 teaspoon salt

½ teaspoon freshly ground pepper

1 pound butternut squash, peeled and cubed (about 3 cups)

1 cup brown vegetable stock

Freshly grated nutmeg for garnish

Preheat the oven to 350°F. In a Dutch oven, heat the oil and butter over medium heat. Add the leeks, carrots, parsnips, sugar, ½ teaspoon of the salt, and ¼ teaspoon of the pepper. Cook, stirring often, until the vegetables are lightly browned, about 5 minutes.

Add the squash, stock, and remaining ½ teaspoon salt and ¼ teaspoon pepper and stir to mix. Bake until the vegetables are tender, about 20 minutes. Sprinkle with nutmeg and serve hot.

tuscan pasta and vegetables

SERVES 4 / Escarole and fennel give this pasta dish an earthy flavor. If escarole is not available, use spinach, kale, or broccoli raab.

2 tablespoons olive oil

1 cup chopped onion

1 cup cored, seeded, and diced red bell pepper

1 cup diced fennel bulb

1 cup diced zucchini

2 medium cloves garlic, minced

1 teaspoon dried oregano

1 cup diced canned tomatoes

1 can (15 ounces) cannellini beans, rinsed and drained

4 cups chopped escarole

1 cup clear vegetable stock

Salt and freshly ground pepper

12 ounces dry penne pasta

Grated parmesan cheese (optional)

Bring a large pot of water to a boil. Meanwhile, in a large skillet, heat the oil over medium-high heat. Add the onion, bell pepper, fennel, zucchini, garlic, and oregano. Cook, stirring often, until the vegetables begin to soften, about 10 minutes. Add the tomatoes and cook, stirring often, for 1 minute. Add the beans, escarole, and stock and cook until the vegetables are tender and the escarole wilts, about 10 minutes. Season with salt and pepper to taste.

Add 1 teaspoon salt to the boiling water, then add the pasta, stirring to prevent sticking. Cook, stirring occasionally, until just tender, 8 to 10 minutes. Drain well. Transfer the pasta to a warm serving bowl. Spoon the vegetable mixture over the pasta and toss to coat. Serve hot with Parmesan cheese, if desired.

roasted vegetable ratatouille

SERVES 6 / Roasting rather than sautéing the vegetables intensifies the flavors in this Provençal classic. The ratatouille is good on its own or served over pasta or couscous.

1 head garlic

12 ripe plum tomatoes, halved and seeded

1 medium eggplant (about 1 pound), cut lengthwise into
**   ½-inch-thick slices**

4 small zucchini, cut in half lengthwise

1 large onion, cut into ½-inch-thick slices

1 large red bell pepper, cut in half lengthwise and seeded

1 large yellow bell pepper, cut in half lengthwise and seeded

⅓ cup chopped fresh basil leaves

3 tablespoons olive oil

1 tablespoon chopped fresh thyme leaves

Salt and freshly ground pepper

Preheat the oven to 450°F. Peel away as much of the papery skin from the garlic head as possible and wrap the head loosely in foil. Roast the garlic until it is very soft, about 30 minutes.

Meanwhile, coat 2 baking sheets with vegetable oil or cooking spray. Arrange the tomatoes, eggplant, zucchini, onion, and bell peppers on the sheets and roast for 20 minutes, turning once, until just tender and lightly browned. Let cool slightly. Reduce the oven temperature to 350°F.

Separate the garlic cloves and squeeze the soft pulp into an ovenproof Dutch oven. Remove the skins from the tomatoes and peppers. Chop all the vegetables and add to the garlic in the Dutch oven. Stir in the basil, olive oil, thyme, and salt and pepper to taste. Cover and bake, stirring occasionally, until heated through and thickened, about 30 minutes. Serve warm or at room temperature.

portobello burgers with pesto-pepper mayo

SERVES 4 / Portobello mushrooms are prized for their firm, meaty texture and rich, earthy flavor. Grilling the mushrooms and serving them as you would a burger is a terrific way to enjoy them.

pesto–pepper mayo
¼ cup chopped roasted red peppers (drain if jarred)
2 tablespoons store-bought pesto
1 clove garlic, minced
¼ cup soy or low-fat regular mayonnaise
Salt and freshly ground pepper

4 large portobello mushrooms (about 1 pound), stemmed
Olive oil, for brushing
4 crusty rolls, split and lightly toasted

TO MAKE THE MAYO: In a food processor, combine the roasted bell peppers, pesto, garlic, and mayonnaise and process until well blended and smooth. Season to taste with salt and pepper. Scrape the mixture into a small bowl and set aside.

TO GRILL THE MUSHROOMS: Prepare a hot charcoal fire, preheat a gas grill to high, or heat a grill pan over medium-high heat. Hold 1 mushroom in your hand, cut-side up. Using a small, sharp knife, carefully cut and scrape to remove most of the dark brown "gills." Repeat with the remaining mushrooms. Set aside.

Brush a little oil on both sides of the mushrooms. Place the mushrooms cut-side down on the grill or in the pan. Cook until golden and tender, turning once, about 10 minutes in all.

Place 1 mushroom on the bottom of each roll. Spoon a little mayo over each, cover with the bun tops, and serve.

grilled vegetables with garlic bread

SERVES 4 / Fellow food writer Patsy Jamieson serves this hearty yet simple salad as a first course or light supper when it's too hot to cook indoors. Be sure you use fresh vegetables and good-quality bread. To make Parmesan shavings, start with a chunk of cheese that weighs at least 4 ounces. Use a swivel-blade vegetable peeler to shave off attractive curls, letting them fall onto a piece of wax or parchment paper.

balsamic vinaigrette

2 tablespoons extra-virgin olive oil

2 tablespoons balsamic vinegar

½ teaspoon Dijon mustard

1 tablespoon water

Salt and freshly ground pepper

8 cups mesclun greens, thoroughly dried

4 portobello mushrooms (about 1 pound total), stemmed and cut into ½-inch-thick slices

2 medium sweet onions, such as Vidalia or Walla Walla (about 1½ pounds total), cut into ½-inch-thick slices

1 large red bell pepper, cored, seeded, and cut into ½-inch-wide strips

16 cherry tomatoes

1 tablespoon extra-virgin olive oil

Salt and freshly ground pepper

8 slices Italian bread, ¾ inch thick

1 clove garlic, cut in half

1 cup Parmesan shavings

Prepare a hot charcoal fire or a preheat a gas grill to high. Set a fine-meshed grill topper on the rack to heat.

TO MAKE THE VINAIGRETTE: In a small bowl, whisk together the olive oil, balsamic vinegar, mustard, and water. Season to taste with salt and pepper.

continued

TO PREPARE THE VEGETABLES: Put the greens into a large bowl and set aside. Spread the mushrooms, onions, bell pepper, and tomatoes on 2 baking sheets. Brush both sides of the vegetables with the oil and season to taste with salt and pepper.

Lightly oil the grill topper. Grill the vegetables in batches until nicely browned and tender, 2 to 4 minutes per side. Transfer the vegetables to the baking sheets as they are done. Grill the bread alongside the vegetables until lightly toasted. Immediately rub the warm grilled bread with the cut sides of the garlic.

Add the grilled vegetables and the vinaigrette to the greens and toss well. Divide the salad among serving plates and sprinkle Parmesan shavings on top. Serve with the garlic bread on the side.

fruits

Nowhere else is nature so lavish as in the provision of fruits. They come in a glorious array of colors and shapes, are juicy and fragrant, and offer us much in the way of nutrition. Fruits are full of complex carbohydrates, vitamins, minerals, and fiber. On top of that, they're low in calories and virtually fat-free.

Of course, eating fruit out of hand is the easiest way to enjoy it. But if you've ever cooked with fruit you know the magic it can work on a dish. Besides adding an unexpected depth of flavor and richness, it also makes food taste fresher and healthier. So don't think of fruit as just a snack or dessert; it's equally at home in an appetizer, main course, or side dish.

apple

Today, throughout the United States, apples occupy the largest fruit segment in supermarket produce sections. Although the varieties change during the seasons to reflect what's available, you'll usually find eight varieties in any given store. Keep in mind that supermarkets will carry only apples that look good, ship well, and store well. The best places to discover and taste different and heirloom varieties are local orchards and farmers' markets.

best way to core and peel an apple

Here's what to do if you're making a recipe that calls for peeled and cut apples: Cut the apple into quarters. Using a sharp paring knife, remove the core by sliding the blade at an angle from one end to the center of the quarter, passing under the core. Turn the quarter and repeat the procedure from the opposite end. Repeat with the remaining quarters (a). Using the paring knife, remove the peel from each quarter. Once all the apples are cored and peeled, cut them as specified in the recipe.

to prepare whole apples for baking: Take out the core and seeds with an apple corer or sharp knife, cutting almost to the bottom but not all the way through (b). Push the corer in straight through the stem end, twist, and pull out. Look inside the cavity and remove any seeds with the tip of a paring knife.

Peel around the apple in one piece with a sharp knife, if the recipe indicates, and rub the surface with lemon juice to prevent discoloration. When ready to use, pat them dry with paper towels.

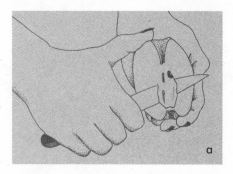
a

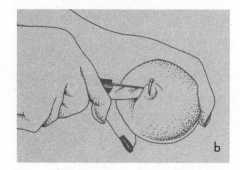
b

what apples should I use?

eating: This is a matter of preference, but the following apples make excellent eating: Fuji, Gala, Golden Delicious, Granny Smith, Gravenstein, Jonathan, McIntosh, Newtown Pippin, Red Delicious, Stayman, and Winesap.

pies and tarts: Use tart or slightly acidic varieties with a good texture: Braeburn, Empire, Gravenstein, Jonathan, McIntosh, Newtown Pippin, Northern Spy, Rhode Island Greening, Stayman, Winesap, and York Imperial.

sauces and butters: Use hearty, full-flavored apples such as Jonathan, McIntosh, Northern Spy, and Winesap.

baked apples: It's important to choose apples that will hold their shape and not fall apart. Use firmer-fleshed varieties, preferably over 3 inches in diameter: Gala, Gravenstein, Mountaineer, Northern Spy, Rome Beauty, and York Imperial.

KITCHEN NOTES

:: When buying apples, check each one to be sure it is free of bruises and soft spots. They should feel firm when you squeeze them gently.

:: When you get your apples home, refrigerate them. They will deteriorate quickly at room temperature.

avocado

Beneath the rough exterior of an avocado lies a storehouse of goodies. They have a wonderfully silky, smooth texture, subtle aroma, and buttery flavor. One medium-sized fruit (yes, it's technically a fruit, not a vegetable) contains generous amounts of vitamins A, C, E, and B_6 as well as potassium, folate, and dietary fiber. And although it's true that they are somewhat high in fat, it is mostly monounsaturated, which helps to decrease the risk of heart disease and stroke by reducing cholesterol.

best way to pit and slice an avocado

Cut the avocado in half lengthwise around the large pit. Twist the halves in opposite directions to separate them. To remove the pit, slide the tip of a spoon gently underneath it and lift it out, or carefully strike the pit with a sharp knife, embedding the knife tip in the pit. Rotate the knife to lift out the pit.

To slice or cube the avocado, hold a half in one hand, cut-side up, and use a large spoon to scoop the flesh out of the skin in one piece. Put the halves, flat-sides down, on a cutting board and cut into slices or cubes. The fruit discolors quickly when cut; to prevent this, dip the cubes or slices into a mixture of lemon juice and water, or stir a little lemon juice into cubed or mashed fruit.

KITCHEN NOTES

:: The two most popular avocado varieties are the small, rough-skinned Hass, grown primarily in California and Mexico, and the larger, thin-skinned Fuerte, grown mostly in Florida. The Hass avocado has a dense, creamy flesh with a creamy consistency; the Fuerte has a watery consistency and fruity, sweet taste.

:: It's essential to use avocados at the proper stage of ripeness to enjoy their fullest flavor. A ripe, ready-to-eat avocado will yield slightly to gentle pressure. Look for avocados that have an even, unblemished texture, that are uniformly hard or soft over their entire surface, and that feel heavy for their size. Avoid any with bruises and those with a hollow between the flesh and skin.

:: Unlike most fruits, avocados ripen only after they are picked, so most of those found on produce shelves are as hard as rocks. Ripen hard avocados by placing them in a brown paper bag. Close the bag and set it in a cool spot for 1 to 3 days. As avocados ripen, those with bright green skin often develop brown patches. That's acceptable because it's an indication that they are almost ripe.

:: Ripe avocados will keep in the refrigerator for 2 to 3 days.

citrus

The juice and zest of lemons, limes, and oranges add a distinct flavor to many dishes. Not only do they balance out other flavors, but their piquancy and aroma also add an incomparable fresh taste.

best way to juice citrus

A bottled product can't match the intense natural flavor of freshly squeezed citrus juice. The simplest way to juice citrus is to cut it in half crosswise and insert a fork into the flesh while squeezing the fruit into a strainer set over a bowl to catch the seeds (c).

A reamer also works well for juicing. Many designs are available, but they all are essentially variations of the same theme—a ribbed, cone-shaped tool that releases the juice when pressed and rotated in the flesh.

c

best way to zest citrus

Zest, the thin citrus peel, adds a fresh, lively flavor to all kinds of dishes, sweet and savory. When you zest, you want only the oily, colored peel, not the bitter white pith underneath.

Although there are many ways to remove zest from citrus fruits, I prefer to use a lemon grater, a small, flat grater with jagged perforations designed to grate only the peel and not the pith. Draw the lemon or lime diagonally across the grater, holding it over a sheet of wax paper to make gathering the zest easier for measuring. To measure zest, place it lightly in a measuring spoon.

best way to segment an orange or grapefruit

This task is made easier if you start by sharpening a medium-size paring knife. Cut the ends off the fruit and stand it upright on a flat surface. Trim all the peel and white pith, using a series of vertical cuts.

Insert the blade of the paring knife between the membrane and the pulp of each segment and cut toward the center. Flip the cutting edge away from you so that the blade is now parallel to the next membrane.

KITCHEN NOTES

:: Not all lemons and limes are created equal. For instance, big varieties with thick skins often yield little juice. Look for medium-sized, smooth, thin-skinned lemons that are free from soft spots and yield gently to pressure. These are much more likely to give juice. Heaviness is also an indicator that lemons and limes are full of juice.

:: Rolling lemons and limes on a hard surface, while pressing down on them with the palm of your hand, is a trick to help them give off more juice. Another technique is to drop them briefly into hot water.

:: The oil in citrus peel is the strongest just after zesting, so always remove the zest just before using it.

:: If you'll be using both the juice and the zest of a citrus fruit, remove the zest first.

:: Oranges can be stored at room temperature for up to 1 week, or store them in the refrigerator for up to 14 days.

:: One medium orange will give you about ½ cup of juice, about 1 tablespoon of grated zest, and 10 to 12 sections.

lemon drops

There's a kitchen tool called a "lemon trumpet" or "lemon faucet" that allows you to extract a small amount of lemon juice without cutting into the fruit. Simply twist it into the fruit, then squeeze the fruit, and the juice will flow through the tube. Another way to achieve this is to pierce the skin with a toothpick and squeeze out the desired amount of juice. Insert the toothpick in the hole to store the fruit.

other tools for zesting

citrus zester: For finely grating zest, the citrus zester has about five tiny sharp-edged holes that lie along the blades in a downward curve. The angle ensures an incision only into the fruit's colored skin, which contains the flavored oils.

citrus stripper: Also called a canelle knife, the citrus stripper has a V-shaped tooth that peels the zest into thin strips. This tools works well to make decorative strips for a garnish.

sharp paring knife or vegetable peeler: You can also use either of these tools for zesting, but be careful not to cut too deep. The zest can then be cut into thin strips or finely chopped.

the new citrus

Although many consumers are reluctant to move away from the familiar navel orange, curious cooks can now play around with a remarkable variety of oranges:

blood orange: A sweet orange with flesh that be deeply red or merely blushed with red. A properly ripened blood orange can have an almost raspberry-like flavor. Great for juicing.

cara cara: A navel orange that has a sweet pink flesh similar to a ruby grapefruit.

kumquat: Like miniature oranges, these citrus fruits have bright orange skin and a sweet-tart flesh. The fruit is eaten whole, skin and all. Common varieties include Meiwa and Nagami.

mandarin oranges: Clementine, Dancy, Honey, and Satsuma are some of the kinds of mandarin oranges you may find in your market. They may be seedless or seedy. A ripe mandarin is fragrant, juicy, and sweet, with a hint of acidity.

Minneola tangelo: This variety looks like a large orange with a knob-like formation at the stem end. Because it is a cross between a tangerine and a grapefruit, its flavor is both sweet and tart.

tangor: Thought to be a cross between an orange and a mandarin, the tangor is sweet-tart, rich in flavor, and juicy, with many seeds. Temple is one of the more common varieties.

kiwi fruit

If you haven't tried kiwi, you're in for a delicious treat. About the size of a large egg, the fuzzy brown fruit doesn't look appetizing until you cut it open and reveal its jade green interior sprinkled with tiny black seeds. The kiwi tastes like a blend of strawberry, peach, and melon. It is also the fruit with the highest level of vitamin C—almost twice that of an orange—and magnesium, a nutrient important for cardiovascular health.

best way to eat kiwi

Take a knife and slice the kiwi in half. While holding one half of the kiwi in your left hand, take a spoon and scoop out a bite of that tangy, tender, sweet, and juicy fruit. Then scoop out another bite, then another.

best way to peel and slice kiwi

Using a small, sharp knife, cut off both ends of an unpeeled kiwi. Insert a soup spoon between the skin and the flesh. Turn the kiwi, pushing the spoon deeper into the fruit, removing the flesh from the skin. Push the flesh out of the skin. Place the kiwi on a cutting board and slice.

KITCHEN NOTES

:: Although most people hesitate to eat the skin of the kiwi fruit, it is completely edible.

:: Select kiwi that are firm and free from bruises. They are ripe when the skin yields when gently pressed.

:: Store unripe kiwi at room temperature. Once ripened, refrigerate for up to 4 days.

mango

A really good mango may be the finest fruit in the world, soft as a peach and dripping with juice. The fruit's luscious flavor, consistent good quality, and abundance in spring and early summer (before peaches and plums hit the farm stands) have contributed to its growing appeal. A ripe mango will have firm, deep orange flesh that yields when pressed lightly. Push aside the little nub at the stem end and sniff; the fruit should give off a spicy, fragrant aroma.

best way to slice and chop a mango

Cutting a mango for the first time is a challenge. The seed of this kidney-shaped fruit is large, with fibers that connect it to the flesh. Leave the peel on and cut a lengthwise slice from either side of the flat pit in the center (d).

Make crisscross sections in the flesh down to, but not through, the peel. Push the peel upward to invert the fruit; the cubes will rise and separate (e).

Slide the knife along the base of the cubes to separate them from the peel.

If you want slices instead of cubes, peel the mango, cut the flesh from the pit in big pieces, then slice it. Don't waste the flesh on the pit; cut as much off as you can with a sharp paring knife.

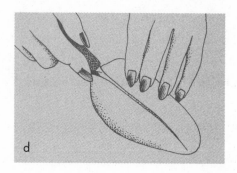 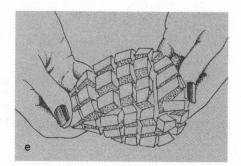

KITCHEN NOTES

:: Always peel mangoes before you eat them—like poison ivy, their distant cousin, mangoes can cause a rash if the skin is eaten.

:: Mangoes can be stored at room temperature for up to 1 week to ripen; refrigerate them if they are very soft. Soft spots or wrinkled skin indicate over-ripeness.

papaya

Sometimes incorrectly called pawpaws, papayas are shaped like an elongated pear, about 5 to 6 inches long, with one bulbous end that holds a cavity of black seeds and juicy orange fruit. Papayas taste like sweet melon with peachy undertones. They are used in countless ways, green and ripe, raw and cooked.

best way to peel and cut a papaya

Using a paring knife, peel the papaya in long strips. Cut a papaya in half and you'll find a mass of gray-black seeds in the center. Scoop out and discard the core of black seeds and gelatin. Cut the papaya halves in slices or cubes and serve.

KITCHEN NOTE

:: Papayas have soft skin and bruise easily, so they must be handled with care. Select ones that are at least half yellow (the rest of the skin will be green) and yield to gentle pressure. Avoid very soft or bruised fruit with a fermented aroma. Refrigerate ripe papaya to use within 1 week.

peach

It's hard to beat the pleasure of eating a peach out of hand. But the fruit's firm flesh and juicy sweetness make it the perfect ingredient for a variety of preparations, both sweet and savory.

best way to peel and slice a peach

Very ripe peaches are usually easy to peel; others may need to be blanched first. To blanch, cut a small X in the rounded end opposite from the stem.

Dip the fruit into boiling water for 30 seconds, then plunge it into ice water. The skins will peel off easily. Peaches oxidize and brown when exposed to air; rub or sprinkle them with lemon juice to prevent browning.

To halve peaches and nectarines, position the knife at a right angle to the crease in the fruit and cut it in half along its equator. Grasp the halves and twist them apart.

KITCHEN NOTES

:: Peaches are picked when mature but firm for their trip to the market. To encourage ripening, store peaches in a loosely closed paper bag or ripening bowl. Trapping the gas the peaches release as they ripen speeds up the process. Check daily; then refrigerate when ripe. In the refrigerator the peach will keep for up to 1 week, but optimum flavor will return only when the peach is brought back to room temperature.

:: Peaches with even a touch of green were immature when picked and will never ripen to their characteristic sweet, juicy flavor.

:: Look for peaches with a creamy-gold or yellow skin and a strong peach aroma. The rosy blush indicates certain varieties, not ripeness.

pineapple

The pineapple has been called the king of fruits, and with its crown of spiky green leaves and imposing shape, it is certainly impressive. These succulent tropical gems don't ripen off the plant, so those you buy are ready to eat. Choose the largest, plumpest one you can find.

best way to prepare a pineapple

If you want to end up with slices to serve fresh, cut off the top of the pineapple with a sharp knife. Cut off the bottom, exposing the flesh. Stand the pineapple on a cutting board. Cut down around the fruit to remove the peel in long slices, cutting deep enough to remove the brown "eyes" that are found on the outside of the flesh (f). (These have an unpleasant, peppery flavor.)

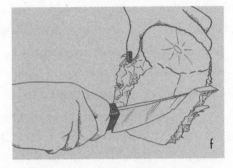

Place the pineapple flat on the cutting board and cut the fruit into rounds or slices. Remove the central core for each slice with a sharp knife, small round cookie cutter, or apple corer (g).

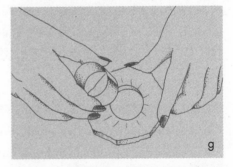

To end up with wedges, begin with the whole, peeled pineapple standing on one end. Cut the pineapple lengthwise into quarters, cutting through the center core (h). Cut the core from each quarter, then cut the quarters into wedges.

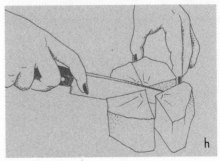

pineapple presentations

Hollowed-out pineapple shells make good receptacles for serving items like fruit salad, salsas, or just cut-up pineapple.

to hollow out a whole pineapple: Start by cutting off the leafy top with about ¾ inch of the crown, setting it aside for the lid. Using a long, sharp knife, cut around the flesh, leaving a shell about ½ inch thick. Cut almost to the bottom but not through the shell. Remove the flesh from the inside and cut the fruit off the core. Fill the hollow pineapple as desired. Use the crown as a decorative lid.

to hollow out a half shell: Hold the pineapple firmly and cut in half lengthwise, cutting through the leaves as well for a dramatic effect. With a sharp knife, cut along one side of the core and then around the inside of the shell to loosen a large section of the fruit. Leave about 1 inch of shell. Repeat on the other side of the core. Remove the fruit, then cut out the core by running your knife under it from one end to the other. Discard the core. Fill the shells as desired.

to make pineapple boats: Cut the pineapple lengthwise into quarters, again including the leaves, then cut out the core from each one. Without removing the flesh entirely, slide a knife between the flesh and skin on each wedge to separate them. Cut the flesh crosswise into slices. Still leaving the flesh on the skin, push alternate slices of pineapple to the left and right.

KITCHEN NOTE

:: Cooks should know that pineapple, as well as kiwi fruit and papaya, contains bromelain, an enzyme that breaks down protein. Because of this, pineapple will cause dairy products to break down and separate.

cooking techniques

dried fruit

Oven-drying is a slow, gentle cooking process that uses dry heat to extract the water from fruit. Left in the oven for several hours at a low temperature, the fruit does not burn, but shrinks and shrivels as the water evaporates. The outside dries while the inside steams, turning the whole fruit soft and chewy. The resulting flavors are surprisingly concentrated, the colors subdued and rich.

best way to dry fruit

Preheat the oven to 225°F. Begin by cutting the fruit into halves, quarters, or slices. Smaller fruits like grapes or berries can be dried whole. Line baking sheets with parchment paper to keep the fruits' abundant juices from sticking to the pans. If desired, you can sprinkle the fruits with chopped fresh herbs, salt and pepper, sugar, lemon zest, red pepper flakes, and other spices.

The fruits will dry in 1 to 6 hours. You can mix any combination of fruit on the same baking sheet; simply remove each fruit when the edges begin to shrivel and dry and the center still remains a little juicy. Store dried fruit in an airtight container in a cool, dry place for up to 1 month.

KITCHEN NOTES

:: Fruits with the highest water content work best for drying. Stone fruits, figs, and grapes dry with juicy centers. Pears and apples cut into ¼-inch slices will have a more chewy, leathery texture.

:: For best flavor, the fruit should be ripe but not overly ripe. It should hold its shape when cut.

:: Used dried peaches and nectarines on fruit tarts and dried figs in salads. All dried fruits are great in compotes.

:: Homemade dried fruit will not keep as long as store-bought varieties. Store homemade dried fruit in airtight containers

grilled fruit

Don't limit the grill to just entrées. You can add delicious flavor to just about any meal with grilled fruits. They can easily replace a sauce, condiment, or vegetable side dish, and, of course, they make fabulous desserts. Most people don't consider preparing fruit this way, but grilling intensifies fruit's natural flavor and sweetness while absorbing an appetizing smoky taste.

best way to grill fruits

Brush fruits with a little mild olive oil or vegetable oil to prevent them from sticking to the grill and drying out.

To facilitate turning, a grill basket works wonderfully. Grill the fruit over medium-low coals until it is soft but not mushy, 2 to 10 minutes.

KITCHEN NOTE

:: When you remove fruits from the fire, brush them again with a little oil or melted butter to revive their vibrancy.

fruit on the grill

....

apples and pears: Peel, core, and cut into 1-inch-thick wedges. Thread onto skewers or lay on a grill basket rack. Brush with melted butter and grill for 10 to 12 minutes, turning once or twice.

bananas: Just before grilling, slice the bananas, still in their skins, lengthwise. Grill cut-side down for 2 to 3 minutes, turn and grill 2 to 3 more minutes. To serve, remove the bananas from their skins.

figs: Halve and grill cut-side down to start, turning once, for about 5 minutes.

mango: Halve and grill cut-side down to start, turning once, for about 5 minutes.

melons and papayas: Halve, peel, and remove seeds from fruit. Cut each half into ½-inch-thick wedges. Grill for about 2 minutes per side.

nectarines and plums: Halve and pit. Grill cut-side down to start, turning once, for about 6 minutes.

peaches: Peel, halve, and pit. Grill cut-side down to start, turning once, for about 8 minutes.

pineapple: Peel, cut into ½-inch-thick slices, and core. Grill until lightly golden, about 2 minutes per side.

poached fruit

When a fruit doesn't seem quite ripe or flavorful, it can benefit from poaching in flavored syrup. Unlike other cooking methods, poaching allows the shape, texture, and basic flavor to remain intact while improving the fruit's texture as well as enhancing rather than masking its flavor. Poaching fruit also allows you to infuse it with an herb or spice. See page 138 for the fruits that are best for poaching.

best way to poach fruit

The most delicious way to poach fruit is by using a simple poaching syrup with some fresh lemon juice and a stick of cinnamon, some crushed fresh ginger, or a liqueur. Other flavorings include citrus zest, vanilla bean, wine, herbs, and spices. I like to use a ratio of 2 tablespoons lemon juice for every 2 cups of syrup. Pour the syrup, along with any flavorings, into a large pot. Bring to a boil, then reduce the heat to low. Peel or halve the fruits as indicated in the box. Then carefully add them to the pot. If necessary, add some more syrup or water to cover the fruits completely. Cook just below simmering until the fruit is fork-tender but not mushy.

When the fruits are just tender, turn off the heat and let them cool in the syrup to absorb as much flavor as possible. If the fruits seem too soft, remove them from the syrup right away and cool them as fast as possible in the refrigerator. To serve, spoon some of the poaching liquid over the fruit. Both can be warm or chilled.

poaching syrup

In a medium pan, combine 2 cups sugar and 2 cups water. Bring to a boil over medium-low heat, stirring occasionally to dissolve the sugar crystals. Remove from the heat. Makes 3 cups.

poaching fruit

· ·

apples and pears: Using a paring knife, quarter or halve the fruit. Core the fruits through the bottom end with a melon baller. As the fruits are peeled, it's a good idea to rub them with lemon juice to prevent discoloration. Poach for 15 to 20 minutes.

apricots and plums: Do not peel. Cut in half and remove pits. Poach for 5 to 8 minutes.

melons: Cut the melon in half and, using a spoon, scoop out the seeds. Cut the flesh off of the skin into large chunks. Add melon chunks to the syrup along with any juices. Poach for 5 to 10 minutes.

oranges: Using a sharp knife, cut away the peel and remove all white pith. Add peeled oranges to the syrup along with any juices. Poach for 5 to 10 minutes.

peaches: Peel peaches, cut them in half (or quarters), and the remove pits. Poach for 8 to 10 minutes.

pineapples: Peel with a knife and remove the eyes (see page 133), quarter, and core.

lemon cornmeal cake

SERVES 12 / This moist, lemony cake is flecked with the pleasant crunchiness of cornmeal. It pairs beautifully with fresh berries, such as blueberries and raspberries soaked in some orange juice or liqueur, or it can simply be served with a dollop of vanilla yogurt. Because it is not overly sweet, this sturdy cake makes an appealing breakfast as well as dessert.

1 cup yellow cornmeal, plus more for dusting

½ cup unbleached all-purpose flour

1½ teaspoons baking powder

¼ teaspoon salt

1 cup sugar

¼ cup vegetable oil

2 tablespoons butter, at room temperature

3 large eggs

½ cup plain low-fat yogurt

2 teaspoons grated lemon zest

1½ tablespoons fresh lemon juice

Preheat the oven to 350°F. Line the bottom of a 10-inch round pan with wax paper. Lightly grease the paper and dust with a little cornmeal, shaking out the excess.

In a medium bowl, mix the cornmeal, flour, baking powder, and salt. Set aside. In a large bowl, mix the sugar, oil, and butter until well blended. Add the eggs, one at a time, stirring just until blended. Add the yogurt, lemon zest, and lemon juice and stir just until blended. Add the dry ingredients and stir just until blended. Do not overmix.

Spoon the batter into the prepared pan and smooth the top with a rubber spatula. Bake until the cake is golden and a toothpick inserted into the center comes out clean, about 40 minutes. Cool the cake in the pan on a wire rack for 10 minutes. Invert the cake onto the rack, peel off the paper, and cool completely.

spiced peach chutney

MAKES 4 CUPS / Garlic and fresh ginger add a lively flavor to this fresh fruit chutney. It will add interest to everyday meals, such as curries, stews, and sandwiches, and can also be served as an appetizer with soft Brie or Camembert cheese on crackers.

2 pounds fresh peaches (about 8 medium), peeled
2-inch piece fresh ginger, peeled and minced
6 cloves garlic, minced
1 small orange
1 cup golden raisins
1 cup cider vinegar
½ cup packed light brown sugar
¼ teaspoon cayenne pepper
½ teaspoon salt
¼ teaspoon ground cinnamon

Coarsely chop the peaches and transfer them to a large pan. Add the ginger and garlic.

Using a citrus stripper or small, sharp paring knife, remove the zest from the orange in long strips and add to the pan. Remove and discard the white pith from the orange. Chop the orange, removing any seeds, and add it to the fruit in the pan.

Add the remaining ingredients and stir well. Bring the mixture to a boil over medium-high heat. Reduce the heat to medium-low, partially cover, and simmer, stirring occasionally, until all the liquid has evaporated and the chutney has thickened, about 45 minutes. Remove the pan from the heat and let cool.

Store the chutney in an airtight container in the refrigerator for up to 3 weeks.

quinoa salad with mango

SERVES 6 / Fresh mango adds an unexpected depth of flavor and richness to this main-dish salad. Fresh papaya and pineapple can also be used here.

2 cups water

1 cup uncooked quinoa

1 tablespoon tahini

2 tablespoons orange juice

1 cup plain low-fat yogurt or soft tofu

½ teaspoon ground cumin

Pinch of ground ginger

½ cup cooked or canned chickpeas

1 large ripe mango, diced

¼ cup golden raisins

¼ cup chopped cilantro leaves

In a medium saucepan, bring the water to a boil. Stir in the quinoa. Return to a boil. Reduce the heat, cover, and simmer until the water is absorbed and the grains are tender, 15 to 20 minutes.

Meanwhile, in a small bowl, mix the tahini and orange juice until blended. In a large bowl, whisk the yogurt until light and smooth. Whisk in the tahini mixture, cumin, and ginger. Stir in the chickpeas, mango, and raisins.

Fluff the quinoa with a fork. Stir into the mango mixture. Add the cilantro and stir until blended. Serve chilled or at room temperature.

guacamole

MAKES 2 CUPS / Besides being a wonderful dip for chips, guacamole is also good spread on sandwiches or served with shredded lettuce as a side dish. Add a little Italian dressing to it and you'll have a fresh-tasting salad dressing within seconds.

2 ripe medium avocados, preferably Hass
2 tablespoons fresh lemon juice
2 cloves garlic, minced
1 medium shallot, minced
½ teaspoon salt
3 tablespoons chopped fresh tomato
1 tablespoon chopped cilantro leaves
Several drops hot pepper sauce

Cut the avocados in half and remove the pits. Scoop out the pulp and place in a medium bowl. Drizzle with the lemon juice and mash with a fork. Add the garlic, shallot, salt, tomato, cilantro, and hot pepper sauce and mix well. Serve right away.

apple-oat squares

MAKES 16 / Charmingly old-fashioned and simple, these wholesome bars pair the comforting flavors of apples and oats. They're the perfect snack to pack in a lunch box or to enjoy with a cup of tea.

> 1½ cups unbleached all-purpose flour
>
> 1 cup old-fashioned rolled oats
>
> 1 cup packed light brown sugar
>
> 1 teaspoon grated lemon zest
>
> ¾ teaspoon baking powder
>
> ½ teaspoon salt
>
> ½ teaspoon ground cinnamon
>
> ¼ teaspoon ground nutmeg
>
> 3 tablespoons vegetable oil
>
> ¼ cup apple juice concentrate, thawed
>
> 2 tart medium apples, such as Granny Smith, peeled, cored, and
>   thinly sliced
>
> ¼ cup coarsely chopped walnuts, toasted

Preheat the oven to 350°F. Lightly grease a 9-inch square baking pan, or coat with nonstick cooking spray.

In a large bowl, mix the flour, oats, brown sugar, lemon zest, baking powder, salt, cinnamon, and nutmeg. Work in the oil and apple juice concentrate with a fork or your fingertips until the mixture resembles coarse crumbs.

Firmly press 2 cups of the oat mixture into the bottom of the prepared pan. Arrange the apples over the crust in three rows. Mix the walnuts into the remaining oat mixture. Sprinkle the mixture evenly over the apples and pat into an even layer.

Bake until the top is golden and the apples are tender when pierced with a fork, 30 to 35 minutes. Cool completely on a wire rack before cutting into squares.

pineapple fried rice

SERVES 6 / This vibrantly colored meal-in-one can be made with either leftover or freshly cooked rice.

5 tablespoons peanut oil

3 large eggs

¼ teaspoon salt

1 large onion, finely chopped

1 clove garlic, minced

1 teaspoon Szechwan hot bean paste

1½ cups cubed fresh pineapple (½-inch pieces)

1½ cups drained, cubed firm tofu (½-inch pieces)

1 tablespoon sugar

1 cup diced celery

4 green onions (white and light green parts), thinly sliced

4 cups cooked brown or white long-grain rice (1½ cups uncooked)

¼ cup tamari or low-sodium soy sauce

¼ cup vegetable stock

Salt and freshly ground pepper

Place a wok or large skillet over high heat and add 1 tablespoon of the oil. In a small bowl, beat the eggs with the salt. Add the eggs to the hot oil and cook, stirring until the eggs are set. Remove to a plate.

Add 2 tablespoons oil to the wok and heat over high heat. Add the onion, garlic, and bean paste and stir-fry for 30 seconds. Add the pineapple, tofu, and sugar and stir-fry until heated through and glazed, about 2 minutes. Add the celery and stir-fry for 1 minute. Transfer mixture to a bowl.

Add the remaining 2 tablespoons oil to the wok and heat over high heat. Add the green onions and stir quickly. Add the rice and stir-fry until heated through, about 2 minutes.

Stir in the tamari and stock until the rice is well coated. Add the scrambled eggs and pineapple-tofu mixture and stir until heated through. Season with salt and pepper and serve hot.

You don't have to be a vegetarian to reap the many benefits that grains and the pastas made from them have to offer. They're easy to digest and loaded with complex carbohydrates, the body's most readily available source of sustained energy. Ounce for ounce, you'll find the greatest nutritional return from these foods. And in terms of meal planning, the mind-boggling array of flavors, shapes, and textures assures that your diet will be varied.

pasta & grains

pasta

Besides its versatile nature, pasta has many other favorable features. It's easy to prepare, inexpensive, and adaptable. And is there anyone on Earth who doesn't just plain love it? Now that we are ardent fans, there is more great news—pasta is good for us. It is an excellent source of complex carbohydrates, which are essential in a balanced diet. So while trendiness may have sent pasta into the limelight, commonsense eating guarantees that it is there to stay.

best way to cook pasta

To cook pasta perfectly, you must start with the right pot. If you are cooking 1 pound of pasta, use a pot that will hold 4 to 5 quarts of water to give the pasta plenty of room to move around. There must be enough water to dilute the starch that leaches out of the pasta; otherwise the pasta will stick together. With an adequate amount of water, there is no need to add oil, which some cooks add with the idea that it will keep the pasta from clumping together.

Adding salt to the water, however, is an essential step that you shouldn't omit. When pasta is cooked in unsalted water, no matter how flavorful the sauce, the dressed pasta will taste bland. Use a coarse-grained salt, adding about 1 tablespoon per pound of pasta. Don't salt the water until it comes to a boil. Salted water has a higher boiling point. Add the salt to the boiling water and return to a boil before adding the pasta, to give it time to dissolve.

When the salted water is boiling, add the pasta all at once and stir with a wooden spoon to help keep the pasta from sticking. Stir the pasta occasionally during cooking. Always time the pasta from the moment the water returns to a boil. The most reliable way I've found to know when pasta is done is to start sampling it about 3 minutes before the package directions suggest it should be done. As a general rule, pasta is perfectly cooked when it has some bite to it but still is tender throughout—also called al dente. Undercooked pasta will have a visible white core and be slightly crunchy, while overcooked pasta will have lost its chewiness.

Drain the pasta right away—it will continue to cook as long as it sits in the water. Pour it into a large colander and give it several shakes. Don't overdrain the pasta; it should be slightly wet so it will coat well with sauce.

toss it right

Have the sauce heated and ready so the pasta can be tossed with it right after it has been drained.

Sauce the pasta in the pot or skillet containing the warm sauce, or in a warmed serving bowl.

Use two large forks and mix the pasta so that every piece is lightly coated with the sauce. Don't oversauce; the pasta should be moistened, not drowned.

glossary of pasta shapes

Pasta is available in literally hundreds of shapes and sizes today, and to increase the confusion, manufacturers often use different names for the same shape. Here are some of the most common pasta shapes.

agnolotti: Small crescent-shaped stuffed pasta.

anelli (anellini): Small pasta rings.

cannelloni: Large, round pasta tubes used for stuffing.

capelli: Also called angel hair. Delicate, long, and extremely fine pasta strands.

capellini: Long, fine strands that are slightly thicker than capelli.

cappelletti: Small, hat-shaped stuffed pasta.

cavatelli: Short, narrow, ripple-edged pasta shells.

conchiglie: Shell-shaped pasta.

ditali: Small macaroni about $\frac{1}{2}$ inch long. Used in soups.

ditalini: Smaller ditali.

elbow macaroni: Small, slightly curved tubes.

farfalle: Bow-tie-shaped pasta.

fettuccine: Long, thin, flat ribbons about $\frac{1}{2}$ inch wide.

fusilli: Spiral-shaped or twisted pasta that comes in either spaghetti-length strands or cut about $1\frac{1}{2}$ inches long.

gnocchi: Small dumplings made from potatoes, flour or farina, and usually eggs and cheese.

lasagne: Long, very broad ribbons with straight or rippled edges.

linguine: Narrow, flat ribbons about $\frac{1}{8}$ inch wide.

macaroni: Tube-shaped pasta of various lengths.

mafalda: Mini lasagne noodles.

manicotti: Very large pasta tubes used for stuffing.

orecchiette: Small disc-shaped or ear-shaped pasta.

orzo: Rice-shaped pasta.

pappardelle: Ribbons about ½ inch wide with rippled sides.

pastina: Tiny star-shaped or round pasta.

penne: Diagonally cut tubes with either smooth or ridged sides.

radiatore: Short, chunky-shaped pasta with rippled edges.

ravioli: Square-shaped stuffed pasta.

rigatoni: Large ridged macaroni about 1½ inches wide.

rotelle: Wagon-wheel-shaped pasta.

rotini: Short spiral-shaped pasta about 1 to 2 inches long.

spaghetti: Long, thin, round strands in various thicknesses.

spaghettini: Thin strands of spaghetti.

tagliatelle: Long, thin, flat ribbons about ¼ inch wide.

tortellini: Small stuffed pasta formed into a ring or hat shape.

vermicelli: Very thin strands of spaghetti.

ziti: Long, thin, straight-cut tubes ranging in length from 2 to 12 inches.

dried vs. fresh

Pasta is sold either dried or fresh. Dried pasta is made from flour and water. The best for flavor and texture is made from 100 percent durum wheat or semolina. The term "enriched" on the label of a package of dried pasta indicates that B vitamins and iron lost in processing have been added back. Fresh pasta, made with eggs and all-purpose flour, is lighter but richer than dried pasta. One is not superior to the other, but each stands up better to different sauces: Dried pasta is better for robust, full-bodied sauces, and fresh pasta requires a lighter treatment.

:: Choose dried or fresh pasta that is made from 100 percent durum wheat (also called semolina), a hard wheat that allows pasta to hold its shape, texture, and flavor while cooking.

:: If the pasta will be used to make a salad, rinse it under cold running water after cooking to remove the excess starch and to keep the pieces from sticking together.

:: Dried pasta will keep, stored airtight in a cool, dark place, almost indefinitely. Whole-wheat pasta is the exception; it will keep for only 1 month.

:: Fresh pasta will keep, stored airtight in the refrigerator, for up to 5 days or frozen for up to 4 months. Do not thaw frozen pasta before cooking.

:: Pasta cools quickly. Heating the serving bowl or plates will help keep it warm. To warm a serving bowl, pour hot water into it and let it stand until ready to use, then pour out the water and dry the bowl. Warm plates by putting them into a 250°F oven for 10 to 15 minutes just before serving.

:: To hold pasta made ahead of time, drain, rinse, toss with a little olive oil, and store at room temperature in a sealed plastic bag or a tightly covered bowl.

asian noodles

It wasn't that long ago that the word "noodle" conjured up just one image—Italian pasta. But today, as we embrace the cuisines of Thailand, Japan, Korea, Indonesia, Vietnam, and the Philippines, we are happily discovering just how diverse noodles can be. Cooks in the Far East and Southeast Asia have long used a wide range of noodles made from wheat flour, rice flour, buckwheat, mung bean, and yam. The good news is that these noodles are more widely available in the United States than ever before, and preparing them is easier than you might think.

asian egg noodles

Asian-style wheat noodles made with egg include lo mein, chow mein, somen, udon, and ramen. Go to any Asian market and you'll find them fresh, frozen, and dried. You'll see varying shapes and sizes, with different noodles called by the same name and similar noodles called by different names. In short, shopping for these noodles can cause confusion. Keep in mind, though, that because they are all made from the same ingredients, the noodles are, for the most part, interchangeable in recipes.

best way to cook asian egg noodles

Due to the variety of Asian wheat noodles available, it is best to follow the cooking instructions on the package and cook them until tender but still firm to the bite (al dente). Drain well.

bean threads

Made from starch extracted from mung beans, these dried noodles, also called cellophane noodles, have a thread-like fineness and, when rehydrated, a clear transparency.

best way to prepare bean threads

Bean threads are also cooked as part of the manufacturing process and require only soaking. Put them in a large bowl and add warm water to cover. Let them soak until softened, about 15 minutes. Because the noodles are typically sold in long strands that are bundled, they should be cut into shorter lengths to be eaten easily. This is best done after they are soaked. Drain well and use scissors to cut through the loops at the end of the bundles, or cut them into the lengths called for in the recipe.

buckwheat (soba) noodles

In Japan, buckwheat flour is used to make noodles known as soba. Soft brown buckwheat flour has an earthy, slightly sour flavor that gives the noodles a rich, robust taste. Some soba are made from just buckwheat, but more often they include whole-wheat flour.

Unless you're in Japan, fresh soba noodles are hard to find, but dried soba noodles with at least 80 percent buckwheat flour are excellent for home cooking. Packages of Japanese dried soba noodles will tell only how much buckwheat is in them in Japanese. The ingredients, however, will be listed in English. Look for ones given in this order: buckwheat flour, wheat flour, and salt, and nothing else.

best way to cook buckwheat noodles

To cook dried soba, bring $2^{1}/_{2}$ quarts of water to a boil in a large pot. Add 1 pound noodles, stir gently, and reduce the heat to medium. Simmer until tender but still firm to the bite (al dente), about 6 minutes. Drain well.

rice noodles

Noodles made from cooked rice are prevalent in Southeast Asia and also can be found in the cuisines of China and Japan. Tender, mildly sweet in flavor, and pale in color, they are excellent with both subtle and spicy toppings.

best way to cook rice noodles

Because they have already been cooked as part of their manufacturing process, preparing rice noodles is fairly simple. Put dried noodles (also called rice sticks) in a large bowl and add cold water to cover. Let soak until soft, about 30 minutes. Drain the noodles and proceed with the recipe.

If using fresh rice noodles, put them in a colander. Bring a pot of water to a boil and pour it over the noodles to rinse, soften, and warm them. The hot water removes an oil coating that prevents them from sticking together in their package.

rice

At the American table, rice is finally coming into its own, as we are discovering the delicious versatility and intriguing taste it can add to many meals. But adding rice to our diet reaps not only flavor benefits but nutritional ones as well. Rich in complex carbohydrates, rice has a mere whisper of fat per 1-cup serving and is packed with fiber and B vitamins. And few foods are so adaptable to so many preparations—from soup to dessert and for every meal from breakfast to late-night snack.

As our interest in rice grows, so does the selection of rices and rice products available to us. There are about 40,000 varieties of rice but only three main types. Long-grain rice includes the aromatic varieties like basmati and jasmine. It cooks up dry and fluffy, making it good for dishes where distinct, separate grains are desirable, such as pilafs and salads. Medium- and short-grain rices remain moist after cooking, with a greater tendency to cling together. They're great for risottos, croquettes, rice puddings, and sushi rolls.

best way to cook rice

There is no reason to rinse domestically grown rice. However, imported varieties or rice bought from a bulk bin benefit from rinsing to remove dust and grit. Put rice in a colander and rinse it under cold running water until the water runs clear.

Start with the right pan; a 2- to 3-quart pan is perfect for cooking 1 cup of raw rice. Bring the required amount of water (see the chart on page 155) to a boil. Stir in the rice and add a little salt, if desired. Return the water to a boil. Cover, reduce the heat, and simmer until the rice is tender and the liquid is absorbed. Simmer white rice for about 15 minutes and brown rice for 40 minutes. Remove the pan from the heat and let it stand, covered, for about 10 minutes. Do not remove the lid of the pot while the rice is cooking; the escaping steam can result in undercooked rice.

To make a rice pilaf, first sauté onions and other aromatic ingredients in butter or oil in a deep skillet and then stir in long-grain rice. Stir until the rice is coated with the butter or oil, about 2 minutes. Pour the required amount of water or stock into the pan. When the rice has absorbed the liquid and is tender, the pilaf is ready.

brown vs. white

All rice starts off brown. The grain is harvested in its hull, a tough, inedible covering. Removing the hull reveals the whole brown, red, or black kernels inside. To get white rice, these kernels are refined—stripped of their husk, bran, and germ to achieve a polished grain that has very little left in the way of nutrition. Refined rice is sometimes enriched after the fact with vitamins and minerals, but the amounts added back pale in comparison to the original. Parboiled or converted rice fares a bit better healthwise. This is because, before hulling, the grains are steamed under pressure, which forces the vitamins and minerals on the outside of the kernels into the center, saving much of the nutritional value.

rice glossary

Navigating the world of rice can be confusing. Here's a rundown of some rice varieties. Some are available in supermarkets, while others have to be purchased in ethnic markets or specialty food stores.

Arborio: A medium-grain Italian variety prized for making the classic dish risotto. This small, round rice cooks to a soft, creamy consistency while maintaining a slightly firm center. For the best texture when cooked, do not rinse the grains.

basmati: A wonderfully nutty-tasting, aromatic long-grain rice from northern India and Pakistan, available in both brown and refined varieties. When cooked, the rice elongates instead of plumping, resulting in long, narrow grains.

black japonica: A cross between a medium- and short-grain rice, this rice is not milled and has the cooking characteristics of brown rice. It has a sticky texture and somewhat grassy flavor. You may find it mixed with a medium-grain mahogany variety.

brown: This rice requires longer cooking than white rice because only the inedible husk has been removed, leaving the outer shell (bran) intact, which acts as a barrier to heat and moisture. The bran layer colors the rice beige and, when cooked, gives the rice a nutty taste and a chewier texture. Although the long-grain variety is most common, medium-grain and short-grain brown rice are also available.

jasmine: A delicately flavored rice with an almost floral fragrance. This long-grain Thai native is now also grown in the United States. It cooks to a slightly stickier consistency than other long-grain varieties and will not harden when refrigerated, as some others will do.

sushi: A white, sticky-textured medium-grain variety often imported from Asia. It is mainly used for Japanese nori-wrapped rolls.

sweet or sticky: A round, starchy, short-grain Asian variety that is exceptionally sticky and sweet. Steaming is the best cooking method to prevent a gluey texture. This rice, which comes in both brown and white versions, is traditionally used for porridge and sweets and to make small Japanese rice cakes called *mochi*.

Texmati: A brand name for a hybrid of basmati and Texas-grown long-grain rice that was developed in the 1970s. Available in both brown and refined forms, it has a somewhat milder flavor than basmati and doesn't elongate as much during cooking. Calmati is a similar hybrid grown in California.

Valencia: A medium-grain variety from Spain, especially suitable for the Spanish dish paella. Look for it in specialty food markets.

Wehani: A long-grained basmati hybrid named for its developers: Wendell, Eldon, Homer, Albert, and Harlan Lundberg, of Lundberg Family Farms in California. This unrefined long-grain rice has a rich russet color, nutty flavor, and "popcorn" aroma when cooked.

wild pecan: Another basmati hybrid, grown in Louisiana and golden brown in color because it retains a bit of bran. Intensely aromatic and flavorful, this rice cooks quickly.

wild rice: This is not a true rice—it's actually the seed of an aquatic grass—but its long, dark grains resemble rice. Indigenous to the northern Great Lakes region and southern Canada, it was a staple food for American Indians in that area. Some is still hand-harvested in the wild, though commercial wild rice cultivation and machine harvesting are increasingly common. Wild rice is higher in protein and B vitamins than regular rice. It has a deeply earthy flavor and fluffy texture when cooked. For economy and a toned-down taste, try mixing it with long-grain brown rice in recipes.

rice cooking chart

grain (1 cup dry)	water	cooking time	approx. yield
Brown Rice			
Long-grain, medium-grain basmati, Wehani, Wild Pecan, Valencia	$2\frac{1}{2}$ cups	35 to 45 minutes	3 cups
Short-grain	$2\frac{1}{4}$ cups	40 to 45 minutes	$3\frac{1}{4}$ cups
White Rice			
Long-grain, medium-grain, basmati, Texmati, jasmine	2 cups	15 to 20 minutes	$3\frac{1}{4}$ cups
Converted	$2\frac{1}{4}$ cups	20 minutes	$3\frac{1}{4}$ cups
Red Rice	$2\frac{1}{2}$ cups	45 minutes	3 cups
Black Japonica	2 cups	45 minutes	3 cups
Wild Rice	4 cups	45 to 50 minutes	3 cups

risotto

Of the world's famous rice dishes, none is cooked like risotto. Slowly, patiently, the cook teases the creamy essence out of the rice to make an irresistible, comforting dish. Making a good risotto is like making good soup. It involves no special tricks, just careful observation. While frequent stirring is necessary to produce the characteristic creaminess of a good risotto, constant stirring is not. Walking over to the pan every minute or two and stirring the rice for about 10 seconds with a wooden spoon is sufficient. The rice does require attention, but it is not all-consuming. Between stirs you can be preparing other items in the recipe or menu.

However, the type of rice you use is critical. Italian medium-grain rices, such as Arborio or Carnaroli, are the best choices. Other medium-grain or long-grain rices are not suitable because they have a different ratio of starches and will not yield slightly chewy grains surrounded by a creamy sauce.

best way to cook risotto

This is a basic recipe for classic risotto that will serve four. Have about 6 cups of a good-quality vegetable stock (preferably homemade) simmering over low heat. In a wide, heavy pot, heat 1 to 2 tablespoons butter and 1 tablespoon olive oil over medium heat. Add ½ cup finely chopped onion and cook, stirring often, until softened, 3 to 4 minutes. Add 1½ cups Arborio rice to the pot and stir it around for a minute or so, until the grains are thoroughly coated with the butter mixture. As you stir, the grains will start to make a clicking noise, which tells you it's time to add the wine, ½ cup dry white or red.

Wine gives risotto an acid note that lifts up the flavors. If you don't want to use wine, add a little lemon juice at the end to achieve the same purpose. When the wine is stirred in, the rice will begin to release some of its starch, turning the liquid slightly milky—a sign of creaminess to come.

After the wine is absorbed, begin adding the warm stock to the rice. Because its flavor will permeate the dish, use stock of the highest quality. Add the stock in small increments, about ½ cup at a time, just enough so that the liquid comes up to the top of the rice. Keep the heat high enough to maintain a lively bubble. Stir the risotto every minute or so, and add more stock when the rice has absorbed the liquid.

After about 15 minutes, begin to taste the rice for doneness. When it is tender, with just a firm bite in the center, it is nearly done. The total cooking time is usually about 25 minutes. When the rice is done, the final step in a great risotto is done off the heat. This involves adding butter to give the risotto a rich texture. Any final notes of flavor—herbs, cheese, or an extra splash of wine—are also added just before serving.

KITCHEN NOTES

:: You will need a wide pot so that the risotto can cook quickly. A tall, narrow pot just doesn't work well. Also, given the relatively long cooking time, it's essential to choose a heavy-bottomed pot to prevent scorching.

:: Never rinse the rice before making risotto or you'll wash off some of the grain's starch, which is essential in creating its noteworthy creaminess.

grains

Whole grains are the perfect food: thoroughly versatile, delicious, filling, low in fat, and packed with nutrients. Besides having a wide range of B vitamins, grains provide ample iron, calcium, phosphorous, potassium, magnesium, and zinc.

To get the most from your grains, use unrefined ones. Refined grains stripped of their bran and germ lack several B vitamins, most minerals, and much of their fiber. Enriching these grains adds back only three B vitamins and iron, resulting in a paler version of the original.

best way to simmer grains

Just before using, rinse the grains well in a fine sieve (pre-steamed, rolled grains such as oats, rye flakes, triticale, and wheat flakes do not need rinsing). Toasting grains in a dry or lightly oiled skillet before cooking will impart a delicious nutty flavor. This technique works great for millet, quinoa, and buckwheat groats.

In a large, heavy saucepan, bring to a boil the amount of water specified (see the chart on facing page). Stir in the grains. Return to a boil. Reduce the heat, cover, and simmer until the water is absorbed and the grain is tender. Do not stir while the grain is cooking. (Bulgur, oats, and couscous do not require simmering; just turn off the stove and let them stand, covered, for the specified time.)

If the grain is still chewy at the end of cooking, add ½ cup water for every cup of grain used, then cover and simmer until the water is absorbed.

KITCHEN NOTES

:: You can reduce the cooking time of wheat and other whole-grain berries by soaking them in cold water to cover overnight. Use the soaking water for cooking them.

:: Whole grains will keep for several months, so for economic reasons, it's wise to buy them in bulk. Make sure the store you are buying from has a good turnover, so you know you are getting the freshest grains possible. Look for grains that are plump, not shriveled, with uniform size and color.

:: Put grains in tightly lidded jars and store in a cool, dry place. Heat and humidity will turn grains rancid and destroy their nutrients. During the warm months, refrigerate grains.

grain cooking chart

grain (1 cup dry)	water	cooking time	approx. yield
Amaranth	3 cups	20 to 25 minutes	2 ½ cups
Barley			
Whole (hulled, pearled)	3 ½ cups	50 to 55 minutes	3 cups
Grits	4 cups	15 to 20 minutes	3 ⅔ cups
Job's tears (hato mugi)	3 cups	40 to 45 minutes	2 ½ cups
Buckwheat groats	2 cups	15 to 20 minutes	2 ½ cups
Kamut			
Whole grain	3 cups	1 hour	3 cups
Rolled	2 cups	15 to 20 minutes	3 cups
Millet	2 ½ cups	35 to 40 minutes	3 ½ cups
Quinoa	2 cups	15 to 20 minutes	3 ½ cups
Rye			
Whole berries	3 ½ cups	50 to 60 minutes	3 cups
Cracked	3 cups	40 to 45 minutes	3 cups
Rolled/flaked	2 cups	15 to 20 minutes	2 ½ cups
Spelt			
Whole grain	3 cups	1 hour	2 ½ cups
Rolled	2 cups	15 to 20 minutes	3 cups
Teff	3 cups	15 to 20 minutes	3 cups
Triticale			
Whole berries	3 ½ cups	50 to 55 minutes	2 ½ cups
Flaked	2 cups	15 to 20 minutes	2 ½ cups
Wheat			
Whole berries	3 ½ cups	50 to 55 minutes	2 ½ cups
Cracked	3 cups	35 to 40 minutes	2 ½ cups
Rolled/flaked	2 cups	15 to 20 minutes	3 cups

polenta

Polenta is a thick, creamy, golden pudding that has inspired Italian cooks to create countless variations. Common throughout northern Italy, polenta can be eaten hot (known as soft polenta), or it can be poured into a pan, cooled until firm, and sliced. In that form, it can be layered with sauces, cheese, and vegetables and baked until bubbly.

best way to cook soft polenta

The traditional method for making soft polenta requires constant stirring and a watchful eye to prevent lumping and scorching. But I've found that cooking it in a double boiler produces soft, fluffy polenta every time, with only occasional stirring.

Fill the bottom half of a double boiler with 2 inches of water. Bring the water to a boil, reduce the heat, and keep the water at a simmer.

Place 4 cups of boiling water in the top half of the double boiler. Whisk in 1 cup medium-grind cornmeal and ½ teaspoon coarse salt (or to taste). Set the top of the pan in its base, cover, and simmer the polenta until soft and tender, 1¼ to 1½ hours, stirring about every 20 minutes with a long-handled wooden spoon.

As it nears doneness, taste the cornmeal as you would pasta. The grains should be tender yet retain a bit of texture. The polenta should also have a distinct corn flavor and be the right consistency—not too thin or too thick. Remove the polenta from the water and let it stand, covered, for 5 minutes before serving.

Once the polenta is cooked, it can be kept for up to 4 hours and reheated. To reheat the polenta, set it in the top of a double boiler over simmering water and stir until heated through.

best way to cook firm polenta

Polenta can also be cooked to a thicker texture, cooled until firm, and then sliced or cut into shapes. To make firm polenta, lightly coat an 8-inch square pan or a 9-by-5-inch loaf pan with nonstick olive oil spray and set aside. In a medium saucepan, bring to a boil 4½ cups water, 1½ cups cornmeal, and 1 teaspoon salt; whisk well. Cook the polenta over medium heat, whisking constantly, until it starts to thicken. Add 1 tablespoon olive oil or butter and cook over low heat, stirring with a wooden spoon until the polenta is thickened and smooth, about 30 minutes. Scrape the polenta into the prepared pan and smooth the top. Cool thoroughly, then cover the pan and refrigerate overnight. The polenta is then ready to be cut into shapes and pan-fried, baked, or grilled.

cornmeal vs. polenta

"Polenta" is the Italian name for cornmeal and also refers to the dish of cooked cornmeal. Cornmeal sold as polenta will have a medium to coarse grind (similar to granulated sugar) that will cook up soft and tender.

Stone-ground cornmeal is usually the right grind for making polenta. The major brands of finely ground cornmeal found in supermarkets are not suited for making polenta. Instant or quick-cooking polenta is made of cornmeal that has been cooked and dried. Its flavor and texture are not as good as the real thing, but it's acceptable in a time crunch.

oatmeal

Many of us think of oatmeal as a ready-to-eat wonder that comes in a box or envelope. But quick and instant oats are relatively modern inventions, all made by processing steamed, flattened oats into very small pieces so they will cook quickly. This process diminishes the flavor and texture of the oats. For the best oatmeal, start with steel-cut oats, also called Irish or Scottish oats. Look for them in natural-food stores and some large supermarkets.

best way to cook oatmeal

Toasting the oats before they are cooked gives the resulting cereal a delicious nutty flavor. In a medium skillet, melt about 1 tablespoon butter and toast 1 cup steel-cut oats, stirring often, until they begin to brown and give off a fragrant aroma, 1 to 2 minutes.

In a large, heavy saucepan, bring 3 cups water and 1 cup whole milk to a simmer. Stir the toasted oats into the simmering liquid, reduce the heat to medium-low, and simmer gently until the mixture is thick and creamy and almost all the liquid is absorbed, about 30 minutes. Stir in ½ teaspoon salt after 20 minutes of cooking. Stir the oatmeal occasionally while cooking; stirring it too often will diminish its texture. Let it stand, covered, for 5 minutes before serving.

toppings

For many, the toppings are the best part of a hot cereal. Try these:

:: Sliced pears or apples sautéed in butter and sugar

:: Cooked cranberries and oranges

:: Toasted hazelnuts

:: Dried fruits like apricots, figs, and raisins plumped in orange juice

:: Honey and cinnamon

:: Warm cream infused with vanilla

penne with eggplant ragu

SERVES 4 / This chunky eggplant sauce with Asian flavors transforms pasta into company fare. It also makes a great topping for udon noodles or soft polenta.

2 medium eggplants, cut into ¾-inch cubes

4 teaspoons salt, plus more to taste

¼ cup hoisin sauce

¼ cup water

¼ cup fresh lemon juice

2 teaspoons dark (Asian) sesame oil

12 ounces dry penne pasta

3 tablespoons olive oil

4 cloves garlic, minced

2 cups cherry tomatoes, halved

Freshly ground pepper

Put the eggplant cubes into a colander, toss with 2 teaspoons of the salt, and set aside. Bring a large pot of water to a boil.

In a small bowl, mix the hoisin sauce, water, lemon juice, and sesame oil and set aside. When the water boils, add 2 teaspoons salt. Return to a boil and add the pasta, stirring to prevent it from sticking. Cook, stirring occasionally, until the pasta is al dente, about 10 minutes.

Meanwhile, in a large skillet, heat the olive oil over medium heat. Add the garlic and cook, stirring often, until fragrant, about 30 seconds. Add the eggplant in batches, squeezing out as much water as possible first. Cook, stirring often, for 5 minutes. Add the tomatoes and hoisin mixture and stir well. Cover and cook, stirring occasionally, until the eggplant is tender, about 10 minutes.

Drain the pasta and transfer to a large, shallow bowl. Add the eggplant mixture and toss to mix. Season to taste with salt and pepper.

baked pasta with arugula

SERVES 6 / This dish evolved from an improvisation with leftovers, but now it's a favorite that I make time and time again. Arugula has a peppery flavor, but you can also use fresh spinach or Swiss chard. You can also substitute smoked mozzarella, or even Monterey Jack or Cheddar—whatever you have on hand.

2 ½ teaspoons salt

1 pound dry rigatoni pasta (or other medium-sized pasta)

2 tablespoons olive oil

1 medium zucchini, cut into 1-inch pieces

1 medium summer squash, cut into 1-inch pieces

2 cups (packed) arugula, coarsely chopped

1 ½ pounds ripe plum tomatoes, halved, seeded, and cut into ½-inch pieces (1 ½ cups)

8 ounces mozzarella cheese, cut into ½-inch pieces

½ cup kalamata olives, pitted and chopped

½ cup grated Parmesan cheese

½ teaspoon red pepper flakes, or to taste

Bring a large pot of water to a boil. When the water boils, add 2 teaspoons of the salt. Return to a boil, then add the pasta, stirring to prevent sticking. Cook, stirring occasionally, until the pasta is al dente, about 10 minutes. Drain the pasta and return it to the pot.

Meanwhile, preheat the oven to 375°F. Lightly grease a 9-by-13-inch baking dish. In a large skillet, heat oil over medium heat. Add the zucchini and summer squash and cook, stirring often, until they are beginning to soften, 5 to 7 minutes. Add the arugula and cook, stirring, until wilted, about 1 minute.

Add the squash to the pasta, then add the tomatoes, mozzarella, olives, Parmesan, remaining ½ teaspoon salt, and red pepper flakes. Toss to mix well, then transfer the mixture to the prepared baking dish. Bake until the cheese is melted and the pasta starts to brown, about 15 minutes. Serve hot.

pasta e fagioli

SERVES 4 / The satisfying combination of pasta and beans is a staple in the Mediterranean diet. This unpretentious Tuscan-style soup contains white beans, pasta, plum tomatoes, garlic, and basil. If you don't have time to cook the beans, you can use canned beans, just substitute one 16-ounce can, rinsed and drained.

⅔ cup dried cannellini beans

3 tablespoons olive oil, preferably extra-virgin

2 cloves garlic, minced

1 can (16 ounces) plum tomatoes, drained and coarsely chopped

1½ teaspoons minced fresh basil leaves, or ½ teaspoon dried

1 cup dry ditalini or elbow macaroni

2 teaspoons salt, plus more to taste

Freshly ground pepper

In a large pot, combine the dried beans with cold water to cover by 3 inches. Let the beans soak for 6 to 8 hours at cool room temperature or in the refrigerator. Drain the beans in a colander and rinse under cold running water. Or, to save time, place the beans in a large saucepan with cold water to cover by 3 inches. Bring to a boil over medium-high heat. Reduce the heat to low and simmer the beans for 2 minutes. Turn off the heat, cover, and let the beans soak until they have softened and swelled, about 1 hour. Drain well.

In a large saucepan, heat the olive oil over medium heat. Add the garlic and cook, stirring often, until fragrant, about 30 seconds. Add the tomatoes and basil and cook, stirring occasionally, for 5 minutes. Add the beans and 4 cups of water; bring to a boil. Reduce the heat and simmer, uncovered, until the beans are tender, about 1 hour. (If using canned beans, add them with just 3½ cups of water; bring to a boil, reduce the heat, and simmer for 10 minutes.)

Transfer half of the soup to a food processor and process until smooth. Return the purée to the pan. Add the pasta and 2 teaspoons salt. Simmer until the pasta is tender, about 10 minutes. Season to taste with salt and pepper, and serve hot.

asian noodle salad

SERVES 6 / The nutty flavor and chewy texture of buckwheat noodles are highlighted in this light and refreshing salad. It's guaranteed to perk you up on a hot summer day.

12 ounces dry buckwheat noodles (soba)

2 cups peeled, julienned carrots

2 cups julienned snow peas, strings and ends removed

1½ cups cored, seeded, and julienned red bell pepper

½ cup tamari or light soy sauce

6 tablespoons rice vinegar

¼ cup dark (Asian) sesame oil

3 tablespoons chopped green onions (white and light green parts)

2 tablespoons rice wine

2 tablespoons sugar

1½ tablespoons peeled, minced fresh ginger

In a large pot, bring 2½ quarts of water to a boil. Add the noodles, stir gently, and reduce the heat to medium. Simmer the noodles until tender but still firm to the bite (al dente), about 6 minutes. Drain well, rinse under cold running water, and drain again. Transfer the noodles to a large, shallow serving bowl.

Add the carrots, snow peas, and bell pepper to the noodles. In a small bowl, combine the tamari, vinegar, sesame oil, green onions, rice wine, sugar, and ginger. Stir until the sugar is dissolved. Pour the mixture over the noodles and vegetables and toss to coat. Serve at room temperature.

simple lemon pilaf

SERVES 6 / This dish is really simple, really good, and very versatile. You can substitute 1 teaspoon fresh thyme for the parsley and add frozen peas or blanched asparagus tips to dress it up.

1 tablespoon olive oil

1 tablespoon butter

1 medium onion, finely chopped

⅓ cup pine nuts (optional)

2 cups basmati rice

3 cups clear vegetable stock or water

¼ cup fresh lemon juice

1 teaspoon grated lemon zest

2 tablespoons chopped flat-leaf parsley

In a large saucepan, heat the oil and butter over medium heat. Add the onion and pine nuts and cook, stirring often, until they are lightly browned, 5 to 7 minutes.

Add the rice and stir for 2 minutes. Stir in the stock, lemon juice, and lemon zest. Bring to a boil, then cover, reduce the heat, and simmer until the liquid is absorbed and the rice is tender, about 20 minutes. Remove the pan from the heat and let stand, covered, for 5 minutes. Stir in the parsley and serve warm.

polenta with tomato-mushroom sauce

SERVES 4 / Using a combination of fresh and dried mushrooms in this sauce gives it a rich, bold flavor. You can use other fresh mushrooms, such as portobello or shiitake, according to your taste. Although the sauce is served over firm polenta in this recipe, it is also good with soft polenta or even pasta.

tomato-mushroom sauce

1 ounce dried porcini mushrooms

1 cup hot water

1 tablespoon olive oil

1 clove garlic, minced

1 large onion, halved and thinly sliced

½ teaspoon dried oregano

8 ounces cremini mushrooms, sliced

1 can (14 ounces) diced tomatoes

Salt and freshly ground pepper

2 tablespoons chopped parsley

polenta

4½ cups water

1½ cups medium-grain yellow cornmeal

1 teaspoon salt

1 tablespoon olive oil

Grated Parmesan cheese, for garnish

TO MAKE THE SAUCE: In a small bowl, soak the dried mushrooms in the hot water for 15 to 20 minutes. Drain, reserving the soaking liquid. Strain the soaking liquid through a paper towel–lined strainer and set aside. Chop the mushrooms and set aside.

In a large skillet, heat the oil over medium heat. Add the garlic and cook, stirring often, until fragrant, 1 minute. Add the onion and oregano and cook, stirring often, until the onion is softened, about 5 minutes.

Increase the heat to medium-high. Add the cremini mushrooms and reserved chopped, soaked mushrooms. Cook, stirring often, until the mushrooms begin to soften, about 5 minutes. Stir in the reserved soaking liquid and tomatoes. Bring to a boil. Reduce the heat to low and simmer, uncovered, until the juices have reduced slightly, 8 to 10 minutes. Season to taste with salt and pepper. Stir in the parsley. Remove the pan from the heat.

TO MAKE THE POLENTA: Lightly coat an 8-inch square pan with nonstick cooking spray and set aside. In a medium saucepan, combine the water, cornmeal, and salt and whisk well. Cook over medium heat, whisking constantly, until the polenta starts to thicken. Add the olive oil and cook over low heat, stirring with a wooden spoon, until the polenta is thickened and smooth, about 30 minutes. Scrape into the prepared pan and smooth the top. Let stand for 30 minutes, or until firm.

To serve, reheat the mushroom sauce if necessary. Cut the polenta into 8 squares and place 2 squares on each serving plate. Spoon the mushroom sauce over the polenta. Serve right away, sprinkled with Parmesan cheese.

sesame ginger bulgur

SERVES 4 / If you are making this salad ahead of time, remove it from the refrigerator about 30 minutes before serving, as the flavors will be more vibrant at room temperature. Also taste and adjust the seasonings before serving.

1⅔ cups water

1¼ cups bulgur

2 cups lightly packed radish sprouts

1 bunch green onions (white and pale green parts), chopped

¼ cup rice wine vinegar

1½ tablespoons tamari or soy sauce

1 tablespoon dark (Asian) sesame oil

1 tablespoon peeled, minced fresh ginger

1½ teaspoons chile paste with garlic

1 teaspoon honey

¼ cup toasted peanut halves

In a medium saucepan, bring the water to a boil. Add the bulgur, cover, and remove from the heat. Let stand for 30 minutes, or until the water is absorbed. Spread the bulgur out on a baking sheet to cool, about 20 minutes.

In a serving bowl, combine the cooled bulgur, sprouts, and green onions.

In a small bowl, whisk together the vinegar, tamari, sesame oil, ginger, garlic, chile paste, and honey. Pour over the salad and toss to coat. Garnish with peanuts and serve.

winter squash risotto

SERVES 6 / Wonderfully rich and creamy, this dish can be served as a meal all by itself. Remember that risotto waits for no one. Pour it into warm serving bowls and serve right away. As it cools, the rice will tighten and lose its semifluid consistency.

5½ to 6 cups clear vegetable stock
1 tablespoon olive oil
1 tablespoon butter
1 medium onion, chopped
1 clove garlic, minced
2 cups Arborio rice
¼ cup white wine
2½ cups peeled, diced butternut squash (1-inch dice)
2 teaspoons minced fresh rosemary or thyme leaves
¼ cup grated Parmesan cheese
Salt and freshly ground pepper

In a small saucepan, bring the stock just to a simmer over medium-low heat.

While the stock is heating, in a large saucepan, heat the oil and butter over medium heat. Add the onion and garlic and cook, stirring often, until softened, 3 minutes. Add the rice and stir constantly for 1 minute. Add the wine and stir until almost completely absorbed, about 1 minute.

Add ½ cup of the hot stock to the rice and cook, stirring almost constantly, until the liquid is almost completely absorbed. Add another ½ cup stock and cook, stirring constantly, until the liquid is almost completely absorbed. Stir in the squash and continue adding stock, ½ cup at a time, making sure that most of the liquid is absorbed before adding more. Remove the pan of stock from the heat when about ½ cup remains. Start checking the rice for doneness by biting into a grain—it should be firm but tender. The total cooking time is 25 to 30 minutes. Stir in the rosemary, Parmesan cheese, and salt and pepper to taste.

Spoon the risotto into shallow serving bowls and serve right away.

wheat berry waldorf

SERVES 6 / Wheat berries add a wonderful crunchy, chewy texture to this healthy apple salad. It's good served on its own, or it can be stuffed into pita pockets with some shredded lettuce for a great sandwich.

4 cups water

1 cup wheat berries, rinsed and sorted

2 medium-sized tart apples, such as Granny Smith

1 stalk celery, chopped

2 green onions (white and light green parts), chopped

½ cup unsweetened dried cherries or cranberries

¼ cup golden raisins

¼ cup walnuts, toasted and chopped

¼ cup chopped fresh mint leaves

3 tablespoons cider vinegar

3 tablespoons orange juice

½ teaspoon grated orange zest

Salt and freshly ground pepper

In a large, heavy saucepan, bring the water to a boil. Stir in the wheat berries. Return to a boil. Reduce the heat, cover, and simmer until the water is absorbed and the wheat berries are tender, about 1 hour. Drain off any excess water. Spread the wheat berries out on a baking sheet to cool.

In a large bowl, combine the wheat berries, apples, celery, green onions, dried cherries, raisins, walnuts, and mint. In a measuring cup or small bowl, mix the vinegar, and orange juice and zest. Pour over the grain mixture. Season to taste with salt and pepper and toss to coat. Serve at room temperature.

soy foods

Soy, which has been popular in Asian cultures for centuries, has finally come into the American spotlight, and its nutritional profile is only part of the attraction. Yes, it's a great source of protein and has many essential vitamins and minerals, including B vitamins, folic acid, calcium, and iron, but it's also linked to lowering cholesterol, reducing heart disease, relieving menopause symptoms, and preventing osteoporosis. With all these claims, it's no wonder that soy, in all its forms, including tofu, tempeh, miso, edamame, and soymilk, is gaining our attention. And as its popularity skyrockets, so does its availability and variety, making it easier than ever to enjoy this once humble legume.

tofu

Tofu is made by separating soymilk into curds and whey (a thin, light-amber liquid), pressing the curds together, cutting the resulting soy cheese into blocks, and packing them into the whey or water. The amount of whey pressed out of the soymilk curds during the tofu-making process is what ultimately determines its texture. Soft tofu (sometimes called Japanese-style tofu) has a soft consistency, which is great for making dips, dressings, and desserts. Firm tofu has a medium density and is the best type to use when making tofu salads and scrambled tofu. Extra-firm tofu is dense, holds sliced or cubes shapes well, and is ideal for cutlets and stir-fried dishes. Silken tofu has a soft, custard-like texture and is packaged aseptically in 10-ounce containers that do not require refrigeration. Although the silken variety comes in soft, firm, and extra-firm textures, they all are fairly soft and tender.

best way to drain and press tofu

Draining tofu simply means pouring off the water that the tofu is packed in. Pressing means to wrap it in cloth or paper towels and then let it sit on toweling, weighted down, to force out the excess water within. There are several reasons for pressing the water out of tofu, including to make it firmer and chewier, to make room for it to absorb other liquids and seasonings, such as marinades and spice rubs, and to avoid diluting sauces and dressings.

To press a slab of tofu, wrap the entire piece in an absorbent dish towel. Set the tofu on a cutting board and weight it down with something heavy, like a large can of tomatoes. Rest one end of the board on a plate or something else so that the board tilts toward the sink. The excess water will drain off and flow into the sink. Drain for about 30 minutes.

best way to crumble tofu

Another way to remove water from tofu is to squeeze it in your hand. This will give it a texture similar to cottage cheese. This technique works great for making tofu fillings, scrambled tofu, and tofu salads. Cut the tofu into small pieces (1 to 2 inches). Gently squeeze one piece at time over the sink until it resembles large- to small-curd cottage cheese, then crumble the tofu into a bowl. You will be squeezing out about half the liquid.

best way to freeze tofu

Freezing tofu completely changes it texture. The whey, which crystallizes into ice when frozen, melts away, leaving a spongy, solid mass of creamy beige tofu. Frozen and thawed tofu has a chewy, meat-like texture that absorbs marinades and flavorings and is great for grilling as slices or for using crumbled in dishes like chili and tacos.

You can freeze extra-firm, firm, or soft tofu. Open and drain the tofu, then wrap it in plastic wrap and freeze it for at least 12 hours or for up to 5 months. To freeze slices, drain and slice the tofu, arrange on a baking sheet, and freeze until firm. Once frozen, the slices can be stored in a plastic freezer bag.

You can thaw frozen tofu in the refrigerator, at room temperature, or by placing it in a bowl of lukewarm water.

best way to dry and firm tofu

Besides draining and pressing tofu, there are other methods to dry out and firm tofu. These techniques will prevent tofu from falling apart when stir-frying, sautéing, or frying.

Cut drained tofu into slices or cubes. Coat a large nonstick skillet with cooking spray and heat over medium-high heat. Cook the tofu, turning once, until the water has evaporated and the tofu is dry and firm, about 8 minutes. Or you can dry and firm the tofu in a 350°F oven. To do so, place sliced or cubed tofu in an oiled pie plate and bake for 15 minutes. Pour off the water from the pan and continue baking for 15 minutes, or until the tofu is firm and dry.

To firm silken or soft tofu, bring about 6 cups of water to a boil in a wide, deep skillet. Add tofu cubes or slices and simmer for 3 to 5 minutes. Remove the tofu with a small strainer or slotted spoon and set it in a towel to dry for 5 to 10 minutes.

best way to marinate tofu

One of the appealing attributes of tofu is its ability to absorb other flavors, and liquid marinades are a good way to achieve this. But for a marinade to really work, for the flavors to penetrate the tofu and not just surround it, you must use heat.

Drain and press the tofu and cut it into slices or strips. Firm or extra-firm tofu works best (as does frozen, then thawed tofu). Place the tofu in a glass baking dish and pour the marinade over it, turning to coat. Bake the tofu at 350°F for 30 minutes. When cooled, the tofu will keep, covered, in the refrigerator for up to 3 days.

tempeh

Tempeh (TEM-pay) is considered one of the most nutritious soy foods, offering as much as 21 grams of protein in one serving. This traditional Indonesian food is made from cooked whole soybeans that are inoculated with a culture and then fermented until the beans are bound together in a cottony white filament called mycelium. The fermentation process makes the soy protein considerably more digestible and gives tempeh its unique flavor. Some tempeh is made just from soy, but more often it includes one or more grains, like millet, brown rice, quinoa, or barley. It can also contain a flavoring such as sea vegetables or sesame.

Besides being high in protein, tempeh is also rich in vitamin B_{12}, calcium, and fiber. It has a dense, chewy texture and a rich, nutty flavor. Like tofu, tempeh will absorb the flavors of the foods with which it is cooked. Its hearty flavor stands up well to assertive flavors like wild mushrooms and barbecue sauce. Don't be put off by its appearance; because it is a live, ripening food, the flat cake may have grayish or black patches of mold, which are safe to eat. Discard tempeh if it develops mold of another color or a strong ammonia smell.

Tempeh is extremely versatile and is good pan-crisped, fried, grilled, braised, sautéed, and served as burgers and kebabs. It is sold in vacuum-packed 8-ounce packages in the refrigerated and frozen foods section of natural-food stores and large supermarkets. Always check the expiration date marked on the package and select the freshest available.

best way to cook tempeh

Tempeh needs to be cooked to be eaten. Cut tempeh when it is still partially frozen or chilled (it can be sliced, cubed, or chopped, depending on how you plan on using it). Many cooks will steam or poach tempeh before using it to make it juicy and milder tasting or to infuse it with a flavor. This is not absolutely necessary, but you may want to experiment with cooking tempeh both ways.

To steam, cut the tempeh into the desired shapes or leave it whole. Set it in a steamer basket. Cover and steam over boiling water for 15 to 20 minutes. Alternatively, you can simmer tempeh in a stock or thin sauce for 15 to 20 minutes.

To marinate tempeh, first steam it, then place it in a glass baking dish. Pour the marinade over the tempeh, turning to coat. Let it stand at room temperature for at least 20 minutes, or refrigerate overnight. Marinated tempeh can be pan-fried, grilled, or cooked in any way you choose.

To pan-fry, heat a little oil in a medium skillet over medium-high heat. Add the tempeh and cook until browned and crusty, about 2 minutes per side. You can use this technique with steamed, marinated, or plain tempeh.

KITCHEN NOTE

:: Frozen tempeh will keep well for months. Fresh tempeh can be stored, covered tightly, in the refrigerator for up to 5 days.

miso

For thousands of years, dedicated Japanese craftsmen have transformed soybeans and grains into a salty, fermented paste called miso, one of Japan's most celebrated culinary staples. Miso, also called fermented bean paste, comes in numerous varieties with differences in flavor, texture, and aroma—as varied, in fact, as wines or cheeses.

There is no Western counterpart for this rich condiment. It is thick and spreadable, with the consistency of peanut butter. Although the methods used in making miso may vary, the basic process remains true to its centuries-old tradition. Cooked soybeans are mixed with salt, water, and *koji* (a yeast mold cultivated in barley, rice, and soybean paste). The mixture is then placed in a large container and left to ferment. The color, texture, and flavor of miso are affected by the length of time the paste is aged, along with the amount of koji, soybeans, and salt used in production.

Misos have a lovely array of earth colors. They range from golden tans and ambers through rusts and russets to a rich, dark chocolate brown. Light-colored misos are milder in flavor and aroma, with a taste that is sweeter than the full-flavored, well-aged misos.

best way to use miso

When adding miso to liquid foods, first mix the miso with a little hot water in a small bowl until it is dissolved. This technique will remove miso's graininess. Add miso near the end of the cooking time and do not boil, because boiling can destroy some of its properties and turn the miso bitter.

:: When experimenting with miso, remember that the subtle aspects of its color and flavor should be used only to balance other ingredients, as its taste can be overpowering. As a general rule, figure on about 2 teaspoons of miso per serving.

:: In addition to being a soup base, miso is also great in sauces, dips, spreads, dressings, and marinades. It can also replace anchovy paste in recipes.

:: *Hatcho* (hot-cho) miso is the most revered miso in Japan, made using a special type of mold and aged longer than other misos.

soymilk

This creamy liquid is made by soaking and cooking whole beans. The beans are then ground and the milky liquid is pressed out. The milk contains no cholesterol, is high in protein, and naturally contains calcium, though more calcium is often added. Soymilk comes in whole, low-fat, or nonfat varieties, as well as plain or with vanilla, chocolate, or other flavorings.

best way to make soymilk

If you are interested in making soymilk at home, you should invest in a soymilk maker. All you do is add soybeans and water to this device and it will crank out 1 quart of fresh, pure soymilk in about 30 minutes (some machines will make tofu as well). If you use a lot of soymilk, it will save you money. But it will also be useful if you're concerned about additives, as you'll know exactly what you're putting into it. Be sure to use organic soybeans.

KITCHEN NOTES

:: The quality and flavor of soymilk vary considerably from brand to brand, so experiment until you find the one you like best.

:: Once it is opened, store soymilk in the refrigerator for up to 1 week.

:: You can substitute soymilk for dairy milk in just about any recipe.

edamame

Fresh green soybeans called edamame or sweet beans make a fun finger food and are great in salads, soups, and stir-fries. The edible beans come in pairs inside a fuzzy pod and have a sweet, nutty flavor. They are easy to digest and are exceptionally high in protein (½ cup contains 16 grams). The beans also provide vitamin A, fiber, calcium, and a mix of phytochemicals, including isoflavins that act as antioxidants.

Although Americans are just starting to take notice of these snappy little beans, the Chinese have been cultivating them for thousands of years. The word "edamame," however, comes from the Japanese, who love to snack on them right from the pod. The availability of edamame in the United States is definitely growing. Today several kinds—frozen and fresh, in the pod and shelled—can be found in some supermarkets, natural-food stores, and Asian markets. You can also find edamame sold as whole plants at farmers' markets from late May through September.

best way to cook edamame

The beans inside the pods are the only edible portions of the plant. Cook 1 pound of fresh pods (or shelled beans) in boiling salted water for 3 to 5 minutes. Drain, spread on a baking sheet, and let cool for a few minutes. Remove the beans from the pods, if necessary. Frozen edamame, in or out of the pod, have been lightly blanched and require less cooking.

KITCHEN NOTES

:: To enjoy edamame as finger food, use your thumb and forefinger to squeeze the cooked beans from the pod.

:: Fresh soybeans in season are sweeter, crisper, and cleaner tasting than frozen ones, which can lack sweetness and have a softer texture.

:: Store fresh pods in a plastic bag in the refrigerator for 1 to 2 days.

braised tofu in barbecue sauce

SERVES 4 / The extra-firm tofu in this appealing dish absorbs the piquant barbecue sauce without adding flavor of its own.

1 pound extra-firm tofu, drained
2 to 3 tablespoons vegetable oil
1 small onion, finely chopped
1 clove garlic, minced
½ cup tomato paste
1 cup brown vegetable stock or water
½ cup orange juice
¼ cup tamari
3 tablespoons brown sugar
2 tablespoons Dijon mustard
1 tablespoon prepared horseradish
1 teaspoon cider vinegar
2 to 3 drops liquid smoke
Salt and freshly ground pepper

Cut the tofu in half lengthwise, into ½-inch-thick slices. Place the slices on paper towels to drain.

In a large saucepan, heat 1 tablespoon of the oil over medium-high heat. Add the onion and garlic and cook, stirring often, until the onion is softened, about 5 minutes. Add the tomato paste and cook, stirring, for 1 minute. Stir in the stock, orange juice, tamari, sugar, mustard, horseradish, vinegar, liquid smoke, and salt and pepper to taste. Cook, stirring occasionally, until the sauce thickens, about 5 minutes.

In a large cast-iron or other heavy skillet, heat 1 tablespoon oil over medium-high heat. Add the tofu and cook until crisp and golden, about 7 minutes on each side. Add more oil to the pan, if necessary, to prevent sticking.

Pour about half of the barbecue sauce over the tofu and cook, uncovered, until the sauce is reduced by two-thirds. Spoon the sauce over the tofu as it cooks. Heat the extra sauce and serve it on the side.

crispy sesame tofu with vegetables

SERVES 2 / This recipe produces tofu with a crisp, flavorful coating. The sautéed bell peppers and onions add a tasty and colorful touch. For the best texture, be sure to use extra-firm tofu and drain it well. The recipe can easily be doubled to serve more.

> ⅓ cup sesame seeds
>
> 1 pound extra-firm tofu, cut lengthwise into 8 slices, well-drained and patted dry
>
> 3 tablespoons vegetable oil
>
> 1 small onion, thinly sliced
>
> 1 medium red bell pepper, cored, seeded, and thinly sliced
>
> 1 medium yellow bell pepper, cored, seeded, and thinly sliced
>
> 1½ tablespoons peeled, minced fresh ginger
>
> 1 teaspoon dark (Asian) sesame oil
>
> 1 tablespoon tamari or soy sauce

Place the sesame seeds on a small plate. Dredge the tofu slices in the sesame seeds to coat them on all sides.

In a large skillet, heat 2 tablespoons of the oil over medium-high heat. Add the tofu and cook until golden brown, about 3 minutes on each side. Transfer the tofu to a serving platter.

Add the remaining tablespoon of oil to the skillet. Add the onion, bell peppers, and ginger and cook, stirring often, until the vegetables are softened, about 8 minutes. Stir in the sesame oil and tamari. Remove from the heat. Serve the vegetables with the tofu.

tofu bean burgers

SERVES 6 / Great taste and texture make these burgers supreme. Serve them in whole-wheat pita pockets with shredded lettuce and a flavored soy mayonnaise.

1 teaspoon cumin seeds

1½ cups cooked adzuki or black beans, or canned beans,
    drained and rinsed

1 pound firm tofu, well drained and cut into 4 pieces

2 cups fresh bread crumbs

1 tablespoon minced fresh ginger

2 tablespoons brown or red miso

½ teaspoon salt

¼ teaspoon freshly ground pepper

2 tablespoons vegetable oil

In a small skillet, toast the cumin seeds over low heat, stirring constantly, until fragrant, 1 to 2 minutes. Set aside.

In a food processor, process the beans until coarsely chopped. Transfer the beans to a medium bowl. Crumble each piece of tofu into the bowl with the beans. Add the bread crumbs, toasted cumin seeds, ginger, miso, salt, and pepper and mix well. Shape the mixture into 6 round patties.

In a large cast-iron or other heavy-bottomed skillet, heat the oil over medium-high heat. Cook the patties, in batches if necessary, until golden brown, turning once, 3 to 4 minutes on each side. Serve hot.

scrambled tofu with asparagus

SERVES 4 / Scrambling is a common way to prepare tofu. The result is similar in texture to scrambled eggs. The combination of fresh asparagus and cheese makes it truly satisfying.

1 pound firm tofu, drained and cut into 16 cubes

1 tablespoon vegetable oil

2 tablespoons finely chopped green onions (white parts only)

¼ teaspoon ground turmeric

½ teaspoon salt

1 cup chopped cooked asparagus

1 tablespoon finely chopped flat-leaf parsley

½ cup grated fontina, Cheddar, or Muenster cheese

Working with one cube of tofu at a time over a sink, squeeze it gently but firmly in your hand until it crumbles slightly and water drips out. This step is important to prevent the finished dish from being watery. When about half its liquid has been removed, put the tofu into a medium bowl. Repeat until all the tofu has been squeezed.

In a medium skillet, heat the oil over medium heat. Add the green onions and cook, stirring often, for 30 seconds. Add the tofu to the pan. Sprinkle with the turmeric and salt and cook, stirring with a wooden spoon, until it is evenly golden and firm, 3 minutes. Add the asparagus, parsley, and cheese and cook, stirring often, until the cheese melts, about 1 minute. Serve right away.

tempeh and broccoli stir-fry

SERVES 4 / This is about as simple a stir-fry as you can make, yet it's very satisfying. Serve it with rice or noodles to spoon the sauce over.

4 ounces 3-grain tempeh, cut into ¾-inch pieces
¼ cup tamari or light soy sauce
1 tablespoon rice vinegar
3 cloves garlic, minced
2 teaspoons peeled, minced fresh ginger
12 ounces broccoli, stems peeled and cut into ½-inch pieces, florets cut
**   into 1-inch pieces**
2 tablespoons water
1 teaspoon honey
1 teaspoon cornstarch
1 tablespoon peanut oil
1 medium red bell pepper, cored, seeded, and cut into thin strips
Salt and freshly ground pepper
2 tablespoons thinly sliced green onions

In a medium bowl, combine the tempeh with the tamari, vinegar, garlic, and ginger. Stir to blend. Let the tempeh marinate at room temperature for 1 hour.

Steam the broccoli until crisp-tender, 3 minutes. Strain the marinade from the tempeh into a small bowl. Add the water, honey, and cornstarch to the marinade and whisk until well blended.

In a wok or large, heavy-bottomed skillet, heat the oil over high heat. Add the tempeh and bell pepper and stir-fry for 5 minutes. Add the broccoli and reserved marinade and stir-fry until the broccoli is heated through and the sauce thickens, about 3 minutes. Season to taste with salt and pepper. Sprinkle with green onions and serve hot.

tempeh bolognese

SERVES 6 / Tempeh gives this pasta sauce a rich, hearty flavor. Serve it over a medium-sized pasta like rigatoni, penne, or fusilli. This version is based on a recipe from Peter Cervoni, a talented vegan chef who resides in New York.

8 ounces 3-grain tempeh
3 tablespoons olive oil
1 medium onion, chopped
2 medium carrots, peeled and chopped
2 cloves garlic, minced
2 teaspoons dried basil
1 teaspoon dried oregano
1 teaspoon salt
½ teaspoon freshly ground pepper
1 can (6 ounces) tomato paste
1 cup dry red wine
1 can (28 ounces) crushed tomatoes
¼ cup finely chopped flat-leaf parsley
2 tablespoons finely chopped fresh basil leaves

Crumble the tempeh into a medium bowl. In a large saucepan, heat the oil over medium-high heat. Add the tempeh and cook, stirring often, for 5 minutes. Add the onion, carrots, garlic, dried basil, oregano, salt, and pepper. Cover and cook over medium heat for 5 minutes.

Add the tomato paste and cook, stirring, for 1 minute. Stir in the wine and cook for 5 minutes. Add the tomatoes and stir well. Simmer the mixture, uncovered, over medium-low heat until slightly thickened and the flavors have blended, 20 to 30 minutes. Stir in the parsley and fresh basil. Serve over the pasta of your choice.

miso soup with tofu

SERVES 4 / To my mind, there's nothing like a bowl of miso soup. It's a warming elixir that soothes and restores the body and soul. This version of the classic Japanese soup includes shiitake mushrooms, tofu, and fresh spinach.

5 cups water
1 ounce dried shiitake mushrooms
1 medium leek, trimmed, rinsed well, and chopped
1-inch piece fresh ginger, peeled and coarsely chopped
¼ cup mellow white miso
12 ounces firm tofu, drained well and cut into ½-inch cubes
1 tablespoon rice wine
4 cups fresh spinach leaves
Thinly sliced green onion tops, for garnish

In a large saucepan, combine the water, mushrooms, leek, and ginger. Bring the mixture to a boil over high heat. Reduce the heat to medium and simmer for 10 minutes.

Using a slotted spoon, remove the mushrooms from the stock to a cutting board and let cool slightly. Remove and discard the mushroom stems and slice the caps. Set aside.

Strain the stock through a fine sieve into a large bowl and discard the solids. Transfer 1 cup of the stock to a small bowl and stir in the miso until well blended. Return the remaining stock to the saucepan.

Add the tofu, rice wine, reserved mushroom caps, and spinach to the stock. Simmer over medium-low heat, stirring occasionally, until the spinach is tender and the tofu is heated through, about 3 minutes. Whisk in the miso mixture until well blended. To serve, ladle the soup into bowls and garnish with the green onion tops.

couscous primavera with miso dressing

SERVES 4 TO 6 / This recipe not only makes a great last-minute dinner, but is a good way to use up leftover vegetables as well. The miso adds an interesting and delicious flavor to this otherwise traditional salad.

1 cup water

⅔ cup couscous

1 medium red bell pepper, cored, seeded, and julienned

1 small red onion, diced

2 cups small broccoli florets, blanched

1 medium zucchini, diced and blanched

¼ cup mellow miso

1 cup clear vegetable stock

1 to 2 tablespoons vegetable oil

6 green onions (white and pale green parts), thinly sliced

2 cloves garlic, minced

¼ cup chopped flat-leaf parsley

Salt and freshly ground pepper

In a medium saucepan, bring the water to a boil. Stir in the couscous, return to a boil, cover, and turn off the heat. Let stand until the water has been absorbed, 5 to 10 minutes.

Fluff the couscous with a fork and transfer to a large serving bowl. Add the bell pepper, onion, broccoli, and zucchini.

In a small cup, mix the miso with about ½ cup of the stock until blended. In a medium skillet, heat the oil over medium heat. Add the green onions and garlic and cook, stirring often, until softened, about 2 minutes. Stir in the miso mixture, then slowly stir in the remaining ½ cup stock. When the miso is well blended, stir in the parsley. Pour the mixture over the couscous. Season to taste with salt and pepper and serve warm or at room temperature.

banana soy smoothie

SERVES 2 / For this light and delicious morning or afternoon treat, you will need to freeze the bananas ahead of time. Place the pieces in a plastic food storage bag and freeze overnight.

1 ½ bananas, peeled, cut into ½-inch pieces, and frozen

1 cup vanilla soymilk

1 cup ice cubes

1 tablespoon honey or maple syrup

Combine all of the ingredients in a blender and process until the mixture is smooth. Pour into 2 glasses and serve right away.

The image problem of beans has begun to reverse itself as a growing number of health-conscious eaters recognize the humble legume as a protein-dense, low-fat food that's easy to prepare. High in fiber and complex carbohydrates, devoid of cholesterol, and incredibly inexpensive, beans make sense for everyday eating. There are at least seventy varieties of legumes available, with flavors ranging from robust and earthy to delicate and subtle. And their versatility doesn't stop there; most legumes (plus grains, seeds, and other foods) can be sprouted, producing flavorful shoots for use in salads, stir-fries, sandwiches, and more.

legumes & sprouts

dried beans and legumes

Soaking beans before cooking reduces the cooking time and helps to break down the indigestible complex sugars found in them. People have a hard time digesting these sugars and in the process can experience flatulence and bloating. Not all beans need to be soaked before cooking (see the chart on facing page). After soaking, most bean varieties will need additional cooking to become tender and ready to eat or use in a recipe.

best way to soak and cook dried beans and legumes

Before you soak dried beans, spread them on a plate or in a baking pan and sort through them, discarding any that are split, broken, or shriveled. Also remove any pebbles you find. Thoroughly rinse the beans under cold running water. The beans are then ready to be soaked.

There are two basic ways to soak beans. For the slow-soak or cold method, combine the dried beans with cold water to cover by 3 inches in a large pot. Let the beans soak for 6 to 8 hours at cool room temperature or in the refrigerator. Drain the beans in a colander and rinse under cold running water.

Alternatively, you can use the warm or quick-soak method. In a large pot, combine the dried beans with cold water to cover by 3 inches. Bring to a boil over medium-high heat. Reduce the heat to low and simmer the beans for 2 minutes. Turn off the heat, cover, and let the beans soak until they have softened and swelled, about 1 hour. Drain the beans in a colander and rinse under cold running water.

Once soaked, the beans are ready to be cooked. In a large pot, cover the beans with tepid water (sometimes aromatic vegetables, like onions and carrots, and herbs are added for flavor) and simmer gently without boiling them. Boiling will cause the cooking liquid to overflow and the beans to break apart. The cooking times for beans will vary, depending on the variety, size, age, and hardness of the beans. Use the chart on facing page as a guide. To test for doneness, bite into a few beans; they should be tender, not mushy.

KITCHEN NOTE

:: Never add salt to beans while they are cooking. Salt will toughen the seed coat and prevent absorption of the water.

bean soaking and cooking chart

type	soak	cooking time
Adzuki	Slow or quick	Simmer $1\frac{1}{2}$ to 2 hours
Anasazi	Slow or quick	Simmer 1 to $1\frac{1}{2}$ hours
Appaloosa	Slow or quick	Simmer 1 to $1\frac{1}{4}$ hours
Black	Slow or quick	Simmer 1 to $1\frac{1}{2}$ hours
Black-eyed peas	Slow or quick	Simmer 40 to 50 minutes
Cannellini	Slow or quick	Simmer 1 to $1\frac{1}{2}$ hours
Cranberry	Slow or quick	Simmer 1 to $1\frac{1}{2}$ hours
Fava	Slow or quick	Simmer $1\frac{1}{2}$ to 2 hours
Flageolet	Slow or quick	Simmer $1\frac{1}{2}$ to 2 hours
Garbanzo (chickpea)	Slow or quick	Simmer 1 to $1\frac{1}{2}$ hours
Great Northern	Slow or quick	Simmer 1 to $1\frac{1}{2}$ hours
Kidney	Slow or quick	Simmer $1\frac{1}{2}$ to 2 hours
Lima (butter)	Slow or quick	Simmer 1 to $1\frac{1}{2}$ hours
Mung	Slow soak, 1 to 4 hours	Simmer 30 minutes
Navy	Slow or quick	Simmer $1\frac{1}{2}$ to 2 hours
Pinto	Slow or quick	Simmer $1\frac{1}{2}$ to 2 hours
Soybean	Slow or quick	Simmer 3 hours
White	Slow or quick	Simmer $1\frac{1}{2}$ hours

glossary of beans

adzuki beans: These small, oval, reddish-brown beans are especially popular in China and Japan, where they are sometimes used in desserts because of their sweet, nutty flavor and smooth, creamy texture.

anasazi beans: The cultivation of these beans can be traced back to the Anasazi Indians, who lived in the southwestern United States almost 1,000 years ago. Anasazi beans are small, reddish-brown, and kidney-shaped, with white markings. The color fades to a uniform dark pink when cooked.

appaloosa beans: These slender New Mexican white beans have burgundy or dark purple markings. The color contrast fades after cooking, but the markings remain distinct. Appaloosa beans have an earthy flavor and hold their shape well when cooked. They may be substituted for pinto beans.

black beans: Also called turtle beans, these small beans are shiny black and kidney-shaped. They have a full, earthy flavor and a meaty texture. Black beans are a staple in Central and South American countries and are closely related to the kidney bean.

borlotti beans: Plump, round beans popular in Tuscany. They have a pinkish-tan background color with crimson streaks and speckles.

butter beans: These flattish beans range in size from the ⅓-inch Dixie Speckled to 1-inch-long Louisiana Speckled. They have a bland, mild flavor and a slightly grainy texture. The larger ones have tougher skins.

cannellini beans: These medium-sized to large plump oval beans are ivory white and have a creamy texture. They are used extensively in Italian cooking.

cranberry beans: Used interchangeably with pinto beans, these beans are a dark rose color with pink markings. They turn a uniform pink when cooked. Fresh cranberry beans are also used as a shelling bean.

fava beans: Also called broad beans, the fava bean is large and flat with a light brown skin. They grow in large green pods with about eight beans nestled inside. Each fava bean is enclosed in a second, thick skin, which is usually removed before eating. The flavor is assertive, almost bitter. They are commonly used in Arabic, Italian, and Portuguese cooking.

flageolet beans: Prized in French cooking, these small, pale green or white beans have a delicate texture and flavor.

great Northern beans: One of the most versatile and popular varieties of beans in the United States, great Northern beans are oblong and white and a have mild flavor and slightly meaty texture. These beans are the mature dried seeds of the green string bean.

Jacob's cattle beans: Plump white beans with reddish-brown speckles, these beans have an earthy flavor and meaty texture. The markings fade but are still visible after cooking.

kidney beans: There are many varieties of kidney beans, but the most common is the dark red-brown type. They are large kidney-shaped beans with a robust, full-bodied flavor and tender texture. They hold their shape well when cooked.

lima beans: Varieties range from large to baby, but all are somewhat flat with a creamy white to pale green color. They have a mild flavor and soft texture. Limas are named after the capitol of Peru, where they were cultivated many centuries ago.

navy beans: Similar to great Northern beans but smaller. The two beans can be used interchangeably. Navy beans have a mild flavor and soft texture. They are called navy beans because they were frequently served to sailors.

pink beans: An oval, pink-skinned bean with a very creamy texture. They can be used interchangeably with pinto beans.

pinto beans: A medium-sized, oval bean commonly used in the American Southwest for chilis and refried beans. It has a mottled beige-brown skin and an earthy flavor.

red beans: These small, round burgundy-red beans are also called Mexican red beans. They are popular among Hispanic people in the United States and are used to make rice and beans and baked beans.

soybeans: There are more than 1,000 varieties of this extraordinarily nutritious and protein-rich bean, including black soybeans and yellow soybeans. They generally have a mild flavor and soft texture. Fresh soybeans, called edamame, are also available and have a pleasing delicate flavor and crunchy texture. Soybeans are made into a wide variety of products, including soy sauce, soymilk, and tofu.

under pressure

Pressure cookers will cook dried beans in as little as 15 to 20 minutes. Be careful to follow the manufacturer's directions, avoid overfilling the pot, and cook with no more than 10 to 15 pounds of pressure. Adding a tablespoon of vegetable oil to the pot will help prevent excessive foaming and bubbling, which may clog the pressure cooker vent.

lentils and dried peas

These tiny lens-shaped seeds are perfect for family meals because, unlike beans, they need no presoaking and they cook more quickly. Their earthy flavor adds a wholesome quality to soups, stews, salads, dips, casseroles, and side dishes. But this ancient food can be admired for more than its ease of cooking and versatility. Lentils are among the most nutritious of foods. One cup of cooked lentils has 18 grams of protein and provides significant amounts of iron, potassium, and dietary fiber.

Small, round pea varieties, also called field peas, are grown specifically for drying. They may be green or yellow, and they have a higher starch content that enables them to dry better and, when cooked, to have a soft, creamy consistency. Dried peas may be whole or split. When they are split, the outer seed coating is removed. Both whole and split peas do not have to be soaked before cooking.

best way to cook lentils

To use lentils, simply pour them into a bowl and rinse with cold water. Pick out any dark or discolored ones, then drain in a colander. Simmer using a ratio of 1 part lentils to 3 parts water or stock until they're the right texture for your recipe. To use in salads, cook green, brown, and French lentils for 15 to 20 minutes, red lentils for 5 to 10 minutes. For soups and purées, increase the time by 5 to 10 minutes.

best way to cook dried peas

Pour split peas into a bowl and rinse with cold water. Pick out any dark or discolored ones, then drain in a colander. Simmer, using a ratio of 1 part split peas to 4 parts water or stock, until tender, about 1 hour.

KITCHEN NOTES

:: The most common variety of lentil is khaki brown in color. There are also green, yellow, red, and small French lentils, called Le Puy after the region where they are grown in France. Regardless of their color, though, all lentils pack the same nutritional punch and the same great flavor.

:: Cooked lentils and whole and split peas will keep in the refrigerator, tightly covered, for up to 5 days.

fresh peas

Hundreds of varieties of peas are grown, and they appear in a vast selection of dishes all over the world. Some varieties, such as English peas and tiny *petits pois,* are valued for their seeds only and are called shelling beans. Other types, like snow peas and sugar snap peas, have tender, edible pods and are eaten in their entirety.

best way to shell and cook peas

Shell peas just before using. Snap off an end of the pod, pulling the stem to strip off the tough string. Snap the pod in half; it should open easily. Scrape out the peas with your thumb. Very fresh small peas can be eaten raw in salads. Cook older and larger peas in lightly salted, boiling water until tender, 5 to 10 minutes.

best way to prepare and cook pea pods

Most edible pods should be strung, although some newer varieties have been bred stringless. To string a pod, break off the stem end and pull the string down the pod. Turn the pod, break off the other end, and pull the string down the other side of the pod. Cook whole pods in lightly salted, boiling water until tender, 3 to 5 minutes. At this point the pods can be eaten hot, or rinsed under cold running water, drained, and patted dry and used in salads or crudités.

KITCHEN NOTES

:: Store both shelling peas and pea pods in an open plastic bag in the refrigerator for up to 2 days.

:: The best way to tell if a pea pod needs stringing is to bite into it.

:: You'll get about 1 cup of fresh peas from 1 pound in the pod.

sprouts and shoots

Tender and fresh tasting, sprouts and shoots are an increasingly popular way to add a refreshing flavor and crunchy texture to a dish. And as the popularity of these microgreens increases, so does their variety. Not that long ago, mung bean and alfalfa were the only sprouts available at the market, but today sprouts and shoots stemming from vegetables, herbs, and grains are easy to find or to grow. (Sprouts are the result of seeds germinated for anywhere from 3 days to a week. Shoots are a little older and more flavorful, starting at 3 to 4 weeks.)

All sprouts begin with a seed, a nutritionally complete food that contains every food element required for the generation of new life. When a seed germinates, it releases its nutrients and uses up some of its stored carbohydrates and fat to manufacture protein, vitamins, minerals, and enzymes. The resulting sprout is a nutritional powerhouse, containing more nutrients than the original seed.

best way to grow your own sprouts

For equipment you'll need several half-gallon Mason or other jars, cheesecloth, and wide rubber bands.

1. Use good-quality organic seeds that are uniform in color, size, and shape. Rinse the measured amount of seeds or beans in a strainer (per half-gallon jar, use 1 cup beans, legumes, or nuts; 3 to 4 tablespoons small seeds; 1 cup large seeds; or 2 cups grains). Once you have measured the appropriate amount in the jar, secure cheesecloth over the opening with a rubber band and fill the jar halfway with water. Allow the seeds to soak for the appropriate amount of time (4 to 6 hours for small seeds and 12 hours for large seeds, beans, nuts, and grains; see "Sprout Varieties" on facing page for information about specific seeds.) It is possible to drown your sprouts—do not soak them for more than 12 hours.

2. Drain the water and rinse the seeds several times, leaving the cheesecloth in place. Place the jar at 45-degree angle, mouth down, where it can drain freely. Make sure the seeds are not pressed against the opening—it's important for air to circulate in the jar. Rinse the sprouts twice a day by filling the jar with running water and allowing it to overflow. It's important to rinse them so they stay moist, which promotes growth. After each rinse, place the jar back at a 45-degree angle and let it drain. Do this until the sprouts are mature, or ready for harvest (See "Sprout Varieties" for information on the harvest size of specific sprouts). If they become crowded, transfer them to a larger container.

3. When the sprouts are mature, rinse by submerging them in cool water, and discard any hulls that rise to the surface. The sprouts can be harvested and used at this time. Keep them refrigerated in sealed containers for 7 to 10 days.

sprout varieties

alfalfa: These thin, green sprouts have a slightly nutty taste and crisp texture. They are commonly served in salads, sandwiches, or wraps. Let the seeds soak for 6 to 8 hours. For harvesting, they should be 1 to 2 inches in length.

clover: Similar to alfalfa sprouts but with a slightly stronger flavor, these sprouts are popular for growing at home. Let the seeds soak for 6 to 9 hours. For harvesting, they should be 1 to 2 inches in length.

garbanzo (chickpea): Their crunchy texture makes these sprouts a perfect snack or salad addition. Let the beans soak for 12 to 16 hours. These taste best when harvested under 1 inch long.

lentil: These sprouts have a somewhat peppery flavor perfect for quick-cooking soups and stews. They require only 4 to 6 hours of soaking and can be harvested when they reach $\frac{1}{2}$ inch or longer.

mung: Most popular in Chinese cooking, mung bean sprouts have short, silvery white stems and light yellow leaves, with a juicy, crunchy, and sweet refreshing flavor. They are best eaten raw in salads or sandwiches or used as a garnish. Let soak for 8 to 12 hours, and harvest when the sprouts are 1 to 2 inches in length.

pea shoots: Available in lengths from 2 to 6 inches, these sturdy shoots have a sweet flavor and are delicious stir-fried, incorporated into steamed dishes, or quickly sautéed. Let soak for 6 to 10 hours.

radish: Radish sprouts resemble larger alfalfa sprouts and have a distinctive peppery bite. Their zesty flavor makes them a wonderful addition to stir-fries, spring rolls, and other Asian dishes. Let the seeds soak for 7 to 12 hours, and harvest them at 1 inch long.

sunflower: Long, bright green sprouts with a nutty flavor. Eat as a snack, or mix with honey for a breakfast spread for toast or muffins. Soak the seeds for 8 to 12 hours, and harvest when the sprouts are $\frac{1}{2}$ inch long.

wheat berry: A pleasantly chewy texture and somewhat sweet flavor characterizes these sprouts. Soak the seeds for 8 to 12 hours, and harvest them at $\frac{1}{2}$ inch in length. They also can be processed into a liquid called wheatgrass juice, one of the richest sources of chlorophyll available. One ounce of wheatgrass juice packs the nutritional punch of $2\frac{1}{2}$ pounds of leafy green vegetables.

:: The best way to reap the nutritional benefits of sprouts is to eat them briefly cooked. Heat can begin to destroy their protein and active enzymes, so it is best to add them to cooked foods only during the last minute of cooking.

:: When purchasing sprouts, look for those that are fresh and vibrant looking, with buds attached; avoid any that are musty smelling or have brown discoloration. Keep sprouts in their original packaging in the refrigerator. Use mung bean sprouts within 3 days. More delicate sprouts, such as alfalfa, should be used within 2 days.

warm tuscan bean salad

SERVES 4 / If you have ever visited Tuscany, you have probably enjoyed some version of this classic dish. It's wonderful served as part of an antipasto buffet with items like roasted red peppers, olives, and marinated artichoke hearts.

1 ½ cups dried white cannellini beans (about 9 ounces)

4 ripe medium tomatoes, peeled, seeded, and chopped

1 small red onion, finely chopped

1 small stalk celery, finely chopped

2 tablespoons chopped flat-leaf parsley

1 tablespoon chopped fresh basil leaves

2 teaspoons minced garlic

6 tablespoons extra-virgin olive oil

¼ cup fresh lemon juice

Salt and freshly ground pepper

In a large pot, combine the dried beans with cold water to cover by 3 inches. Let the beans soak for 6 to 8 hours at cool room temperature or in the refrigerator. Drain the beans in a colander and rinse under cold running water. Or, to save time, place the beans in a large saucepan with cold water to cover by 3 inches. Bring to a boil over medium-high heat. Reduce the heat to low and simmer the beans for 2 minutes. Turn off the heat, cover, and let the beans soak until they have softened and swelled, about 1 hour.

Drain the beans in a colander and rinse under cold running water. Return the beans to the pot and cover with tepid water. Bring to a simmer and simmer gently, partially covered, until the beans are tender but still hold their shape, about 45 minutes.

Drain the beans well and transfer to a medium bowl. Stir in the tomatoes, onion, celery, parsley, basil, garlic, and 4 tablespoons of the olive oil. Allow the beans to cool to room temperature, then stir in the lemon juice and season to taste with salt and pepper. Just before serving, drizzle with the remaining 2 tablespoons olive oil.

curried chickpeas and potatoes

SERVES 4 / This dish is very simple to make, and it can be made with canned chickpeas if time is an issue. If desired, serve the spicy chickpeas with a cooling topping of plain yogurt mixed with a little chopped fresh mint and finely chopped cucumber.

1½ cups dried chickpeas

2 tablespoons vegetable oil

1 large onion, finely chopped

1 tablespoon peeled, minced fresh ginger

2 cloves garlic, minced

1½ tablespoons curry powder, preferably Madras

2 teaspoons ground cumin

1 pound russet potatoes (2 to 3 medium), peeled and cut into 1-inch dice

1½ cups water

⅓ cup currants or raisins

½ teaspoon salt, plus more to taste

¼ cup chopped cilantro leaves

In a large pot, combine the dried chickpeas with cold water to cover by 3 inches. Let them soak for 6 to 8 hours at cool room temperature or in the refrigerator. Drain the chickpeas in a colander and rinse under cold running water. Or, to save time, place the chickpeas in a large saucepan with cold water to cover by 3 inches. Bring to a boil over medium-high heat. Reduce the heat to low and simmer the chickpeas for 2 minutes. Turn off the heat, cover, and let them soak until they have softened and swelled, about 1 hour.

Drain the chickpeas in a colander and rinse under cold running water. Return them to the pot and cover with tepid water. Bring to a simmer and simmer gently, partially covered, until the chickpeas are tender but still hold their shape, 1 to 1½ hours. Drain well and let cool.

In a large skillet, heat the oil over medium heat. Add the onion, ginger, and garlic and cook, stirring often, until the onion is softened and lightly golden, about 10 minutes. Add the curry powder and cumin and cook, stirring constantly, for 1 minute.

Add the potatoes, water, currants, and ½ teaspoon salt. Bring the mixture to a boil. Reduce the heat to medium-low, cover, and simmer until the potatoes are tender, about 10 minutes. Stir in the chickpeas and cilantro. Cook, uncovered, until the mixture is heated through, stirring occasionally, about 1 minutes. Season to taste with more salt and serve warm.

three-bean chili

SERVES 6 / You can use whatever combination of beans you'd like for this chili. Serve it with warmed tortillas or cornbread for a hearty dinner. If you are pressed for time, this chili can also be made with canned beans.

1 tablespoon olive oil
1 tablespoon coriander seeds
1 tablespoon cumin seeds
¼ teaspoon crushed red pepper flakes
1 large onion, chopped
3 medium bell peppers (one each red, orange, and yellow), cored, seeded, and chopped
2 tablespoons chili powder
1 teaspoon dried oregano
1 can (14 ounces) diced tomatoes
2 cups cooked pinto beans
2 cups cooked black beans
2 cups cooked white beans
Salt and freshly ground pepper
½ cup chopped fresh cilantro or parsley

In a large pot, heat the oil over medium heat. Add the coriander, cumin, and pepper flakes and cook, stirring often, until the seasonings darken slightly, about 1 minute.

Add the onion, bell peppers, chili powder, and oregano and cook, stirring often, until the vegetables begin to soften, about 5 minutes. Stir in the tomatoes and beans and bring the mixture to a boil. Reduce the heat to medium-low and simmer, stirring occasionally, until the vegetables are tender, about 30 minutes, adding water or tomato juice as needed if the mixture seems dry. Season with salt and pepper to taste.

Just before serving, stir in the cilantro. Serve the chili in shallow bowls.

lentil and escarole soup

SERVES 4 / This is one of my all-time favorite soups. It's so easy to make and very satisfying. You can substitute other greens for the escarole, such as Swiss chard, spinach, or mustard greens.

1 tablespoon olive oil

1 medium onion, chopped

1 medium stalk celery, chopped

1 medium carrot, peeled and chopped

1 clove garlic, minced

1 can (14 ounces) plum tomatoes, drained and chopped

8 ounces brown lentils, picked over and rinsed (1¼ cups)

6 cups water

Salt and freshly ground pepper

1 medium head escarole (about 1 pound)

½ cup grated Parmesan cheese

In a large pot, heat the oil over medium heat. Add the onion, celery, carrot, and garlic and cook, stirring often, until the vegetables are soft, about 10 minutes. Add the tomatoes, reduce the heat to low, and cook, stirring often, for 5 minutes.

Add the lentils and water to the pot. Bring to a boil. Reduce the heat and simmer, partially covered, until the lentils are tender, about 45 minutes. Season to taste with salt and pepper.

Meanwhile, separate the escarole leaves and rinse well. Stack the leaves and cut them crosswise into ½-inch-wide strips. When the lentils are tender, stir in the escarole. Return the soup to a simmer and cook, stirring occasionally, until the escarole is tender, about 10 minutes.

To serve, ladle the soup into bowls and sprinkle each serving with Parmesan cheese.

japanese noodles with sprouts

SERVES 4 / Packed with flavor, texture, and nutrition, this easy one-dish meal is exotic without being challenging to make.

8 ounces udon noodles or thin spaghetti
1 tablespoon cornstarch
3 tablespoons water
⅓ cup tamari or soy sauce
1 tablespoon dark (Asian) sesame oil
1 tablespoon rice vinegar
2 teaspoons peeled, minced fresh ginger
2 teaspoons minced garlic
1 teaspoon sugar
½ teaspoon crushed red pepper flakes
1 package (10 ½ ounces) firm silken tofu, drained, pressed, and cut into 1-inch cubes
4 ounces mung or lentil sprouts
4 ounces snow pea shoots or clover sprouts

Bring a large pot of water to a boil. Add the noodles, stirring to prevent sticking. Cook according to package directions, stirring occasionally, until tender.

Meanwhile, in a small bowl, mix the cornstarch with the water until smooth. Stir in the tamari, sesame oil, vinegar, ginger, garlic, sugar, and pepper flakes until well blended.

Heat a large skillet over medium-high heat. Add the tamari mixture and bring to a simmer. Add the tofu and stir-fry until it is heated through and the sauce thickens, 2 to 3 minutes. Add the sprouts and stir-fry just until they are heated through, about 1 minute.

Drain the noodles and transfer to a serving bowl. Add the tofu mixture and toss well to mix.

Nuts and seeds play an important part in our diets, especially for vegetarians, because they are a good source of protein as well as other nutrients. Recently they have been spurned for being too high in fat and calories, but most of the fat is the healthy monounsaturated kind, the same type found in olive oil, which fights "bad" (LDL) cholesterol and keeps arteries clear. One exception is the coconut, which has a relatively high saturated fat content, but in light of its unique taste, it's worth an occasional indulgence.

In addition to beneficial fat, nuts and seeds supply essential fatty acids that help the body function properly. They are also packed with calcium, potassium, vitamin E, and the B vitamins. The key to incorporating these tempting tidbits into your diet is to consume them in place of other fatty foods, not in addition to them, so you can reap all the health benefits and not expand your waistline.

nuts

best way to shell and peel nuts

Peeling nuts refers not to removing the shell, but rather removing the thin skin that covers the shelled nut. Not all nuts require peeling, and some are more difficult to peel than others. As a general rule, peeled nuts cost more than those with the shell or peel still on, so knowing how to do it yourself can save you some money.

almonds: To shell, cover almonds with boiling water and let stand for 15 to 20 minutes. Drain and let cool, then crack with a nutcracker. To peel, drop shelled almonds into boiling water and boil for 30 seconds, then drain and rinse under cold water. Pinch one end of the skin and the nut will slip out the other end. This process is also called blanching.

Brazil nuts: To shell, drop Brazil nuts into boiling water and boil for 3 minutes. Drain and cool, then crack with a nutcracker. To peel, drop the shelled nuts into boiling water with ¾ teaspoon baking soda for every 2 cups of water. Boil for 2 minutes. Drain, and while the nuts are still warm, slip off their skins.

chestnuts: To peel and shell, with a small, sharp knife, cut an X on the flat side of each chestnut. Roast in a shallow baking pan at 375°F until the chestnuts feel soft, about 20 minutes. Let them cool slightly. Using a small, sharp knife, pull off the shell and as much of the skin as possible. Chestnuts with stubborn peels can be reheated for about 5 minutes, then peeled again.

hazelnuts: Use a nutcracker to shell hazelnuts. To peel, spread the shelled hazelnuts in a single layer on a baking sheet with rimmed sides or in a shallow baking pan. Roast in a 350°F oven until the skins begin to flake and the nuts appear golden brown, about 15 minutes. Remove from the oven and wrap in a kitchen towel. Rub the hazelnuts together in the towel, rubbing off as much skin as possible. The hazelnuts are now toasted as well.

peanuts: You can usually shell and peel peanuts easily by hand, either before or after roasting. If, however, removing the brown skin proves difficult, cover the shelled peanuts with boiling water and let stand for 5 minutes. Drain, and the skins should then slip off easily. Spread the skinned peanuts on a rimmed baking sheet or in a shallow baking pan and let dry for several hours, or toast in a 350°F oven for 5 to 8 minutes.

pecans: To shell, pour boiling water over the pecans and let stand until cool or soft, about 30 minutes. Crush the shells with a nutcracker. Use a nut pick or other sharp object to remove difficult pieces of shell from the creases.

pistachios: Pistachios can be shelled by hand, because the drying process after harvesting causes the shells to open slightly. To peel, drop shelled pistachios into boiling water and boil for 5 to 10 minutes. Drain and rinse under cold water, then slip off the skins. The nuts will retain their color better after blanching. Spread the skinned pistachios on a rimmed baking sheet or in a shallow baking pan and let dry for several hours, or toast in a 350°F oven for 8 to 10 minutes.

walnuts: Use a nutcracker to shell walnuts. If you want to remove the outer shell while keeping the nutmeat intact, gently press in the middle of the shell with the nutcracker, rotating it 3 or 4 times as you do.

best way to toast nuts

Many recipes call for untoasted nuts, but I don't know why, because toasting nuts greatly enhances their flavor. Toasted nuts become stale more quickly than raw nuts, so toast only as much as you need just before you are going to use them. Also, always toast nuts before chopping.

Spread shelled nuts in a single layer on an ungreased rimmed baking sheet and place them in a preheated 350°F oven. Toast until fragrant and golden brown, stirring occasionally, for 10 to 15 minutes. The nuts should taste slightly crunchy, with a pronounced toasted flavor and no burnt aftertaste. Let the nuts cool completely before using them.

best way to chop and grind nuts and seeds

Chopped nuts add texture and flavor to almost every category of dish, from breakfast foods to desserts. Some recipes call for ground nuts as an ingredient or thickener for soups and stews, and others may use them for a garnish. Because they have a high oil content, most nuts and seeds can also be ground into a thick spreadable paste or "butter."

Use the food processor to make quick work of chopping or grinding nuts and seeds. Never chop more than 1 cup of nuts at a time, and process with on/off pulses until the nuts are the desired texture. Scrape the bowl, stirring from the bottom, occasionally. Adding 1 tablespoon of flour, cornstarch, or sugar will help keep them from clumping.

nut and seed butters

Butters made by grinding nuts and seed to a paste offer a delicious whole-food alternative to butter and margarine, and they also make nutritious additions to soup, sauces, dips, spreads, and cookies. Toasting the nuts and seeds before grinding not only increases the flavor of the butter but also prolongs shelf life. Homemade butters are easily prepared with your favorite seed or nut, or a combination. Grind the toasted nuts or seeds in a nut mill or food processor until a paste forms. Add oil, a little at a time, to create the desired consistency. A pinch of salt will add flavor. You can also add a little honey or maple syrup.

nut milk

Most any kind of nut can be made into a delicious alternative to dairy milk. Nut milks can be chilled and served as a beverage or poured over hot and cold cereals. They can also be substituted cup for cup in baking for dairy milk. Add them to soups and sauces toward the end of cooking to prevent separation.

best way to make nut milk

To make nut milk, soak ½ cup shelled raw nuts in water to cover. Drain and discard the soaking water. If necessary, rub the nuts between your hands to remove any peels. Put the nuts into a food processor fitted with the metal blade. Add 2 cups water and 1 teaspoon honey or maple syrup, if desired, and process until the mixture is smooth. Add 1 more cup of water, if desired, and process until blended. For a smoother consistency, strain the milk through a fine sieve set over a bowl.

KITCHEN NOTES

:: The high fat content of nuts means they go rancid rapidly. Heat, light, and moisture promote oxidation, so store nuts in a cool dark place or in the refrigerator or freezer. Shelled nuts will keep unrefrigerated for up to 2 months, refrigerated for up to 4 months, and frozen for up to 8 months.

:: The oil of natural peanut butter and tahini (raw sesame paste) will separate to the top of the jar. To make stirring these butters easier, before opening, turn the jar upside down and leave it for about 30 minutes. Turn right-side up, open, and stir to blend. Keep opened jars in the refrigerator.

brining nuts

Soaking in a brine (salted water) gives nuts and seeds a nice salty flavor without a sticky coating. Cover raw nuts or seeds with cold water. Add enough salt so that the water tastes salty but is not overpowering (about ½ teaspoon per 1 cup of water). Let stand overnight. Drain the nuts or seeds and toast in a preheated 250°F oven until they are dried and golden, about 1 hour.

seasonings

It's easy to add extra flavor to toasted nuts and seeds. Try sprinkling them with kosher salt (table salt is too fine to stick to nuts and sea salt is too large) or other spices such as chili powder, curry powder, garam masala, ground ginger, cinnamon, and cumin. First, toss the nuts with oil so they are lightly coated. You can use olive oil or vegetable oils, or the same oil as the nuts you are seasoning—walnut, peanut, or hazelnut. Toast nuts as directed, then toss them with the seasoning (or seasoning mix) of your choice.

seeds

Seeds are often grouped together with nuts, which are the seeds of trees, and they can be used to replace nuts in many recipes. Like nuts, seeds can be ground into pastes and butters and even made into milk-like beverages. They can be sprinkled on soups, salads, and desserts and are easily incorporated into casseroles or pasta or grain dishes, as well as other recipes. For example, 2 tablespoons of ground seeds added to your favorite pie crust recipe results in a more nutritious and flavorful crust.

best way to toast seeds

To toast seeds, spread them in a single layer on a rimmed baking sheet. Bake in a preheated 350°F oven until they are lightly browned, stirring occasionally. The time will vary depending on the type of seed (usually between 3 and 7 minutes), so watch them closely. Toasting seeds brings out their natural flavor.

KITCHEN NOTE
:: Because of their high oil content, seeds can go rancid quickly. It is best to store them in an airtight container in the refrigerator, where they will keep for several months. They can also be frozen for up to a year.

top seeds

flaxseeds: Known as linseed in Europe, flaxseeds are prized by health-conscious eaters everywhere, owing to their abundant omega-3 content. For best digestion, flaxseeds should be ground before using. In addition to sprinkling them on cereals, salads, casseroles, and desserts, you can use ground flaxseeds in baking to boost the nutritional content. Flaxseeds combined with water in a blender become quite viscous and can be used to replace eggs in many recipes.

hemp seeds: These seeds have the highest amount of essential fatty acids of any plant and also provide plenty of protein. They can be purchased hulled for better digestibility. Like other seeds, hemp seeds can be added to baked goods and other recipes or sprinkled on cereals, desserts, and salads.

pumpkin seeds: Extremely high in protein, pumpkin seeds also offer up iron, zinc, vitamin A, and other nutrients. They are great tossed in salads, mixed with grains, or ground up and added to salad dressings, casseroles, and baked goods. Hulled pumpkin seeds are enjoyed as a dry-roasted snack food. Green hulled pumpkin seeds are called pepitas and are often used in Southwestern and Mexican cooking.

sesame seeds: Rich in iron; protein; calcium; and vitamins A, B, and E, sesame seeds come in shades of black, brown, and yellow as well as the more common creamy white variety. Sesame *gomashio,* a mixture of sesame seeds and a small amount of sea salt, is used as a seasoning on grains, pasta, and vegetables.

sunflower seeds: In the shell, we might think of them as birdseed or a snack food, but hulled (shelled), they find their way into breads, cookies, veggie burgers, and pilafs. Hulled sunflower seeds, sometimes called kernels, are a popular garnish for salads. They are rich in omega-6 fatty acids, necessary for health of skin and hair, and are a good source of protein, calcium, iron, and other nutrients.

coconut

The soft, translucent flesh of the young green coconut is considered a delicacy throughout the tropics. But the imported fruits that are available in most supermarkets are mature, hairy, and hard as rocks. When buying a coconut, be sure it feels heavy and that you can hear the water sloshing around inside when the fruit is shaken.

best way to prepare a coconut

To open a whole coconut, puncture 1 or 2 of the round "eyes" near the stem with a screwdriver or ice pick. Let the interior liquid drain out. Some people drink this watery liquid, but more often it is discarded. Put the whole coconut in a baking pan and bake in a preheated 350°F oven for about 15 minutes. Let cool slightly, then wrap in a kitchen towel so it won't shatter, and tap it in several places with a hammer until it cracks apart. Break the meat away, using a small, sharp knife to peel or scrape off the brown inner skin. Grate the fruit to make flakes, or cut it into chunks and process it in a food processor fitted with the metal blade until finely ground.

To toast coconut, spread grated or flaked coconut in a single layer on a rimmed baking sheet. Toast in a preheated 350°F oven, stirring occasionally, until golden brown, about 10 minutes. Let cool before using. Toasted coconut makes a great garnish for Asian dishes and fruit salads.

KITCHEN NOTE

:: Baby coconuts, called *coquitos*, are sold without their husks and have a smooth, dark brown shell the size an acorn. Serve coquitos whole to enjoy like nuts, or crack them in half and serve in a cocktail.

coconut milk and cream

Coconut milk is used to enrich soups, stews, sauces, beverages, puddings, and rice dishes. It is not the liquid found in the center of coconuts—that is coconut water and is not strongly flavored. Coconut milk is made by soaking shredding coconut meat in a hot liquid. You can find it, in cans, in Asian and Latino markets or in these sections of some large supermarkets. Be sure you buy coconut milk that has not been sweetened.

To make coconut milk yourself, combine equal amounts of freshly grated coconut and hot water in a food processor fitted with the metal blade or in a blender; process until well blended. (If using dried coconut, substitute warm milk for the hot water.) Pour the mixture into a bowl and let stand for 30 minutes. Strain the mixture through a fine sieve, pressing down on the pulp with the back of a spoon to extract as much liquid as possible. Discard the pulp. Repeat, using the same coconut but fresh water. The resulting liquid is rich coconut milk. The richer liquid that rises to the top as the milk cools is coconut cream, which you can be spoon off and use separately or stir into the milk to enrich it. Homemade coconut milk and cream should be used within 1 day.

hazelnut-fig bread

MAKES 1 LOAF (16 SLICES) / This quick bread is delicious served plain or spread with a nut butter to accompany tea or coffee. To concentrate their flavor, the hazelnuts are sprinkled over the batter instead of being mixed in. When you prepare this loaf, be ready to hand out the recipe, because someone always asks.

1 cup chopped dried figs
¾ cup fresh orange juice
½ cup sugar
2 tablespoons vegetable oil
1 tablespoon grated orange zest
1 large egg
1 large egg white
1 cup all-purpose unbleached flour
½ cup whole-wheat flour
1½ teaspoons baking soda
¼ teaspoon salt
⅓ cup hazelnuts, toasted, skinned, and chopped

Grease an 8½-by-4-inch loaf pan, or coat with nonstick cooking spray. Place the figs in a medium bowl. In a small saucepan, bring the orange juice to a boil. Pour the hot juice over the figs and let stand for 15 minutes.

Preheat the oven to 350°F In a small bowl, whisk together the sugar, oil, zest, egg, and egg white. Stir into the fig mixture.

In a large bowl, mix both the flours, the baking soda, and salt. Make a well in the center of the mixture. Add the fig mixture to the flour mixture, stirring just until moist. Spoon the batter into the prepared pan and sprinkle with the hazelnuts.

Bake the bread until a wooden toothpick inserted into the center comes out clean, about 45 minutes. Cool for 10 minutes in the pan on a wire rack. Remove from the pan and cool completely on the rack.

nut shake

SERVES 4 / You will be amazed at how rich and delicious this dairy-free shake is. It's important to soak the nuts and dates so they will be soft enough to blend. You can also make this shake with ¾ cup raw cashews soaked in water to cover for 1 to 2 hours. Other flavorings may include carob powder, fresh berries, and ground cinnamon.

¾ cup natural almonds

4 dried dates

3 cups cold apple juice or water

3 to 4 medium peeled bananas, frozen

1 teaspoon vanilla extract

Put the almonds in a small bowl. Cover them with water and let soak for 2 to 8 hours at room temperature. Put the dates in a small bowl. Cover them with cold water and let soak at room temperature for 1 to 2 hours. Drain the almonds and discard the water. Drain the dates and reserve the water.

In a food processor or blender, combine the soaked nuts, soaked dates, juice, and reserved date soaking water, and process until smooth. Break the frozen bananas into pieces, add to the mixture, and process until smooth. Add the vanilla and process to blend. Pour into serving glasses.

pasta with spicy peanut sauce

SERVES 4 / Peanut sauces are quick and easy to make and will greatly enhance the simplest of foods such as noodles and grilled tofu or tempeh. I call for pasta here, but you could easily substitute soba or udon noodles.

12 ounces dry tubular pasta such as penne, freshly cooked

1 small cucumber, halved lengthwise and thinly sliced

½ medium red bell pepper, cored, seeded, and thinly sliced

3 medium green onions (white and light green parts), thinly sliced

3 tablespoons chopped cilantro leaves

peanut sauce

¼ cup plus 2 tablespoons natural peanut butter

¼ cup fresh lime juice

3 tablespoons water

2 tablespoons tamari or low-sodium soy sauce

2 teaspoons brown sugar

2 cloves garlic, minced

¼ teaspoon cayenne pepper

Rinse the cooked pasta under cold water to cool. Drain well. In a large bowl, combine the pasta, cucumber, bell pepper, green onions, and cilantro. Set aside.

TO MAKE THE SAUCE: In a medium bowl, whisk together the peanut butter, lime juice, water, tamari, brown sugar, garlic, and cayenne until well blended.

Add enough peanut sauce to the pasta to season it to taste, and toss well to coat. Serve at room temperature.

toasted walnut-garlic dip

MAKES ABOUT 3 CUPS / This garlicky dip is based on the Greek version of aioli called *skordalia*. Serve it with assorted raw vegetables such as carrots, radishes, endive, and red and green bell peppers.

1 large russet potato (about 12 ounces), peeled and quartered
¾ cup walnuts, toasted
⅔ cup olive oil, preferably extra-virgin
⅓ cup fresh lemon juice
3 cloves garlic, coarsely chopped
2 teaspoons chopped fresh oregano leaves
2 tablespoons cold water
⅓ cup finely chopped fresh parsley
Salt and freshly ground pepper

Cook the potato in a medium saucepan of boiling salted water until tender, about 15 minutes. Drain and let cool completely.

In a food processor, combine the nuts, ⅓ of the cup oil, lemon juice, garlic, and oregano and process until almost smooth. Add the potato, the remaining ⅓ cup oil, and the water. Pulse on and off just until the potato is blended and the mixture is creamy (do not overprocess or the mixture will become sticky).

Transfer the mixture to a medium bowl. Mix in the parsley and season to taste with salt and pepper.

sunflower-sesame patties

SERVES 4 / Serve these protein-packed patties in whole-wheat pita pockets topped with raita (yogurt-cucumber sauce) and chopped tomatoes.

½ cup hulled sunflower seeds

½ cup sesame seeds

1 cup cooked lentils

4 green onions (white and light green parts), finely chopped

1 tablespoon finely chopped flat-leaf parsley

2 teaspoons finely chopped mint leaves

1 tablespoon tahini

½ teaspoon salt

Pinch cayenne pepper

¼ cup plain dry bread crumbs

2 tablespoons olive oil, or more as needed

In a food processor, combine the sunflower seeds and sesame seeds and process until coarsely chopped. Add the lentils, green onions, parsley, mint, tahini, salt, cayenne, and bread crumbs, and process until the mixture is blended.

Shape the mixture into 4 patties and place on a platter. Cover and refrigerate for 30 minutes. In a large skillet, heat the oil over medium heat. Cook the patties until golden brown, about 3 minutes per side. Serve warm.

Turning a few simple ingredients—water, flour, and yeast—into a nourishing food is the art of bread making. This centuries-old process has changed little over time, and the end result remains one of our most elemental and essential foods. Beyond baking a handsome loaf, try making your own crisp and chewy pizza dough. Homemade pizza is always a favorite, and making it at home allows you to create just the kind you or your family likes best. You can whip up a homespun batch of fragrant muffins or a whole-grain quick bread with minimal effort for a delightful addition to almost any menu. The range of techniques and recipes offered in this chapter demonstrates the diverse role that bread and baked goods play in our meals and in between.

baked goods

yeast bread

There's nothing more irresistible than fresh-from-the-oven bread. Yet there is much misinformation about the baking of bread. Many people view it as a laborious process, something pursued only by die-hard bakers. What they don't realize is that homemade bread calls for only about 20 minutes of hands-on activity. Beyond that, the dough is either rising or baking, neither of which requires any effort on the part of the cook. Once you learn the basics, you'll find that bread baking is not only easy but is also one of the most satisfying of all culinary techniques.

best way to make yeast bread

proof the yeast: Yeast, a living organism that converts the natural sugars in flour to gases, is the most commonly used leavener in bread making. Making sure yeast is alive is a process known as proofing. It is a crucial step in bread making because if the yeast is not alive, it can't leaven your bread. Active dry yeast is easy to find in the refrigerated or baking section of supermarkets. Be sure to check the expiration date on individual packages, and keep it refrigerated until ready to use.

When you're proofing yeast, the temperature of the liquid is critical—it should be warm enough to activate the yeast, but not so hot that it kills it. The water temperature should be comfortable to the touch—not too hot but not too cool. The temperature of the water should be between 105° and 110°F.

Pour ¼ to ½ cup (depending on what the recipe calls for) of lukewarm water into a small glass or ceramic bowl. Sprinkle the yeast over the water, then gently stir to dissolve. Set the yeast mixture in a warm place; the mixture should appear slightly bubbly within 5 to 10 minutes. This indicates that the yeast has been activated and is now ready to be added to the flour.

make the dough: In a large bowl, mix the proofed yeast with the liquid, salt, and oil called for in the recipe, then gradually add the flour, stirring with a wooden spoon until the mixture pulls away from the sides of the bowl. Dump the dough onto a floured surface and you're ready to knead.

knead the dough: Kneading performs a crucial function in preparing the dough to rise. It completes the mixing process, but it also allows the flour's protein to develop into gluten.

To properly knead dough, turn it out onto a lightly floured surface and shape it into a ball. Keep a little additional flour on the side and lightly dust the dough as necessary to keep it from sticking. Using the heel of your hand, gently push the dough away from you. At the same time, use your other hand to rotate the dough slightly toward you, guiding the dough slowly around in a smooth, rhythmic, circular motion. Continue this process for approximately 10 minutes, or until the dough is smooth and satiny and has a springy quality.

let the dough rise: Place the dough in a lightly oiled glass or ceramic bowl and cover it with a damp dish towel to keep the surface from drying out. Put the bowl in a warm, draft-free place (a gas oven warmed by the pilot light or the top of the refrigerator are good spots) and allow the dough to rise until it is doubled in size. The rising time depends primarily on the amount of yeast used and the room temperature. Most dough will rise in about 1 to 2 hours. During this period, the yeast multiplies and the gluten in the flour begins to stretch and strengthen. The key process of fermentation also begins. In the absence of oxygen, the yeast organisms begin to break the starch down into simple sugars. This yields carbon dioxide gas, which leavens the dough.

The dough is ready when it springs back slowly when you gently press the surface with a fingertip. (Too long a rising time will permanently weaken the gluten structure and cause it to collapse.) Once the dough has risen completely, punch it down once to deflate it. Turn it out onto a lightly floured surface and gently knead it about 5 times to release the built-up carbon dioxide and to reinvigorate the yeast and gluten. Form the dough into a ball and let it rest, uncovered, for another 5 to 10 minutes.

shape the dough and let it rise again: The last step is to shape the dough according to the recipe and let it rise for the final time. The second rising will take less time than the first, about 45 minutes, because the gluten structure has already been formed. (Note: The finger-poke method is useful only for the first rising.) Before you put the shaped and risen dough into the oven, make several slashes in the top of the loaf, using a sharp knife or razor blade. The slashes will allow the dough to expand rapidly without tearing. You can also brush on a glaze, such as beaten egg, or sprinkle it with seeds at this time.

:: Hard as it is to do, you really should wait until a loaf has cooled thoroughly to the touch before slicing it. The center of a fresh-from-the-oven loaf is still doughy, because the baking process isn't complete. If hot bread is absolutely too tempting to resist, make a few rolls out of part of the dough and bake them along with the loaf. These you can eat almost immediately.

:: Steaming is a great way to revive or reheat bread. Set a slice on a piece of baking parchment on the rack of a regular or improvised steamer, and steam it gently for several minutes, until it rehydrates and softens. Slices will miraculously regain their fresh flavor and moist texture.

:: By the way, the best way to store your loaves (if any are left over, that is), is to keep them unwrapped in a large ceramic bowl with a plate or tray on top at room temperature. Freezing bread is better than refrigerating it (which robs flavor), but freeze sliced loaves rather than whole ones so that you can take out just what you need at any one time.

bread ingredients

Flour, water, and yeast are the three essential ingredients that go into bread. Flour ground from hard wheat is best for risen breads because it contains a considerable amount of gluten, a protein with the capacity to stretch and form a strong elastic structure. Whole-wheat flour makes a slightly heftier loaf than refined (white) flour but provides more nutrients and a richer flavor.

Fats, such as oil, butter, and eggs, are not necessary, though they do give the dough a soft, tender texture and a richer flavor. Sugar and other sweeteners are optional and may mask the subtle flavor of whole grains. Too much sweetener will impair optimal dough development. Salt is used in most breads to add flavor and to control the rate of fermentation.

specialty bread flours

Adding flours milled from other grains besides wheat adds flavor, texture, and nutrients to homemade breads. But these flours can't be used alone, as they almost always produce flat, dense breads because of their low gluten content. For light-textured loaves, use these flours in correct proportion with wheat flour. Here are some recommendations for using specialty flours based on the classic white-bread method.

barley flour: Barley flour should not exceed 20 percent of the wheat flour in bread recipes. It has a nutty, earthy flavor, but it is poor in gluten and will produce a flat, gray bread if not used in the correct proportions.

brown rice flour: This flour contains the germ and bran of the grain. It cannot be used alone in bread making, but can replace up to 20 percent of the wheat flour. Rice flour absorbs liquids slower than wheat flour, so it may take longer to mix a dough with this flour in it.

buckwheat flour: Buckwheat is actually not a grain but a member of the rhubarb family. For best results in bread making, replace up to 30 percent of the wheat flour with buckwheat flour. The resulting loaves will have a fine, moist crumb and a slightly sweet, nutty flavor.

oat flour: Oats are richer in fats and minerals than wheat and have a low gluten content. Adding 15 percent oat flour to bread adds a sweet, nutty flavor as well as nutrients. Doughs made with oat flour will be fairly stiff and take longer to rise.

potato flour: Mixing potato flour and wheat flour makes a wonderful bread with a crisp crust and flavorful interior. Potato flour can be used for up to 20 percent of the wheat flour and adds vitamin C, thiamin, iron, and potassium to breads.

rye flour: After wheat, rye flour is the most suitable for breads. It can come in light, medium, and dark varieties. The light and medium flours can be used all alone for breads; the dark flour, however, is heavier and should replace up to 50 percent of the wheat flour.

soy flour: Soy flour is made from raw soybeans, and soya flour uses lightly toasted soybeans. Both flours produce loaves with a moist, tender crumb and slightly sweet flavor. They have no gluten in them and may replace up to 20 percent of the total quantity of wheat flour in bread. Loaves that contain soy flour will brown quickly and need a lower than usual temperature for baking.

sponge method

The sponge method is the first step in a simple and successful bread-making technique, producing loaves with a tangy, yeasty flavor and good texture. Made by beating air into a mixture of yeast, liquid, and a small quantity of the flour in the bread recipe, the sponge rises before the rest of the ingredients are added. It succeeds because it gives the dough a head start by providing the perfect conditions for the dough to ripen and ferment before shaping and baking. During ripening, enzymes in the yeast break down the starch in the flour to carbon dioxide gas and alcohol, and fermentation is necessary to develop the dough's elasticity.

best way to make a sponge

You can convert any bread recipe to the sponge method by making a sponge first with the warmed liquid, the sweetener, the yeast, and about one-third of the recipe's total flour. Using a whisk or wooden spoon, whip the mixture until it is billowy (about 50 strokes). Cover the bowl with a warm, damp towel or plastic wrap so the sponge does not lose moisture, and set it aside at room temperature for 45 minutes to 2 hours. A shorter or longer rise will not harm the bread, but after 8 hours the yeast in the sponge will have died. Once the sponge has rested, simply add the remaining ingredients and then proceed with the recipe instructions.

sourdough starter

Sourdough starters are easy to develop and to maintain. When used properly, they produce baked goods with a distinctive, subtle flavor and appealing texture.

best way to make a starter

When making a starter, be sure to use a nonmetal container, because the starter will corrode metal. Also, select one that is large enough to allow the mixture to triple in volume. In a container, mix 1 tablespoon active dry yeast, 2 cups unbleached all-purpose flour, 1½ cups warm water or milk, and 1 tablespoon honey or sugar. Let it stand, loosely covered with a kitchen towel or plastic wrap, until it is frothy, bubbly, and smells slightly sour. The bubbles will begin to form in about 3 hours; it could take a few days for fermentation and sourness to develop. After the mixture has reached the sour stage, stir it down and age it for at least 3 days, loosely covered, in the refrigerator. A crock is ideal for storage. Bring the starter to room temperature before using it, and use the sponge method of bread baking (see facing page).

best way to maintain a starter

To maintain your sourdough starter indefinitely, refresh it once a week as follows: Stir the clear liquid that collects on the top back into the starter. Pour half of the starter out, and then add 1 cup water or milk and 1 cup flour. Stir well and let the starter stand, loosely covered, at room temperature for 4 to 5 hours or overnight before storing it in the refrigerator.

KITCHEN NOTES

:: If you seldom use the starter, you can put it into plastic freezer bags or containers in 1 cup quantities and freeze it. Thaw the starter and bring it to room temperature before using.

:: If you neglect a starter for so long that it turns dark and has a very sour-smelling liquid on top, you can try to revive it by combining ¼ cup starter with equal amounts of flour and warm water and milk and letting it stand at room temperature. If it is still alive, it will begin to bubble in a few hours.

pizza

Sure, it's easy to order pizza out, but making it at home offers some satisfying rewards. You can create just the kind of pizza you like best, varying the crust too with some whole-grain flour. For the home baker, one thing is clear: The key to a great pizza is the crust.

best way to make pizza

Make or buy pizza dough and let it rise according to the recipe or package instructions. For a great pizza crust, you need a very hot oven and a pizza stone or quarry tiles. These unglazed stones or tiles imitate the inside of a traditional pizza oven; they absorb moisture from the dough, making it crisp, and they distribute the heat evenly. If you are using a pizza stone or tiles, place them on the bottom rack in the oven. Preheat the oven to 425°F for 25 minutes so the stones will be evenly heated. If you're not using a stone or tiles, you can still make a good pizza crust by baking it on an inverted baking sheet.

Transfer the dough to a lightly floured work surface and gently knead it into a ball. Begin to form the pizza by pressing the dough into a flat circle. Press from the center and work your way out until the dough forms a 7- to 8-inch circle. At this point you can use a rolling pin to roll the dough into a 12-inch circle, or you can stretch the dough the Italian way.

If using a rolling pin, roll the dough from the center outward, rotating it as you go. Lift the dough edges occasionally to prevent sticking. To stretch the dough, place it centered on your two fists, held about 2 inches apart. (Flour your hands if the dough is sticky.) Rotate and stretch the dough, pulling your fists farther apart (about 6 to 8 inches) until the dough is several inches larger. Pull and stretch the dough into a 12-inch circle.

Transfer the dough to a pizza peel, dusted with cornmeal to prevent sticking. Brush the dough very lightly with olive oil, then add the topping. Transfer the pizza to the preheated pizza stone, tiles, or baking sheet. If using a peel, use a slight jerking motion and tilt to slide the pizza from the peel onto the hot stone. Be fast and determined when you do this and the pizza will cooperate. Pizzas baked on stones or tiles will take about 8 to 10 minutes; on a baking sheet they can take 10 to 15 minutes. Check the bottom of the crust to be sure it has browned. When the pizza has finished baking, use the peel as if it were a big spatula to remove it. Transfer the pizza to a cutting board and cut it into wedges with a pizza wheel or serrated knife.

KITCHEN NOTE

∷ A pizza peel is a flat, shovel-like tool made of hardwood that's used to slide pizzas and bread onto stones or baking sheets. A clay baking stone absorbs and distributes heat evenly, giving pizza dough a crisp, chewy crust. Look for these tools at kitchenware stores and housewares departments.

whole-wheat pie pastry

Many people think whole-wheat pastry must be dense and heavy. But when you use the right whole-wheat flour with the correct ratio of white (all-purpose) flour, the result is a light, tender pastry with far more flavor than pastries baked purely with white flour.

best way to make whole-wheat pastry

There is a difference between whole-wheat flour and whole-wheat pastry flour, especially when making pie crusts. Whole-wheat pastry flour is milled from soft wheat that contains less protein than other types of wheat. Less protein means that it produces a lighter, more tender pastry than regular whole-wheat flour. I like to use a mix of whole-wheat pastry flour and white flour.

Mixing the flour and fat is key when making any pastry, and whole-wheat pastry is no exception. The idea is to coat the fat particles with flour so they retain moisture—not to break down the fat so that it is completely incorporated into the flour. For this reason, many recipes suggest mixing the flour with the fat only until it resembles coarse meal. The heat in the oven releases the moisture in the fat, which causes steam. The steam leavens the dough, causing it to expand and become flaky. Milk is also added to many pastries because it adds flavor, texture, and tenderness. If you want to make a dairy-free crust, soymilk works well also. When making pastry, it is important not to overmix the dough. If you choose to make the dough in a food processor, which makes for easy and thorough blending of the flour and oil, pulse it on and off to mix, and scrape the bottom and sides of the bowl occasionally.

Wrap the finished dough in plastic wrap and refrigerate it for 30 to 60 minutes before rolling. The dough won't become very firm, like a butter pastry, but the gluten will relax to ensure easy rolling.

For best results, always roll out pastry made with oil between two sheets of lightly floured wax paper. Also lightly oil the pie pan to help prevent sticking. After the dough has been rolled out, remove and discard the top sheet of wax paper. Center an inverted pie pan over the dough. Slide your hand under the bottom sheet of wax paper and carefully invert the paper, dough, and pie pan in one motion. Remove and discard the wax paper and press the dough into the edges of the pan. For a single-crust pie, trim the excess dough to within ¼ inch of the rim and flute as desired. For a double-crust pie, roll the remaining dough between sheets of wax paper, removing the top sheet. Slide your hand under the bottom sheet and carefully invert the dough over the filling. Trim the excess dough to within ¼ inch of the rim, and flute as desired.

If you need to prebake the pie shell, prick the bottom of the crust with a fork several times to release steam and prevent the crust from bubbling. Bake at 425°F until the pastry is lightly browned, about 15 minutes. If the pie is to be filled and then baked, do not prick the crust. Cover with plastic wrap and chill for 1 hour, or until the filling is ready.

KITCHEN NOTES

:: For easier rolling, press the dough into a flattened, round disk before you chill it.

:: Always roll out the pastry from the center away from you, never back and forth, to keep from stretching the crust.

:: Glass or dark metal pans make crisper crusts. Shiny pans make paler crusts.

pancakes and waffles

Pancakes and waffles are simple foods that are familiar and comforting. Neither is difficult to make, but both rely on some basic principles that, once understood, will elevate ordinary pancakes and waffles to a heavenly delights.

best way to make pancakes

One of the most important things to keep in mind when making pancake batter is not to overmix. Too much mixing overdevelops the gluten in the flour, making the batter elastic—which translates into rubbery pancakes. Overmixing also breaks up the air bubbles, making the pancakes flat.

Begin by mixing the dry ingredients in one bowl and the wet ingredients in another. That way, you'll need to mix the batter less once they are combined. The consistency of the batter is also crucial: If the batter is too runny, it will spread out too much on the griddle, resulting in thin pancakes. If it's too thick it won't spread properly and the pancakes may be doughy in the center. When the consistency is just right, the batter spreads into rounds that rise and cook uniformly.

There are many types of pans to use for cooking pancakes. Today, many stoves have built-in griddles that work great. You can also use a griddle pan, cast-iron stove-top griddle, freestanding electric griddle, well-seasoned cast-iron skillet, or heavy-bottomed nonstick skillet. All that is needed for these surfaces is a light coating of vegetable oil, brushed onto the cooking surface with a paper towel. Nonstick cooking spray also works well. Oil the surface and heat for a few minutes, then test the temperature by sprinkling a few drops of cold water on the griddle. When the water droplets jump on the griddle, you're ready to make pancakes.

Gently pour the batter onto the griddle using a spoon, a measuring cup, or a small ladle. Use ¼ cup of batter to make about a 4-inch pancake. The batter will spread out in circles, so leave enough space so the pancakes will not merge. Cook the pancakes, undisturbed, until the surface is covered with bubbles and the edges look dry, 2 to 3 minutes. Before you flip the pancake over, use a spatula to lift a corner to make sure the first side is golden. After flipping, cook for 1 to 2 minutes more. Never flip them more than once.

best way to make waffles

Waffle and pancake batters are similar, so mixing batter for waffles involves the same principles given earlier for pancakes. Make sure to spray the surface of the waffle iron with cooking spray before each round of waffles. To gauge how much batter to use for each waffle, consult the instructions that came with your waffle iron (usually between ½ and ¾ cup per waffle). You want to use enough batter to cover the surface, so the waffles will be fully formed. If you use too much batter, however, it will seep out over the edges.

KITCHEN NOTES

:: Avoid using self-rising flour, which contains added salt and baking powder—ingredients that will already be included in your recipe.

:: To make lighter pancakes or waffles, separate the eggs and incorporate the yolks into the batter. Beat the whites until they are stiff but not dry, and fold them into the batter as a final step.

:: To keep the first few pancakes or waffles warm while the rest of the batch cooks, place them in a single layer on a baking sheet inside a 200°F oven. They will stay fresh in the oven for about 30 minutes—plenty of time to finish the batch.

:: If you're using melted butter in the batter, it's useful to have the other liquid ingredients at room temperature. If they're too cold, the butter will harden into lumps.

:: Store any leftovers in a plastic bag in the freezer, placing plastic wrap between each pair of pancakes or waffles to keep them from freezing to each other. To serve, thaw and heat in a toaster oven or on a baking sheet in a 350°F oven for 6 minutes, or until hot.

muffins and quick breads

These baked goods are so simple and quick to mix together that the only thing to remember is to go easy. They will be spoiled if you overmix the batter.

best way to mix muffins and quick breads

In one medium bowl, mix the dry ingredients. In a separate bowl, mix the liquids—eggs, milk, and melted butter or oil. Make a well in the flour mixture, add the liquid all at once, and then stir just enough to moisten the dry ingredients. This is where you should avoid overmixing the batter. It should look a little lumpy.

Spoon the batter into the prepared pan. If the batter was mixed correctly, the top of the baked product will be rounded and pebbly looking. If you have overmixed, it will be tough and have tunnels throughout.

Muffins and quick breads are done baking when a wooden toothpick inserted into the center comes out clean.

croutons

These crunchy chunks of bread are extremely easy to make and taste so much better than the store-bought version. They're also a great way to make use of day-old bread.

best way to make croutons

Cut day-old French or Italian bread into cubes (½ to 1 inch) so you have about 2 cups. Heat 1 tablespoon olive oil and 1 tablespoon butter in a medium skillet over medium-low heat. Add 2 minced garlic cloves and 1 teaspoon mixed dried herbs for flavor and cook, stirring, for 30 seconds. Drizzle the mixture over the bread cubes, tossing to coat. Transfer the cubes to the skillet and cook over medium-low heat, stirring occasionally, until the cubes are lightly browned and crisp, about 8 minutes. Let cool, then store in an airtight container for up to 1 week.

rustic oatmeal bread

MAKES 2 LOAVES / These plump, round loaves have a richness that makes them a satisfying part of a soup or salad supper. Store the bread tightly wrapped at room temperature for up to 4 days. Or wrap the cooled loaves in plastic wrap and then in foil, and freeze for up to 3 months; thaw at room temperature. This rustic bread dough can also be made into 24 rolls. Let the rolls rise for about 30 minutes, then bake until golden brown, about 20 minutes.

> **2 envelopes active dry yeast (2 tablespoons)**
> **½ cup warm water (105° to 110°F)**
> **1 ¼ cups boiling water**
> **1 cup old-fashioned rolled oats, plus more for topping**
> **½ cup molasses**
> **6 tablespoons butter or margarine, at room temperature**
> **1 tablespoon salt**
> **6 to 6¾ cups unbleached all-purpose flour**
> **2 large eggs**
> **Egg wash (1 large egg white beaten with 2 teaspoons water)**

In a small bowl, sprinkle the yeast over the warm water and stir to dissolve. Let stand until foamy, about 5 minutes.

In a large bowl, combine the boiling water, oats, molasses, butter, and salt. Mix well and let cool to room temperature. Stir in 2 cups of the flour, the yeast mixture, and eggs until well blended. Add enough of the remaining flour to make a soft dough.

Turn the dough out onto a lightly floured surface. With floured hands, knead the dough for 5 minutes, or until smooth and elastic. Oil a large bowl. Put the dough into the bowl, turning to coat. Cover with greased plastic wrap and let rise in a warm, draft-free place for 1½ to 2 hours, or until doubled in volume.

continued

Lightly grease a baking sheet. Punch down the dough and divide it in half. Shape each half into a round loaf. Place the loaves 5 inches apart on the prepared baking sheet. Loosely cover the loaves with greased plastic wrap or a kitchen towel and let rise in a warm place for no more than 1 hour, or just until doubled in volume. Meanwhile, preheat the oven to 375°F.

Remove the plastic wrap. Gently brush the egg wash over the loaves. Sprinkle each loaf with some oats. Bake the loaves until the tops are golden brown and they sound hollow when the bottom is tapped, 35 to 45 minutes. Transfer the loaves to a wire rack and cool completely.

date-nut bread

MAKES 2 LOAVES / Spicy and moist, date-nut bread makes a fine and somewhat unconventional accompaniment to hearty soups and is also great just for munching. The flavor will improve if, after cooling, you wrap it tightly in foil and let it stand for a day.

> 2½ cups unbleached all-pupose flour
> 1 cup whole-wheat flour
> 2 teaspoons baking soda
> 1 teaspoon baking powder
> 2 cups pitted, chopped dates
> 1½ cups toasted, chopped walnuts
> ½ cup old-fashioned rolled oats
> ¾ cup (1½ sticks) butter, melted
> ¼ cup vegetable oil
> 1 cup packed light brown sugar
> 3 large eggs, beaten
> 1½ cups milk
> ½ cup molasses

Preheat the oven to 350°F. In a large bowl, mix both flours, baking soda, and baking powder. Stir in the dates, walnuts, and oats.

In a medium bowl, whisk the butter, oil, brown sugar, eggs, milk, and molasses. Make a well in the dry ingredients. Add the milk mixture to the dry ingredients all at once and stir just until evenly moistened.

Coat two 8½-by-4-inch loaf pans with nonstick cooking spray. Spoon the batter into the prepared pans, dividing evenly. Bake until a toothpick inserted into the center comes out clean, 45 to 55 minutes. Set the pans on a wire rack to cool for 15 minutes. Turn the loaves out onto the racks and let cool completely.

olive and herb flatbread

SERVES 12 / In addition to baking this flatbread in a flat pan as described in the recipe, you can divide the dough into 6 equal pieces and press them into rounds. The topping also lends itself to many variations, including using crumbled Gorgonzola cheese and caramelized onions.

1½ cups warm water (105° to 115°F)
1 envelope active dry yeast (1 tablespoon)
3 cups unbleached bread flour
½ cup whole-wheat flour
2 teaspoons coarse salt
7 tablespoons olive oil, preferably extra virgin
2 large cloves garlic, minced
¼ cup finely chopped kalamata olives
1 teaspoon chopped fresh herbs, such as rosemary or thyme

To make the sponge, pour the water into a large bowl. Sprinkle the yeast over the water and stir. Let sit for 2 minutes. Stir in 1 cup of the bread flour. Cover the bowl with plastic wrap and let it sit for 2 hours.

Stir the sponge. In a separate bowl, mix the remaining 2 cups bread flour, the whole-wheat flour, and 1 teaspoon of the salt. Add 4 tablespoons of the olive oil, then the flour mixture, 1 cup at a time, to the sponge, stirring well after each addition. When the dough begins to come away from the sides of the bowl, turn it out onto a lightly floured work surface. Knead in the garlic, olives, and ½ teaspoon of the herbs. Continue kneading, adding more flour as necessary, until the dough is shiny, elastic, and no longer sticky, about 10 minutes.

Transfer the dough to a lightly oiled bowl and turn to coat all sides with oil. Cover the bowl with plastic wrap and set aside until the dough triples in volume, about 2 hours.

Punch the dough down and place it on a greased 13-by-9-inch baking sheet. Press and pat the dough until it covers the entire surface of the pan. Cover with a towel and let it rise until the dough reaches the top of the rim, about 45 minutes.

Preheat the oven to 400°F. Just before baking, press dimples into the dough with your fingertips and drizzle the surface with 2 tablespoons of the olive oil. Sprinkle with the remaining ½ teaspoon herbs and 1 teaspoon salt. Transfer to the middle oven rack. Put an empty baking dish on the lower rack. Quickly pour 1 cup boiling water into the empty dish and close the door. Bake until the bread is well risen and golden, 20 to 25 minutes. Remove the bread from the pan to a wire rack. Brush the surface with the remaining 1 tablespoon oil. Cut into squares and serve warm.

whole-wheat pizza dough

MAKES TWO 12-INCH PIZZA CRUSTS / Wheat berries are added to this dough for texture and a chewy consistency. It's a great all-purpose pizza dough that can also be used for calzones and hearty turnovers.

½ cup wheat berries
1 cup cold water
2 cups warm water (105 to 115°F)
2 teaspoons honey
2 envelopes active dry yeast (2 tablespoons)
1 tablespoon olive oil
½ teaspoon salt
⅔ cup whole-wheat flour
3½ cups unbleached all-purpose flour

In a small bowl, combine the wheat berries with the cold water. Cover and let soak for 8 hours or overnight. Drain and set aside.

In large bowl, combine the warm water, honey, and yeast. Let stand until foamy, about 5 minutes. Stir in the oil and salt.

With a wooden spoon, gradually stir in whole-wheat flour and enough all-purpose flour to make a soft dough. Turn out onto a lightly floured surface and knead for 8 to 10 minutes, or until the dough is smooth and elastic, adding additional all-purpose flour as needed to prevent it from sticking.

Put the dough in a greased bowl and turn to coat. Cover with plastic wrap and let rise in a warm, draft-free place until doubled in bulk, 1½ to 2 hours. Use as directed in recipes for pizza.

caramelized onion pizza

MAKES TWO 12-INCH PIZZAS / The best types of onion for caramelizing are the sweet varieties, such as Vidalia, Maui, and Walla Walla. If none of these are available, use yellow onions. Cut into small pieces, this pizza makes a great appetizer.

> **2 tablespoons olive oil, plus more for brushing crust**
> **2 tablespoons packed brown sugar**
> **2 large sweet onions, sliced into ¼-inch-thick rings**
> **Whole-Wheat Pizza Dough (facing page)**
> **1 cup grated part-skim mozzarella**
> **1 tablespoon chopped fresh rosemary leaves, or 1 teaspoon dried**

In a large skillet, heat the oil and sugar over medium heat, stirring, for 1 minute. Add the onions and cook, stirring occasionally, until browned and caramelized, about 18 minutes. Remove from the heat and set aside.

Place a pizza stone, baking tiles, or an inverted baking sheet in the oven. Preheat the oven to 450°F. Gently punch down the dough, divide it in half, and knead each half into a ball. Roll each half out into an 8-inch circle. Use your hands to pat and stretch the dough into a 12- to 14-inch circle. Brush evenly with olive oil.

Leaving a ½-inch edge, sprinkle ½ cup of the grated mozzarella over each pizza crust. Top with the onions and rosemary. Carefully slide the pizzas onto the pizza stone, baking tiles, or baking sheet and bake until the bottoms are crisp and browned, 10 to 14 minutes.

cornmeal pancakes

MAKES 12 PANCAKES / These pancakes are tender and fluffy, thanks to the addition of buttermilk. The cornmeal makes them sturdy enough to serve with a fresh fruit topping like sautéed peaches or apples.

1 cup unbleached all-purpose flour
1 cup yellow cornmeal
2 tablespoons sugar
2 teaspoons baking powder
½ teaspoon salt
1½ cups buttermilk
¼ cup vegetable oil
2 large eggs
Butter and maple syrup or honey for topping.

Preheat the oven to 200°F. In a medium bowl, mix the flour, cornmeal, sugar, baking powder, and salt. In a small bowl, beat the buttermilk, oil, and eggs with a fork until blended. Add to the flour mixture and stir just until smooth.

Heat a lightly greased griddle or large, heavy skillet over medium-high heat until hot, or until a few drops of water dance on the surface. Stir the batter. For each pancake, pour about ¼ cup of batter onto the hot griddle. Cook for about 2 minutes, or until the tops are covered with bubbles and the edges look dry. (Before turning the pancakes, lift the edges to check that the undersides are golden brown.) Turn the pancakes and cook for 1 to 2 minutes more, or until the other side is golden brown.

Transfer the pancakes to a heatproof plate or baking sheet, cover loosely with foil, and keep warm in the oven. Repeat with the remaining batter. Serve topped with butter and maple syrup or honey.

cinnamon-apple waffles

MAKES 6 WAFFLES / The flavors of apple and cinnamon have a natural affinity for one another and make a great breakfast waffle. Oats lend a chewy texture and nutty flavor to the batter.

> 1 ¼ cups unbleached all-purpose flour
> ¾ cup quick-cooking rolled oats
> 1 teaspoon baking powder
> ½ teaspoon baking soda
> ½ teaspoon ground cinnamon
> 1 cup buttermilk
> 2 large eggs, separated
> ½ cup unsweetened applesauce
> 2 tablespoons butter, melted
> 2 tablespoons light brown sugar
> Butter and maple syrup for topping

In a large bowl, mix the flour, oats, baking powder, baking soda, and cinnamon. In a medium bowl, whisk the buttermilk, egg yolks, applesauce, melted butter, and brown sugar until well blended. Stir the buttermilk mixture into the dry ingredients until just evenly moistened. Let stand for 5 minutes.

Meanwhile, in a small bowl, beat the egg whites with an electric mixer until soft peaks form when the beaters are lifted. With a rubber spatula, gently fold the egg whites into the batter just until combined.

Heat a waffle iron. Lightly grease the grids of the iron. Pour ½ to ⅔ cup of the batter (or the amount recommended by the manufacturer) into the center of the grids, spreading the batter almost to the corners. Close the lid and bake according to the manufacturer's instructions or until the iron opens easily.

Transfer the waffles to the oven, placing them directly on the oven rack so they will remain crisp. Repeat with the remaining batter.

Place the waffles on warm serving plates and top with butter and maple syrup. Serve right away.

whole-wheat pie crust

MAKES I SINGLE-CRUST 9-INCH PIE SHELL / This wholesome pie crust can be used for any pie or tart recipe. Be sure to use whole-wheat pastry flour, which is made from softer wheat than regular whole-wheat flour.

> 1 cup unbleached all-purpose flour
> ¾ cup whole-wheat pastry flour
> 2 tablespoons sugar (optional)
> ½ teaspoon salt
> 5 tablespoons mild vegetable oil, such as canola
> 5 tablespoons regular soymilk, chilled

In a large bowl, mix both flours, sugar (if using), and salt. Slowly add the oil and stir with a fork until blended. The mixture will look like pea-sized crumbs. Add the soymilk, a little at a time, and stir until the mixture comes together.

Turn the pastry out onto a lightly floured work surface and gently knead 2 or 3 times into a ball. Place the dough on a large sheet of plastic wrap and flatten into a round disk, about ¾ inch thick. Wrap in plastic wrap and refrigerate for 30 to 60 minutes before rolling.

peach crunch pie

SERVES 8 TO 10 / Fruit pies like this one are in season all year, since you can use frozen, unsweetened fruit if fresh fruit is not available. Take advantage of the packaged frozen fruit that comes already peeled, sliced, and pitted. Or freeze your own fruit when it's in season.

Whole-Wheat Pie Crust (facing page)
6 cups peeled, pitted, sliced peaches (6 large)
½ cup sugar
¼ cup unbleached all-purpose flour
Finely grated zest of 1 lemon
1 ½ tablespoons fresh lemon juice
¼ teaspoon ground nutmeg

crumb topping
2 ¾ cups old-fashioned rolled oats
¼ cup rice flour
¾ cup chopped pecans
2 ½ tablespoons mild vegetable oil, such as canola
¼ cup maple syrup
½ teaspoon salt

Lightly grease a 9-inch deep-dish pie pan. Between two sheets of lightly floured wax paper, roll the pastry out into a 12½-inch circle. Remove and discard the top sheet of wax paper. Invert and center the pie pan over the dough. Slide your hand under the bottom sheet of wax paper and carefully invert the paper, dough, and pie pan in one motion. Remove and discard the wax paper and press the dough into the edges of the pan. Trim the excess dough to within ¼ inch of the rim, and flute as desired.

Preheat the oven to 400°F. Place a baking sheet on the center rack of the oven. In a large bowl, combine the peaches, sugar, flour, lemon zest and

continued

juice, and nutmeg, and mix well. Let stand for 5 minutes, stirring occasionally. Spoon the peach filling into the crust and smooth the top. Place the pie on the baking sheet and bake for 30 minutes.

Meanwhile, make the topping: In a medium bowl, combine the oats, rice flour, pecans, oil, maple syrup, and salt. Stir until the mixture forms large crumbs.

After 30 minutes, remove the pie from the oven and spoon the topping evenly over it. Press down lightly to compact the filling. Reduce the temperature to 350°F and bake until the juices bubble thickly, about 30 minutes. Transfer the pie to a wire rack and let cool.

and more

This chapter contains a collection of items that don't quite fit into the other chapters of the book but are nonetheless important for the vegetarian cook to know how to use. From the familiar, such as eggs and honey, to the relatively unknown, such as sea vegetables and agar, you'll learn techniques that will round out your knowledge of vegetarian cooking.

eggs

The egg is one of the most ubiquitous foods in the kitchen, with Americans eating an average of 225 per year. It's an essential ingredient in many of the foods that we love, including cakes, cookies, sauces, and puddings, and it also endures as a food in itself. In a pinch, a couple of eggs, boiled, scrambled, or fried, make a satisfying meal, and a healthful one, too, despite many fears to the contrary. Stored inside the smooth shell is a complete protein and every vitamin except C. And although the yolk contains saturated fat and cholesterol, the American Heart Association reports that a healthy diet can include 4 eggs per week.

best way to hard-cook eggs

Place eggs in a saucepan large enough to hold them in a single layer. Fill the pan with cold water to cover the eggs by about 1 inch. Bring to a boil over medium-high heat. Cover the pan, turn off the heat, and let the eggs stand for 11 to 12 minutes. Remove the eggs from the pan and place them in the bowl of cold water. Let stand for 3 minutes. This will make peeling easier and prevent the yolk from turning green, a sign of overcooking. Crack the shell by gently pressing it against a hard surface, and peel under cold running water.

For soft-cooked eggs, follow the same procedure but let the eggs stand for only 2 minutes. Remove the eggs from the water with a slotted spoon and serve in egg cups.

best way to scramble eggs

For each serving, combine 2 eggs with 2 teaspoons water or milk and salt and pepper to taste. Beat the eggs briskly with a fork, whisk, or egg beater until the whites and yolks are blended and the mixture is frothy. Melt a little butter in a skillet over medium-high heat. Add the eggs and reduce the heat to medium. Do not disturb the eggs for 30 seconds; then, with a rubber spatula, gently stir the mixture, lifting the cooked portions and letting the uncooked eggs flow underneath. Cook just until the eggs are set but still moist and shiny.

best way to fry eggs

Use a skillet just large enough to hold the number of eggs to be cooked. Add ½ teaspoon butter to the pan for each egg, and melt it over medium-high heat until it sizzles, tilting the pan to coat it evenly.

Carefully break the eggs into the pan. Reduce the heat to medium and cook, uncovered, until the whites are set and a pale, translucent film covers the yolks, about 1 minute. Turn off the heat and let the eggs stand for 1 minute.

For eggs over easy, follow the same procedure, but after cooking for 1 minute, use a spatula to carefully flip the eggs over, and cook for another 30 seconds.

best way to poach eggs

Immerse eggs, in their shells, in boiling water for 5 seconds, then remove them with a slotted spoon and set aside. Fill a large, wide saucepan with water about 2½ inches deep and bring to a boil. Reduce the heat to medium so the water is just simmering. Break the eggs, one at a time, into the water. Cover the pan. Turn off the heat and let stand until the whites are firm, about 3 minutes. Using a slotted spoon, remove the eggs from the water, one at a time, and set the spoon with the egg inside on paper towels or a kitchen towel to drain briefly. Trim away ragged edges with kitchen scissors before serving, if desired.

If you will not be serving poached eggs right away, place them in a bowl of cold water, cover, and refrigerate for up to 8 hours. To reheat the eggs, transfer them to a bowl of water that is just hot to the touch and let stand for 10 minutes; then serve.

best way to make a frittata

Frittatas are the Italian answer to the omelet, a baked egg dish that takes any number of fillings. Begin by heating 1 tablespoon olive oil in a 12-inch ovenproof skillet. Add 3 to 4 cups of sliced or chopped vegetables such as onion, bell pepper, cooked potatoes, or tomatoes. Cook, stirring occasionally, until tender, 5 to 10 minutes.

In a medium bowl, whisk together about 8 large eggs, 1 tablespoon chopped fresh herbs, and salt and pepper to taste. At this point you could also add some grated cheese. Pour the egg mixture over the vegetables and cook undisturbed for 2 minutes. Transfer the skillet to a 350°F oven and bake until set, about 15 minutes. Run a spatula around the edge of the frittata to loosen it from the skillet. Slide it out onto a platter and serve hot or at room temperature.

best way to make an omelet

Many novice cooks view omelet making as intimidating. But once you learn to turn an omelet, and all you need is practice for this, this delicious egg dish will become a quick and simple technique. One of the nicest things about omelets is that they can be filled with virtually anything.

For each omelet, beat 3 eggs with 1 tablespoon water and some salt and pepper. Heat 1 tablespoon butter in an 8-inch omelet pan or skillet over medium-high heat. (If using a nonstick pan, lightly coat with nonstick cooking spray.) Pour the egg mixture into the pan. Slide the pan back and forth over the heat to keep the omelet from sticking. As the bottom begins to set, slip a thin spatula under the eggs, tilting the pan and lifting the cooked portion to let the uncooked egg mixture flow under it to the center.

When most of the omelet is set but the top is still a little moist, spoon the filling down the center. Loosen the omelet from the pan and fold one-third from the far side toward the center. Tip the pan over a serving plate so the unfolded side begins to slide out. Flip the omelet so it folds into thirds.

best way to separate eggs

When separating eggs, do not use the old-fashioned method of pouring the yolk back and forth between the halves of the broken shell. This is a good way to pick up microscopic bacteria still on the shell. For the same reason, it is not a good idea to separate eggs in your hands. Instead, invest in an inexpensive egg separator, a small perforated gadget that allows the egg whites to drain while holding the yolk.

best way to beat egg whites

When beating egg whites, begin with room-temperature whites without a speck of yolk in a clean, dry glass or metal bowl, and use clean, dry beaters or whisks. Whites can increase 6 to 8 times in volume, but even a tiny bit of fat will inhibit them. If the recipe calls for soft peaks, beat the whites only until they pile softly or the peaks curl over slightly when you lift the beater. If the recipe calls for stiff peaks, beat the whites until they no longer slip when you tilt the bowl and until the peaks stand straight up when you lift the beater. An acidic stabilizing agent such as cream of tartar or lemon juice added at the beginning of beating will make the whites more stable—helpful if you will be folding them into a batter. If adding sugar, begin adding 1 or 2 tablespoons at a time once the whites begin to foam. Add it slowly so that it does not weigh down the whites.

designer eggs

Eggs are now being marketed with less fat and cholesterol and more vitamin E and omega-3 fats than regular eggs. Hens are fed special diets, including flaxseed, sea kelp, and rice bran, that alter the nutritional profile of eggs and, producers contend, make them healthier for humans. Considering the ups and downs of eggs' fortunes over the past two decades, it's no wonder that producers are trying to spruce up their nutritional image. But are designer eggs truly an improvement over ordinary eggs? Yes, but not a dramatic one. Specialty eggs contain about 190 milligrams of cholesterol compared to regular eggs' 215 milligrams. Some have about 6 times the vitamin E of regular eggs, and that's useful, and others show a 10-fold increase in omega-3 fatty acids. You should weigh the benefits of specialty eggs against their higher cost—about one-third to one-half more than ordinary eggs, depending on the brand.

egg basics

:: Eggs on the market are sold by grade and size. Standards for such are established by the United States Department of Agriculture. The grades, in descending order, are Grade AA, Grade A, and Grade B. Grade AA eggs spread less and have a slightly firmer and higher yolk and white than Grade A eggs. Eggs that are Grade B will spread more than the other two grades and have a flattened yolk. Eggs are also sold by size—jumbo, extra large, large, medium, small, and peewee. Price differences are based largely on egg size, with larger eggs costing more per dozen than smaller ones.

:: To prevent the growth of potentially harmful bacteria such as salmonella, select clean eggs from a refrigerated case. Don't buy any that are dirty, cracked, or leaking. Slightly move each egg in the carton to make sure it isn't stuck to the bottom because of a crack that you cannot see.

:: Refrigerate eggs in their carton (not the slot in the refrigerator door) as soon you get home. Storing eggs in the carton keeps them from losing moisture and absorbing odors.

:: Always store eggs large-end up. It keeps them fresher and helps the yolk stay centered.

:: Do not leave eggs in any form at room temperature for more than 2 hours, including preparation and serving time.

:: When cracking eggs, try to avoid getting any eggshell into the raw eggs, to keep any bacteria present on the shell from contaminating the egg.

:: Be sure to wash your hands, utensils, equipment, and countertop after working with eggs.

:: Use raw eggs in their shell within 5 weeks and hard-cooked eggs in their shell within 1 week. Use leftover raw yolks or whites within 2 days.

yogurt

By draining the liquid whey from yogurt, you can make a delicious soft "cheese" with the texture of soft cream cheese. It can be used in place of sour cream and cream cheese in recipes with excellent results. Try it as a spread on crusty slices of bread, as a base for a dip, or as a topping for tacos and burritos. You can also whip yogurt cheese with sugar and vanilla for a delicious dessert topping.

best way to make yogurt cheese

You can spend money buying a deluxe yogurt cheese maker or a yogurt funnel, but you can also achieve the same results with simple cheesecloth. Line a sieve or colander with three layers of 100-percent-cotton cheesecloth. Suspend the lined sieve over a bowl. Spoon in yogurt. The amount of yogurt cheese you get will be approximately half the amount of the yogurt you began with.

Cover with plastic wrap and refrigerate for 4 to 24 hours, until the cheese is the desired consistency. Remove it from the refrigerator and discard the liquid. Gather the edges of the cheesecloth together, gently squeeze out any remaining liquid, and transfer the yogurt cheese from the cheesecloth to a container.

KITCHEN NOTES

:: You can use all kinds of plain yogurt to make yogurt cheese, including low-fat, nonfat, or whole-milk yogurt. Avoid yogurts containing additives like modified food starch, vegetable gums, or gelatin; these thickeners will inhibit the release of the whey.

:: Store yogurt cheese in an airtight container in the refrigerator for up to 1 week. Freezing affects its consistency, turning it slightly grainy, although it is still fine to use.

ginger

While referred to as a root, ginger is technically an underground stem or rhizome. As the ginger plant grows, the stem branches underground into stubby protrusions. Fresh ginger is used as an aromatic, like garlic, whose function is to impart its essence into dishes. Ginger has a clean, slightly sweet flavor with a distinctive bite.

best way to mince fresh ginger

Ginger's oil is highly volatile, meaning that it vaporizes when exposed to air. So when using ginger, slice off just what you need from the root. Peel away the brown outer layer with a paring knife or vegetable peeler, then slice it across the grain into thin rounds. Cut the rounds into thin strips and then cut crosswise into small pieces. To grate ginger, peel it and then grate it using the small holes of a cheese grater.

best way to extract ginger juice

The juice is the most potent part of the ginger root. To extract it, place grated or minced ginger in a square of cheesecloth. Gather the edges of the cheesecloth together and squeeze over a bowl.

KITCHEN NOTES

:: When you buy fresh ginger, select hard rhizomes that are smooth, unblemished, and firm. Wrinkling means it has started to dry out. The larger the "hand," the older and more pungent the flavor. Young ginger, which typically comes from North America or Jamaica in late spring and early summer, has a milder flavor, as do the smaller tubers. Large pieces are often broken into lengths of different sizes.

:: Fresh, unpeeled ginger keeps for up to 3 weeks in the refrigerator. Wrap it in a paper towel, then place it in an airtight container or plastic bag.

forms of ginger

crystallized ginger: One of the world's oldest candies, crystallized ginger is made by slow-cooking fresh ginger in sugar water, then rolling it in granulated sugar. Also called candied ginger, it has a gentle, warming bite.

dried ginger: You can buy dried ginger in Indian or Chinese markets to keep on hand to grind as the need arises. The dried form provides a surprisingly true ginger taste.

pickled ginger: A familiar accompaniment to sushi, pickled ginger is made by marinating fresh ginger in a rice vinegar solution and then slicing it paper-thin along the grain.

powdered ginger: The mainstay of baking, ground ginger is a rich, warm spice. Its aroma and flavor are fragile, so buy it in small quantities if possible.

preserved ginger: A delicious spicy-sweet condiment made from fresh ginger that's mellowed in a sugar syrup. Chinese preserved ginger is often flavored with licorice and a touch of salt.

honey

Dozens of varieties of honey are marketed in the United States, but all are three basic kinds: comb honey, straight from the hive; chunk honey, which contains bits of the honeycomb; and extracted honey, the most commonly packaged form, that has been heated, strained, and filtered for clarity. As a rule, the lighter the color of the honey, the milder the flavor. Select mild honeys, such as clover or alfalfa, for use in recipes with delicate flavors. Use more distinctly flavored honeys, such as orange or sage, in spreads or other recipes where a more pronounced flavor is desired.

best way to use honey

Honey has more sweetening power than sugar, so it's best to use it in recipes that call for it specifically. If you want to experiment with honey as a sugar substitute, start by using it in place of up to half the sugar called for in the recipe. (When doing this with baked goods, decrease the amount of liquid by ¼ cup per cup of honey used, and reduce the oven temperature by 25° to prevent overbrowning.)

KITCHEN NOTES

:: Honey is sold by weight. The contents of a 12-ounce jar will fill an 8-ounce (1-cup) glass measure.

:: Keep honey from sticking to measuring cups by spraying the cups with non-stick cooking spray. Or if oil is used in the recipe, measure it before measuring the honey.

:: Store honey at room temperature, even after opening it.

:: If honey crystallizes, remove the lid and place the jar in warm water until the crystals dissolve, or microwave it in an uncovered microwave-safe jar or container on High, stirring every 30 seconds, until the crystals dissolve. Don't let the honey boil or scorch.

natural thickeners

Agar and kudzu make excellent natural alternatives to gelatin, which is derived from animal products. Their natural jelling properties add thickness and stability to puddings and other desserts.

agar

Agar is a nutrient-rich jelling and thickening agent made from a sea vegetable. It is colorless, odorless, and basically tasteless, making it perfect for producing puddings, custards, mousses, and other desserts.

best way to use agar

Agar comes in bar and sticks (also called kanten), powdered, or as flakes. With some practice, it is easy to work with. The flake and powder forms are the easiest to use. Both must be dissolved before being added to a recipe. In a small saucepan, combine the agar flakes or powder with a liquid that can be boiled, such as a nonacidic fruit juice or water. Do not use acidic liquids like vinegar or wine. Bring it slowly to a simmer over medium-low heat and simmer, whisking often, until it is completely dissolved, about 10 minutes for flakes and 5 minutes for powder. Boiling the agar mixture will reduce its thickening power.

Bars and sticks of agar need to be soaked in water for at least 30 minutes and for up to 24 hours before using. The longer you soak it, the easier it will be to dissolve. Remove the agar from the water and squeeze it dry. If it is still in large pieces, shred it finely; then dissolve it as you would the flakes and powder.

substituting agar for gelatin

To replace gelatin with agar in recipes, use these measurements as a general rule of thumb:

1 package gelatin (4 teaspoons) = 2 tablespoons agar flakes, 2 teaspoons agar powder, 1 agar (kanten) bar

kudzu

This powdery, chalky starch is made from the root of the kudzu plant. Also known as kuzu, it is prized for its thickening qualities, imparting a translucent, creamy texture to foods without affecting their flavor or color.

best way to use kudzu

Crush the lumps in powdered kudzu with the back of a spoon, then measure as needed. Dissolve the kudzu in a small amount of cold water before adding it to the liquid being thickened. Be sure that it is all dissolved. The dissolved kudzu works best if you add it to the liquid when it's heated to just below a simmer. When first added, the kudzu will turn the liquid a chalky white, but the color will dissipate after a couple of minutes. The longer you cook the kudzu, the thicker the mixture will become.

KITCHEN NOTES

:: When buying kudzu, check to be sure that it consists of 100 percent organic kudzu root. Some lower-quality brands are a mix of kudzu and potato starch.

:: Store kudzu powder in an airtight container in a cool, dry place, and it will keep for up to 1 year.

:: Store agar (in all forms) in an airtight container in the refrigerator.

:: Foods made with agar don't require refrigeration to firm up.

:: Many cooks use both kudzu and agar together. The agar produces a firm texture and the kudzu contributes a creamy, soft consistency.

sea vegetables

Most people wrinkle their noses at the thought of eating sea vegetables or sea-weed, but these nutritious foods have been consumed for hundreds of years. In fact, many of us have been eating sea vegetables without knowing it, as they are used in products like ice cream, baked goods, salad dressings, and toothpaste. Ounce for ounce, sea vegetables are higher in vitamins and minerals than any other class of food. They are a rich source of protein and are packed with 13 vitamins, 20 amino acids, and 60 trace minerals. They are particularly high in iodine, iron, phosphorus, and calcium and have been linked to helping dissolve fats and cholesterol deposits created from other foods.

best way to rehydrate sea vegetables

Although you can harvest sea vegetables yourself or buy them fresh from rep-utable natural-food stores, more commonly they are sold packaged in a dehydrated form. Most sea vegetables need to be soaked before using to make them tender and easier to cook. Soaking will also make the flavor milder. If a sea vegetable is to be soaked, place it in a bowl large enough for it to expand, and cover with warm water. The soaking time varies depending on the type of sea vegetables (see pages 258–259), and some expand more than others do when soaked, from 2 to 5 times in volume. Once soaked, use sea vegetables within 2 to 3 hours, as they will lose their freshness. Many cooks save the soaking water to use in the recipe they are preparing. If you do this, be sure to let any sand particles settle to the bottom, and pour off the liquid slowly.

KITCHEN NOTES

:: When purchasing sea vegetables, it's best to buy organic varieties—their superior quality is worth the extra money.

:: Store sea vegetables in an airtight container in a cool, dark place, and they will keep indefinitely.

:: It's okay if white crystals form on your sea vegetables during storage. This is only the salt from evaporated seawater, and you can just brush it away.

:: Some people are concerned that as the oceans become more polluted, sea vegetables will become harmful. But testing shows that pollutants don't become concentrated in sea vegetables.

guide to sea vegetables

Here is a description of the sea vegetables most commonly used in cooking.

alaria: A sea vegetable cultivated wild along the coast of Maine, alaria is high in calcium, vitamin A, and the B vitamins. Alaria is almost identical to Japanese wakame biologically and nutritionally, with a black or dark-green color, but it has a more delicate taste than wakame, which is cultivated. It also needs to cook longer than wakame. It is excellent in miso soup and goes well in any dish that needs to cook for more than 20 minutes. The word "alaria" is Latin for "wings," since its leaves look somewhat like wings.

arame: A good source of protein, iodine, calcium, and iron, arame is a dried sea vegetable that comes in strands. It has a mild, sweet taste and is available in natural-food stores. It is especially good in stir-fries, salads, stews, and pasta and rice dishes. Soak for 3 to 5 minutes, or add it to dishes 3 minutes before the end of cooking.

dulse: Reddish in color, with a soft, chewy texture, dulse can be eaten right out of the package or cooked quickly and added to recipes. It has a salty, spicy flavor and can be added to salads and stir-fries or lightly fried and eaten as a snack. It is native to the North Atlantic coasts and has a long history in Northern European cultures. Extremely high in protein, iron, and vitamin B_6 (one cup provides 100 percent of the Recommended Dietary Allowance for iron and B_6), dulse is also rich in vitamin B_{12}, potassium, and fluoride. Its appealing taste makes it a good introductory sea vegetable for beginners and children. When fried, it makes a delicious alternative to bacon in a BLT sandwich.

hijiki (hee-jee-kee): Also called hiziki, this glossy black sea vegetable is one of the strongest-tasting varieties and one of the richest in minerals. It is extraordinarily high in calcium and iron. In its dehydrated form, hijiki resembles curly black strands, and it expands up to 5 times its dry volume when soaked. Let hijiki soak for about 10 minutes, and cook it for about 30 minutes. It is often sautéed with vegetables or used in soups, and it pairs particularly well with onions and root vegetables.

kelp: Kelp is a large brown seaweed that grows in the underwater forests. It is sold in dried crinkled sheets or in packages of strips. It is used in soups and stews, stir-fried with vegetables, or cooked with beans or grains. Soak it before cooking, or add it dry to soups and other liquids, where it will expand up to 5 times in volume. Kelp is high in calcium, potassium, magnesium, and iron and is a good source of chromium and iodine.

kombu: This sea vegetable is a member of the kelp family and is important in Japanese cooking. Sold in dried strips or sheets, it is dark green, almost black, in color. Kombu is a natural tenderizer and is good cooked with dried beans because it reduces cooking time and improves digestibility. In Japan it is best known for making dashi, a soup stock used for soups and sauces. It is also sometimes pickled.

laver: Indigenous to the North Atlantic, laver is purplish black in color and related to nori. It's especially good dry-roasted to bring out its nutty flavor. It can then be crumbled and used as a nutritious condiment to sprinkle over soups, salads, or grain dishes. Laver has a long history in the British Isles, where it is combined with rolled oats and fried as a breakfast bread.

nori: Rich in protein, calcium, vitamins, iron, and minerals, nori is a paper-thin sea vegetable that has a sweet ocean taste. It is usually used as a wrapper for Japanese sushi or crumbled as a garnish for soups and salads. If purchased toasted, it is known as yakinori. Nori that has been brushed with soy sauce is called ajijsuke-nori.

wakame: Wakame is a mild-flavored sea vegetable that can be used in a variety of recipes. It is sold dried in a thick, wide, brown strip, but when rehydrated, it unfurls into a delicate green leaf attached to a thick mid-rib section. Traditionally added to miso soup, wakame is also good with other vegetables or in salads, stir-fries, or rice dishes. It is rich in calcium, with high levels of B vitamins and vitamin C.

olives

In our expanding appreciation of Mediterranean cuisines, Americans have begun to explore the vast variety of olives. In just the past five years, the demand for olives has increased tremendously, with the result that many kinds are now available. As our interest increases, more and more types will be imported as well as grown domestically.

When first picked, olives have a strong, bitter taste and are basically inedible. They must be cured before they can be consumed. Curing softens and preserves the olives and develops their flavor: Curing can be done in several ways, including brine curing, dry curing, oil curing, and lye curing. Brine-cured olives, such as kalamata, niçoise, and picholine, are fermented in a salt solution and have a complex flavor and slight bitterness. Dry-cured olives, such as gaeta and nyons, are packed in salt and dried, developing a strong flavor and shriveled appearance. Mildly flavored olives with even-colored skin, like those found canned on grocery store shelves, are cured in a water-lye solution. Olives cured in oil are often too strong and leathery to eat out of hand but add a great flavor to sauces and stews.

best way to pit olives

When you need to pit a large quantity of olives (and you don't care whether the olives are crushed), this is a way to quickly tackle the job. Spread the olives on a sheet of paper towels or a kitchen towel, and then cover them with another towel. Run a rolling pin over the top, pressing down gently—it will then be easy to remove the pits from the crushed olives.

KITCHEN NOTE
:: Unopened jars of olives can be stored in a cool, dark place for up to 1 year. Once opened, they need to be refrigerated and will keep for up to 1 month.

basque scrambled eggs

SERVES 4 / This quick and nourishing meal is full of bell peppers, onions, and tomatoes, making it one of the most colorful egg dishes to prepare.

2 teaspoons olive oil

1 medium onion, thinly sliced

2 medium green bell peppers, cored, seeded, and cut into thin strips

1 clove garlic, minced

3 to 4 ripe plum tomatoes, chopped

6 large eggs

3 tablespoons water

2 tablespoons finely chopped green onions (white and light green parts)

¼ teaspoon salt

¼ teaspoon freshly ground pepper

In a large, ovenproof skillet, heat the oil over medium-high heat. Add the onion and bell peppers and cook, stirring often, until softened, 6 to 8 minutes. Add the garlic and tomatoes. Cook, stirring often, for 2 to 3 minutes, or until the liquid has evaporated.

Preheat the broiler. In a small bowl, beat the eggs with the water, green onions, salt, and pepper. Pour the egg mixture over the vegetables and cook for 1 minute. Stir the mixture gently for 1 to 2 minutes more, or until the eggs are set but still shiny and moist. Place the skillet under the broiler for 1 to 2 minutes, or until lightly browned. Transfer the mixture to a serving platter and serve right away.

spinach-mushroom omelet

SERVES 2 / One of the nicest things about omelets is that they can be filled with virtually anything you have in the refrigerator. The spinach and mushroom combination used here is good served with whole-wheat toast and freshly squeezed orange juice.

filling
3 tablespoons butter
1½ cups sliced cremini or button mushrooms (4 ounces)
½ cup thinly sliced red onion
½ teaspoon dried thyme
Salt and freshly ground pepper
4 cups fresh spinach leaves, rinsed and patted dry

omelet
3 large eggs
2 teaspoons water
¼ teaspoon salt
¼ teaspoon freshly ground pepper
1 tablespoon butter or margarine

TO MAKE THE FILLING: In a medium skillet, melt the butter over medium-high heat. Add the mushrooms and onion and cook, stirring often, until the mushrooms are lightly browned and the liquid has evaporated, about 8 minutes. Stir in the thyme and salt and pepper to taste. Add the spinach, stirring over medium heat just until the leaves are wilted, about 2 minutes. Remove from the heat.

TO MAKE THE OMELET: In a small bowl, beat the eggs with the water, salt, and pepper. Heat an 8- to 10-inch nonstick omelet pan or skillet over medium-high heat. Melt the butter in the pan. Pour in the beaten eggs. Swirl the pan by the handle to distribute the eggs evenly over the surface. Cook, without stirring, for 10 seconds, or until the bottom and edges begin to set. As the bottom begins to set, lift the cooked portion of the omelet with a thin spatula to let the uncooked egg mixture flow under it. Repeat until most of the omelet is set but the center is still moist and creamy.

Spoon the filling down the center of the eggs. Loosen the omelet from the pan and fold one-third from the far side toward the center. Tip the pan over a serving plate so the unfolded side begins to slide out. Flip the omelet so it folds into thirds. Slide the omelet onto a plate and serve right away.

herbed yogurt cheese

SERVES 4 / This delicate, fresh cheese makes a sensational appetizer. Serve it with crusty fresh bread or crackers.

4 cups plain low-fat yogurt
¼ cup extra-virgin olive oil
2 cloves garlic, minced
3 tablespoons chopped flat-leaf parsley
1 tablespoon chopped fresh basil leaves
½ teaspoon chopped fresh thyme leaves
1 teaspoon chopped fresh rosemary leaves
Herb sprigs for garnish

Line a sieve or colander with two to three layers of cheesecloth. Suspend the lined sieve over a bowl. Spoon in the yogurt. Cover with plastic wrap and refrigerate for 8 to 24 hours, until the cheese is the desired consistency. Remove from the refrigerator and discard the liquid. Gather the edges of the cheesecloth together, gently squeeze out any remaining liquid, and transfer the yogurt cheese from the cheesecloth to a medium bowl.

In a small bowl, combine the olive oil, garlic, and chopped herbs and mix well. Divide the yogurt cheese into four rounds, shaping it into patties with your hands. Place the rounds in a shallow bowl. Pour the herb mixture over the cheese, and let it stand at room temperature for 30 minutes. Cover and refrigerate overnight.

Remove the cheese from the refrigerator 30 minutes before serving. Transfer to a serving platter and garnish with sprigs of fresh herbs.

honey-ginger sauce

MAKES 1¹/₂ CUPS / Here's a good all-purpose sauce to use as a marinade for vegetables, tofu, or tempeh, and as a flavorful sauce for stir-fries.

4-ounce piece fresh ginger
¹/₂ cup mirin
¹/₂ cup honey
¹/₂ cup tamari or soy sauce
2 green onions (white and light green parts), finely chopped

To extract the juice from the ginger, grate the piece of ginger. Tie the grated ginger in a piece of cheesecloth and squeeze the juice into a small bowl. You should have 2 tablespoons.

Add the mirin, honey, tamari, and green onions and mix until well blended. Pour the sauce into an airtight container and store in the refrigerator until ready to use.

chinese vegetable and arame stir-fry

SERVES 4 TO 6 / You won't be able to resist this fragrant and interesting dish, which combines both sweet and sour Asian flavors. It is based on a recipe from vegan chef Peter Cervoni, who likes to use sea vegetables in many of his preparations.

1 cup arame

5 cups broccoli florets

3 tablespoons olive oil

3 cups sliced fresh shiitake mushrooms

1 medium carrot, peeled and thinly sliced

5 ounces snow peas, cut into 2-inch pieces (2 cups)

4 cups chopped napa cabbage (2-inch pieces)

4 cups chopped bok choy (2-inch pieces)

1 teaspoon salt

¼ cup clear vegetable stock or water

4 medium cloves garlic, minced

3 green onions (white and light green parts), thinly sliced

2 tablespoons peeled, minced fresh ginger

1 cup fresh orange juice

2 teaspoons chickpea miso (or other favorite variety)

1½ teaspoons kudzu dissolved in 1 tablespoon fresh orange juice

2 tablespoons tamari or soy sauce

1 teaspoon dark (Asian) sesame oil

In a large bowl, combine the arame with 3 cups cold water. Let stand until softened, about 10 minutes. Drain and set aside.

In a wok or large, heavy-bottomed skillet, bring 2½ quarts lightly salted water to a boil over high heat. Add the broccoli and cook just until dark green, about 30 seconds. Drain and set aside.

Return the wok to high heat and add 1 tablespoon of the olive oil. Add the mushrooms and stir-fry until lightly browned and liquid evaporates, about 3 minutes. Transfer to a medium bowl and set aside.

Return the wok to high heat and add 1 tablespoon of the olive oil. Add the carrot and snow peas and stir-fry for 1 minute. Add the cabbage, bok choy, and salt and stir-fry for 1 minute. Gradually drizzle the stock around the outer perimeter of the vegetables. Cover and cook for 1 minute. Transfer to a large bowl and set aside. Rinse the wok.

Set the wok over medium-high heat and add the remaining 1 tablespoon olive oil. Add the garlic, green onions, and ginger and stir-fry for 1 minute. Add the orange juice, any liquid that has exuded from the vegetable mixture, and the miso and stir vigorously with a whisk to break up the miso.

As the liquid comes to a boil, add the kudzu mixture and whisk vigorously until well blended, about 1 minute. Reduce the heat to medium-low and add the tamari, reserved mushrooms, broccoli, vegetables, and arame. Stir-fry until heated through, about 2 minutes. Stir in the sesame oil and serve hot.

tapenade

MAKES ABOUT 1 CUP / This classic French olive spread is mellow and rich and is great served with toasted baguette slices.

1 cup good-quality brine-cured olives like kalamata or niçoise, pitted
2 tablespoons drained capers
½ cup extra-virgin olive oil
1 ½ teaspoons chopped fresh thyme leaves, or ½ teaspoon dried
1 small clove garlic, crushed
1 ½ teaspoons fresh lemon juice
½ cup fresh bread crumbs
Freshly ground pepper

In a food processor, combine the olives, capers, olive oil, thyme, garlic, and lemon juice. Process until the mixture is finely chopped.

Add the bread crumbs and pulse on and off until blended. Season to taste with pepper. Serve right away, or transfer to an airtight container and refrigerate for up to 1 week.

mail-order sources

Bean Bag
818 Jefferson Street
Oakland, CA 94607
Phone: 800-845-BEAN (2326)
Beans and bean products.

Bob's Red Mill Natural Foods, Inc.
5209 SE International Way
Milwaukie, OR 97222
Phone: 800-349-2173
www.bobsredmill.com
Grains, grain products, seeds, and beans.

Bridge Kitchenware
214 East 52nd Street
New York, NY 10022
Phone: 212-688-4220
www.bridgekitchenware.com
Cookware and utensils.

Country Life Natural Foods
P.O. Box 489
Pullman, MI 49450
Phone: 800-465-7694
www.CLNF.org
Soy foods by mail order.

Dean & DeLuca
560 Broadway
New York, NY 10012
Phone: 800-221-7714
www.deandeluca.com
Specialty foods.

Delftree Farms
234 Union Street
North Adams, MA 01247
Phone: 800-243-3742
Fresh and dried shiitake mushrooms.

Diamond Organics
P.O. Box 2159
Freedom, CA 95019
Phone: 888-ORGANIC (674-2642)
www.diamondorganics.com
Fresh and organic produce.

Gold Mine Natural Food Company
7805 Arjons Avenue
San Diego, CA 92126
Phone: 800-475-FOOD (3663)
www.goldminenaturalfood.com
Full-service whole food supplier.

**Gourmet Mushrooms and
Mushroom Products**
P.O. Box 515
Graton, CA 95444
Phone: 800-789-9121
www.gmushrooms.com
Fresh and dried mushrooms.

The King Arthur Flour Baker's Catalog
RR2, Box 56
Norwich, VT 05055
Phone: 800-827-6836
www.kingarthurflour.com
*Special bread and baking equipment and
ingredients.*

Lundberg Family Farms
P.O. Box 369
Richvale, CA 95974
Phone: 530-882-4551
www.lundberg.com
Brown rice and brown rice products.

The Mail Order Catalog
P.O. Box 180
Summertown, TN 38483
Phone: 800-695-2241
www.healthy-eating.com
Soy foods by mail order.

Maine Coast Sea Vegetables
3 George's Pond Road
Franklin, ME 04634
Phone: 207-565-2907
www.seaveg.com
Domestic and imported sea vegetables.

Melissa's World Variety Produce, Inc.
P.O. Box 21127
Los Angeles, CA 90021
Phone: 800-588-0151
www.melissas.com
Exotic and specialty fruits and vegetables.

Mendocino Sea Vegetable Company
P.O. Box 1265
Mendocino, CA 95460
Phone: 707-937-2050
www.seaweed.net
Sea vegetables.

Miracle Exclusives
64 Seaview Boulevard
Port Washington, NY 11050
Phone: 800-645-6360
www.miracleexclusives.com
Grain mills, soymilk makers, pressure cookers, and cookware.

Organic Provisions
P.O. Box 756
Richboro, PA 18954
Phone: 800-490-0044
www.orgfood.com
Full-service whole food supplier.

Oriental Pantry
423 Great Road
Acton, MA 01720
Phone: 978-264-4576
www.orientalpantry.com
Asian foods.

Penzey's Spices
Brookfield, WI 53150
Phone: 800-741-7787
www.penzeys.com
Herbs and spices for all ethnic cuisines.

The Sprout House
P.O. Box 754131
Parkside Station
Forest Hills, NY 11375
Phone: 800-777-6887 (SPROUTS)
www.sprouthouse.com
Sprouts and sprouting supplies.

Sultan's Delight
P.O. Box 090302
Brooklyn, NY 11209
Phone: 800-852-5046
www.sultansdelight.com
Middle Eastern and Mediterranean foods.

index

table of equivalents

The exact equivalents in the following tables have been rounded for convenience.

liquid/dry measures

u.s.	metric
¼ teaspoon	1.25 milliliters
½ teaspoon	2.5 milliliters
1 teaspoon	5 milliliters
1 tablespoon (3 teaspoons)	15 milliliters
1 fluid ounce (2 tablespoons)	30 milliliters
¼ cup	60 milliliters
⅓ cup	80 milliliters
½ cup	120 milliliters
1 cup	240 milliliters
1 pint (2 cups)	480 milliliters
1 quart (4 cups, 32 ounces)	960 milliliters
1 gallon (4 quarts)	3.84 liters
1 ounce (by weight)	28 grams
1 pound	454 grams
2.2 pounds	1 kilogram

length

u.s.	metric
⅛ inch	3 millimeters
¼ inch	6 millimeters
½ inch	12 millimeters
1 inch	2.5 centimeters

oven temperature

fahrenheit	celsius	gas
250	120	½
275	140	1
300	150	2
325	160	3
350	180	4
375	190	5
400	200	6
425	220	7
450	230	8
475	240	9
500	260	10